Slavery and Religious Conversion
in Portugal's Indian Empire, 1500–1700

Indian Ocean Studies Series

Richard B. Allen, series editor

Richard B. Allen, *European Slave Trading in the Indian Ocean, 1500–1850*

Erin E. Stiles and Katrina Daly Thompson, eds., *Gendered Lives in the Western Indian Ocean: Islam, Marriage, and Sexuality on the Swahili Coast*

Jane Hooper, *Feeding Globalization: Madagascar and the Provisioning Trade, 1600–1800*

Krish Seetah, ed., *Connecting Continents: Archaeology and History in the Indian Ocean World*

Pedro Machado, Steve Mullins, and Joseph Christensen, eds., *Pearls, People, and Power: Pearling and Indian Ocean Worlds*

Burkhard Schnepel and Julia Verne, eds., *Cargoes in Motion: Materiality and Connectivity across the Indian Ocean*

Jane Hooper, *Yankees in the Indian Ocean: American Commerce and Whaling, 1786–1860*

Daren E. Ray, *Ethnicity, Identity, and Conceptualizing Community in Indian Ocean East Africa*

Stephanie Hassell, *Slavery and Religious Conversion in Portugal's Indian Empire, 1500–1700*

ADVISORY BOARD

Slavery and Religious Conversion in Portugal's Indian Empire, 1500–1700

Stephanie Hassell

OHIO UNIVERSITY PRESS
ATHENS, OHIO

Ohio University Press, Athens, Ohio 45701
ohioswallow.com

Printed in the United States of America
Ohio University Press books are printed on acid-free paper ∞ ™

Library of Congress Cataloging-in-Publication Data

Names: Hassell, Stephanie, 1985– author.
Title: Slavery and religious conversion in Portugal's Indian empire, 1500–1700 / Stephanie Hassell.
Description: Athens, Ohio : Ohio University Press, 2025. | Series: Indian Ocean studies series | Includes bibliographical references and index.
Identifiers: LCCN 2024054813 (print) | LCCN 2024054814 (ebook) | ISBN 9780821425947 (paperback) | ISBN 9780821425930 (hardback) | ISBN 9780821425954 (pdf)
Subjects: LCSH: Slavery—India—Goa (State)—History. | Portuguese—India—Goa (State)—History. | Slavery and the church—India—Goa (State)—History. | Conversion—Catholic Church—History. | Christianity and other religions—India—Goa (State)
Classification: LCC HT1249.G63 H37 2025 (print) | LCC HT1249.G63 (ebook) | DDC 306.3/620954/7809031—dc23/eng/20250127
LC record available at https://lccn.loc.gov/2024054813
LC ebook record available at https://lccn.loc.gov/2024054814

For my mother,
Linda Greene Hassell,
who is also a writer

Contents

Preface

This book probes the relationship between slavery, religion, and empire while simultaneously examining enslaved lives in the early modern Indian Ocean region. The core source base comprises records from the Goa Tribunal of the Portuguese Inquisition. Such records present opportunities but also challenges for the reconstruction of slavery, and I have discussed some of the methodological issues in previous work.[1] Most importantly for this study, the records document the voices and lives of enslaved people whose experiences are vastly understudied in the Portuguese Empire in India. Inquisition cases and case summaries contain biographical details that would otherwise be lost to us. They also reiterate the significance of religious identity in the sixteenth and seventeenth centuries. Race was certainly a marker of difference. However, it does not prominently factor into this study of enslaved Catholics' role in the Portuguese imperial-religious project or their experience of slavery as Catholic coreligionists of their enslavers.[2]

Identifying enslaved individuals was a concern driving this study. Contemporary records used many terms to indicate slave status. The terms "captive" and "slave" were used interchangeably. Other indicators of slave status were the words *moço/moça* (young man/woman) or an ethnonym followed by a possessive and the enslaver's name, as will be discussed in chapter 1. Enslaved individuals often lacked Portuguese surnames; however, ethnonyms often took their place as descriptors. While ethnonyms did not pinpoint precise origins, they did provide a general geographical provenance. Thus, Maria Jaoa was presumably of Javanese descent, while Isabel

Guzarata was likely from Gujarat. Another way of marking ethnicity was the use of the word *casta* (caste) followed by an ethnonym. Hence, "Maria Jaoa" was synonymous with "Maria casta Jaoa," and "Isabel Guzarata" could appear as "Isabel casta Guzarata." Some ethnonyms were modified in Portuguese to reflect gender. For instance, masculine forms of the abovementioned ethnonyms were "Jao" and "Guzarate." As will be discussed in chapter 1, certain ethnonyms protected some groups from enslavement, albeit in theory rather than consistent practice.

Multiple monetary units appear in the text. While this book is not an economic history, it does occasionally mention prices paid for enslaved individuals as well as fines assessed by the Portuguese Inquisition. Currencies referenced in the text include the *real* (plural: *reis*) as well as the *cruzado, pardao, tanga,* and *xerafim* (plural: *xerafins*). One cruzado was worth between 360 and 400 reis. One pardao was worth between 300 and 360 reis. One tanga was worth 60 reis, and one xerafim equated to 300 reis.[3] Given the status of enslaved individuals in the Portuguese Empire in India as human property, the monetary values affixed to them opens up compelling lines of inquiry for future research beyond the scope of this study. It is with excitement and great anticipation that the exploration of slavery in Portuguese India will continue to enrich the fields of Indian Ocean history and slavery studies.

Acknowledgments

Sitting in a seminar at the University of Virginia, I decided I wanted to write a book. I had no idea as an undergraduate how long that journey would take or the countless people who would participate in the process. The following is an attempt to at least mention some of the individuals who were instrumental. To those whom I have inadvertently forgotten, my apologies and sincere gratitude.

At UVa, Joe Miller and J. D. La Fleur introduced me to the history of slavery in the Indian Ocean world. At Stanford University, I owe much thanks to Richard Roberts, Sean Hanretta, and Jim Campbell, whose guidance shaped the dissertation in which I used the Inquisition cases forming the bulk of this book. Thank you for believing in me and in my work.

I was blessed with a provost's postdoctoral fellowship at Duke University in the History Department, where Bruce Hall's mentorship and countless conversations enhanced the ideas in this book. Besides Bruce, I want to especially thank Jan Ewald, Sally Deutsch, Philip Stern, Adriane Lentz-Smith, John Martin, and Sumathi Ramaswamy. Tatiana Seijas, Colleen Kriger, and Mariana Dantas, then at the National Humanities Center, asked probing questions that helped push the book forward. Laurie Benton, Jon Glassman, Sandra Greene, and David Schoenbrun likewise cheered me on.

Colleagues at Clemson University kindly commented on portions of the book. Many thanks to Stephanie Barczewski, Lee Wilson, Katie Langenfeld, and members of the Humanities Hub Workshop for sharing feedback as well as Billy Terry for lending his mapmaking skills. Also, a heartfelt thanks to Anne Grant in the library as well as the indefatigable interlibrary loan staff.

Many archivists, librarians, and local historians in Goa and Lisbon aided the project in essential ways. In Goa, many thanks to Blossom Medeira, Lilia Maria de Sousa, Celsa Pinto, and the Central Library staff. In Lisbon, I am grateful for the help of librarians and archivists at the Arquivo Histórico Ultramarino, Arquivo Nacional da Torre do Tombo, and Biblioteca Nacional. Without their collective expertise and conversations, this project would not have come to fruition. Moreover, I am indebted to the research assistance of Mark Sebastian Pinto. This book was enhanced by his transcriptions collected in Goa during the pandemic as well as his database entry of parish records, manumission records, and material from the Cadernos do Promotor (Prosecutor's Notebooks). In Goa I also had the great benefit of a wonderful roommate, Ananya Chakravarti, whose kindness and generosity knew no bounds. I am glad our research stints overlapped.

Generous funding facilitated the research over the years. The Social Science Research Council International Dissertation Research Fellowship, the Ric Weiland Graduate Fellowship, and the Stanford History Department supported the foundational research. A wealth of funding from Clemson was instrumental afterward, including the History Department's professional development funds, the Lightsey Fellowship, the Humanities Hub Fellowship, multiple Faculty Research Development Program grants, and additional professional development funds from the Humanities Hub and the Pathways in the Humanities and Social Sciences Initiative. Last but not least, I am grateful to my parents, who always made sure I had a financial cushion when overseas.

This book benefited from much substantive feedback from Richard Allen and the anonymous readers who read the manuscript in its entirety. In the copyediting stage, Don McKeon and Tyler Balli likewise invested their time and effort. Many thanks for all your comments; any remaining errors are mine. Above all, I hope this study encourages others to continue the project of filling the silences inherent in the study of slavery.

To my friends and family who heard over and over about the book, thank you for your abundant patience, pep talks, and prayers. This book is dedicated to my mother, Linda Greene Hassell. Thanks to you, Dad, LJ, and Jo, for your past and present encouragement and support along the way.

Slavery and Religious Conversion in Portugal's Indian Empire, 1500–1700

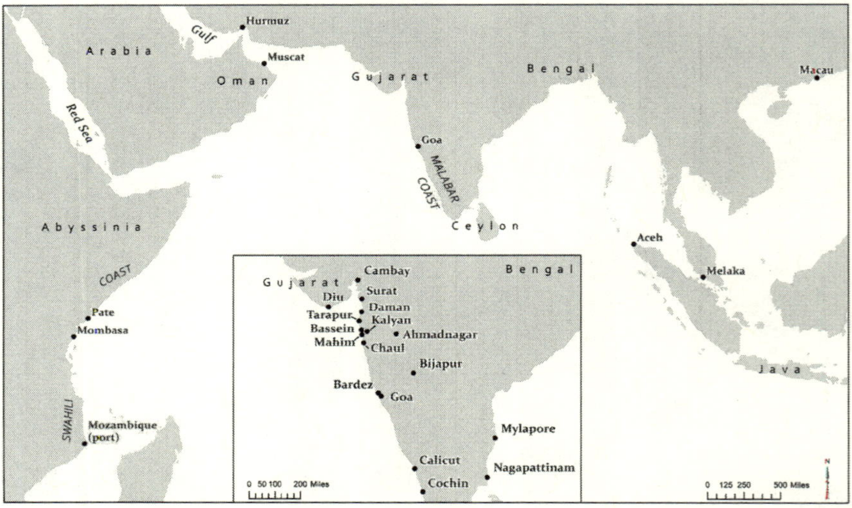

India in the Indian Ocean World, 1500–1700.
Prepared by William Terry.

Introduction

Slavery and Religious Conversion

IN 1557 ILENA MACHADA appeared before an inquisitorial judge in Goa, the capital of the Portuguese Empire in the Indian Ocean (Estado da Índia), and she denounced her former owners for practicing Judaism. She was a freed woman, previously enslaved to the married couple Diogo Soares and Leonor Fernandes. She had also worked as a slave in the household of Guiomar de Oliveira and Estevão Lopes, the sister and brother-in-law of Leonor Fernandes. In both households, she claimed she had been treated well, yet she also claimed her mistresses hated her. Both Leonor Fernandes and Guiomar de Oliveira had accused Ilena of having an affair with their husbands.[1] Moreover, both sets of households—husbands and wives alike—claimed they had tortured her as a punishment for being "perverse" and sneaking male lovers into the house to sleep with them.[2] Whatever the case may be, she was eventually sold to a friend, gained her freedom, and married. She resumed working for her former owners, but her return did not bode well for them. She had reputedly sworn an oath of vengeance.[3] It would seem Ilena made good on her promise to take revenge. She denounced her former owners and their relatives for practicing Judaism, a particularly weighty religious offense for someone of their status as New Christians.[4] Snared by the Portuguese Inquisition, they found themselves at the mercy of enslaved and freed Catholic witnesses.

These inquisitorial encounters reflect the imperial and social significance of religious conversion in Portuguese India. Enslaved individuals were part of the larger Portuguese project of making and retaining a Catholic empire. The crown and the church penetrated households to shape the relationship between the enslaved and their enslavers. Responsible for their enslaved dependents' conversion to Catholicism, slaveholders became religious stewards whose spiritual duties toward their slaves helped expand the Christian population. Moreover, this converted population was part of the imperial security apparatus: enslaved Catholics were conceptualized as loyal allies against neighboring Muslim states. By their conversions to Catholicism, enslaved individuals became members of the broader Catholic colonial community. Their conversion, though not always mapping onto their religious beliefs, enabled them to belong. The act of baptism created social incorporation, solving the remedy of social death.[5] Their religious status also conveyed rights that enabled slave agency and provoked household struggles, similar to conflicts over "fractional freedoms" claimed in Latin America.[6] Thus, the making of a Catholic empire was a contested process tied to the complex relationships between slaveholders, enslaved individuals, and the church.

SLAVERY IN EARLY MODERN EUROPEAN EMPIRES IN THE INDIAN OCEAN

The study of slavery in this empire underscores the Estado as a Catholic state in the Indian Ocean. Multiple scholars have probed this convergence of empire and religion. Collectively they demonstrate that the Estado was an overtly religious state, although religious considerations were not the only factors behind imperial policies. Glenn Ames tracks religious policies from 1600 to 1700, showing the state's concerted effort to spur Catholic conversions as well as the economic repercussions of religious policies.[7] Just as Ames points to economic pressures weakening religious policies, G. V. Scammell assesses seventeenth-century imperial pragmatism, as discriminatory religious policies yielded to financial and labor needs.[8] Patrícia Souza de Faria examines contemporary seventeenth-century debates over the allocation of resources and manpower for the church versus the military.[9] Teotonio R. de Souza examines the diplomatic role of missionaries.[10] Moreover, Ângela Barreto Xavier probes the relationship between local conversions in Goa and the preservation of the empire.[11] Missing from these discussions of the Estado as a Catholic state is an analysis of slavery in the Indian Ocean world—the imperial role of enslaved people as Catholics, the ways in which religious conversions shaped their status in the empire, and the meaning of religious conversions for the lived experience of slavery.

The Estado's concerns about slaves' religious conversions exemplify its commitment to creating a Catholic empire. Inquisition records particularly detail that commitment. The Portuguese Inquisition was a hybrid ecclesiastical and state institution. Accordingly, inquisitorial encounters bring conversion, slavery, and empire into one field of vision. While most of the trial records of the Goa Tribunal were destroyed, this book relies on extant sixteenth- and seventeenth-century cases containing enslaved defendants and witnesses. The broader inquisitorial context is enabled by Inquisition case summaries that show prosecutorial trends reflecting the anxieties of the Portuguese imperial state. Parish records, ecclesiastical council records, and municipal council records, among other sources, likewise emphasize the significance of religious conversion.

Slavery in Portuguese India is an underexplored topic. Despite slavery's connection to state building, studies of the Estado generally overlook enslaved people or mention them incidentally as supporting actors or as objects of trade.[12] Similarly, social histories of Portuguese India speak to the presence of slaves without featuring them as subjects of their own history.[13] Jeanette Pinto's work is trailblazing as the first monograph on slavery in Portuguese India. It provides an essential overview that strongly establishes and condemns the presence of slavery. Yet it is missing an analytical framework, treats enslaved people as passive, and lacks connections to the broader Portuguese imperial-religious and Indian Ocean contexts.[14] Ann Pescatello and Timothy Walker show the Estado's military reliance on slaves, yet their analyses miss the connection between slaves' religious identity and imperial security.[15] Most literature on slavery in the Portuguese Empire on the Indian subcontinent concerns either enslaved Africans and their descendants or the slave trade from Africa, with a focus mainly on the eighteenth and nineteenth centuries.[16] This monograph focuses instead on the sixteenth and seventeenth centuries, and it includes both Asian and African slaves.

The centrality of slavery in South Asian history is well established. Historians have delved into the subcontinent's many forms of slavery as well as its presence within Hindu, Muslim, and European polities.[17] Most importantly for this study, Indrani Chatterjee and Richard M. Eaton emphasize the need to situate South Asian slavery within broader geographic contexts and the larger literature on slavery studies.[18] Yet their important coedited volume *Slavery and South Asian History* included only one case study from Portuguese India, with a singular focus on military slavery.[19] This monograph demonstrates that the broader history of slavery in the Portuguese Empire in India is inextricably tied to the South Asian context while simultaneously connected to imperial and Indian Ocean geographies. The very presence of enslaved Indians within Portuguese India, the empire's roles as an importer and exporter of slaves, and the mobile lives of border-crossing fugitive slaves all make it imperative to deepen the scholarship of the Portuguese colonial presence on the subcontinent. Doing so will simultaneously expand the scholarship on slavery in European empires in India, a topic that has grown but remains understudied.[20]

All early modern European empires in the Indian Ocean relied on slavery and the slave trade; the Portuguese Empire was no exception.[21] The inseparability of slavery in early modern European empires from the broader Indian Ocean context demands that we include these colonial empires in the examination of Indian Ocean slavery studies. Such work enables comparative and connective histories of slavery.[22] Moreover, the significance of European slave trading in the Indian Ocean is clear from the standpoint of numbers, although it is difficult to reconstruct the full trade. In the sixteenth to mid-nineteenth centuries, at least 1,016,373 to 1,125,780 enslaved Africans and Asians circulated in the Indian Ocean and even beyond through European slave trading in the region.[23] The Portuguese slave trade included the export of at least 53,875 to 101,750 enslaved Africans and Asians from 1500 to 1834, per Richard Allen's revised estimates.[24] Additionally, recent scholarship has illuminated the significance of European slave trading from the Indian subcontinent itself.[25] Raiding, famines, warfare, and kidnapping all produced slaves for export from India.[26] While there is a dearth of consistent data, the Portuguese exported thousands of slaves from India from 1550 to 1600.[27] These numbers of exported individuals reflect not only economic transactions but also forced migrations that changed the lives of the enslaved and the lives of those left behind. Yet the scale and impact of Portuguese slave trading certainly exceeds their role in exporting individuals overseas. A reconstruction of internal slave trading within the Indian subcontinent would further add to the Portuguese colonial impact. Unfortunately, there are not any studies of the workings of the internal slave trade in India; this is a topic beckoning more research.[28] The vast range of Indian forms of slavery undoubtedly produces difficulty in the trade's reconstruction.

Overall, the Portuguese slave trade fit within the broader Indian Ocean pattern of multidirectional slave trading observed by Gwyn Campbell.[29] Enslaved individuals shipped across the Indian Ocean arrived in the Portuguese imperial network of port cities, as Portuguese slaving activities encompassed East Asia, South Asia, Southeast Asia, and East and Southern Africa.[30] From 1580 to 1640 during the Iberian Union of Crowns, Portuguese slave traders also transported enslaved individuals to the Spanish Philippines.[31] In addition, the Portuguese exported enslaved individuals back to the metropole, linking the Indian Ocean slave trade to Europe.[32] Enslaved individuals from the Estado also entered the transatlantic slave trade, connecting the Indian Ocean and Atlantic worlds of slavery.[33]

Given this history of slavery and slave trading, the need for more research on Portuguese India is clear. The relative neglect is problematic, given the empire's role as the first early modern European empire in the Indian Ocean. By comparison, the history of Dutch slavery and slave trading is far better studied.[34] There is a growing interest in slavery under the British East India Company.[35] In addition, colonial slavery at the Cape of Good Hope and Mauritius have garnered substantial scholarly attention.[36]

Examining slavery in the Portuguese Empire shows the need for a comparative discussion of slavery in European empires in the Indian Ocean. The Spanish Philippines constituted the only comparable empire with its similar religious project and simultaneous reliance on slavery.[37] This particularly Iberian approach to religious empire building distinguished the Portuguese from the French. The widescale conversion of slaves to Catholicism was not a high priority for the French, notwithstanding the Code Noir. This legal code regulated slavery in the French Atlantic colonies and eventually extended to the French Mascarenes in 1723. Religious provisions included mandates for baptism, Christian instruction, and the observance of Catholic holy days. However, the plantation context created a formidable barrier.[38] Forming an even starker contrast, the Portuguese Empire's Protestant competitors did not attempt to create religious empires. Gert Oostindie and Bert Paasman note this distinction for the Dutch.[39] Moreover, Protestant empires generally did not target slaves for conversion because of the conceptual link between freedom and Christian conversion.[40] These empires tended to eschew mass conversions of enslaved people out of the fear that conversion to Christianity could entitle them to freedom. A tantalizing exception raised by Michael Bennett is the East India Company's brief commitment to slave conversion in the late seventeenth century.[41] Such conversions accompanied manumissions, which he suggests may have reflected contemporary English concerns about the perceived incompatibility between slavery and Christian conversion. Thus, the conceptual link between freedom and conversion observed by other scholars is present. However, Bennett also suggests that the English may have been influenced by the Portuguese, who had a medieval precedent of conditional freedom tied to conversion to Christianity.[42] This potential connective history of Indian Ocean slavery merits further examination. While the Portuguese practiced conditional freedom in Goa, Portuguese Catholicism did not create moral qualms about the continued enslavement of Christian converts.[43] At the very least, though, it is probable that there were partial transfers of ideas about slavery and conversion between the two empires.

Moreover, despite Protestant empires' lack of prioritization of slave conversions, some enslaved individuals did convert to Christianity. This raises other possibilities for future comparative work. What was the significance of religious conversion in their lives? Were those conversions ever significant to states that did not merge conversion and empire building? We know that religious conversion could create a change in political subjecthood, which provided opportunities for fugitive slaves. Matthias van Rossum, Alexander Geelen, and Merve Tosun provide an example for the Dutch Indian Ocean.[44] This seems similar to the role of Catholic conversion for fugitive slaves fleeing to the Portuguese Empire. Both examples speak to the acquisition of colonial subjects and changes in imperial jurisdiction through religious conversion. While beyond the scope of this book, more research is needed to examine the significance of the religious conversions and religious identities of enslaved individuals in other early modern European empires.

SLAVERY IN THE ESTADO: A BRIEF INTRODUCTION

In the sixteenth and seventeenth centuries, Europeans established empires in the Indian Ocean. The Portuguese were the first, after rounding the Cape of Good Hope in Vasco da Gama's 1497–99 journey to India. Capturing strategically located port cities soon thereafter, the Portuguese established the Estado da Índia, an empire that stretched at its height from Mozambique to Macau. Goa became the colonial capital in 1530, and from there the annual voyage (*carreira da Índia*) connected the Estado to the Portuguese metropole of Lisbon. Backed by papal authority, the Portuguese conceptualized the Indian Ocean as a closed ocean (*mare clausum*). Instituting a spice monopoly to the rest of Europe in addition to attempting to control and tax oceanic trade more broadly, the Portuguese created a new type of trading empire in the Indian Ocean upheld by state violence.[45] While the Portuguese were never able to control Indian Ocean trade, their economic successes in the sixteenth century inspired a wave of seventeenth-century European competitors, including but not limited to the English, Dutch, and French.[46] The Dutch East India Company (Verenigde Oostindische Compagnie, or VOC) would pose the gravest threat, creating a sprawling empire and conquering many Portuguese imperial possessions in the process.[47]

Similarly to enslaved individuals in other early modern European empires in the Indian Ocean, those in Portuguese India labored in an array of occupations. Empire building was a messy, contested process, and enslaved individuals provided military labor in the context of manpower shortages. Surrounded by rival Muslim states and competitors, Catholic slaves were particularly seen as loyal.[48] In addition to temporary military labor, enslaved individuals performed sexual labor, domestic work in households, and farmwork, although not in a plantation context. They also worked in religious institutions.

Estimating the scope of the slave population is challenging for the sixteenth and seventeenth centuries. More consistent population records are available for the late eighteenth century and beyond.[49] Yet the prevalence of slavery, particularly in Goa, is clear. Contemporary travelers in the sixteenth and seventeenth centuries estimated slaveholders in Goa owned a minimum of six slaves to as many as forty.[50] António Bocarro's population survey, discussed more in chapter 3, estimated that slaveholders in Goa generally owned ten. Outside of Goa, he tended to quantify only slaves capable of military service, leading to lower slave estimates in other Portuguese settlements elsewhere on the subcontinent.[51] Rudy Bauss suggests that 2,153 enslaved individuals lived in Goa in 1719; however, this estimate is potentially problematic because of its conflation of the ethnic term *cafre* (which the Portuguese applied to East and Southern Africans, from the Arabic term *kaffir,* or unbeliever) with "slave." In his demographic reconstructions, he also interprets the term *pardo* to mean "free."[52] Perhaps these equivalencies worked for the eighteenth century, but we are still left with a lack of documentation of the non-African enslaved population, which could not have utterly vanished. Overall, Bauss estimates that in the early eighteenth century only 1 percent of the population was enslaved in the Goan districts of Ilhas, Bardez, and Salcete.[53] Paulo Teodoro de Matos estimates an enslaved percentage of 4.8 specifically in Ilhas in 1753, remarking that the Portuguese were the predominant slaveholders.[54] While late eighteenth- and nineteenth-century records are more consistent, one possible pathway forward for future research is a demographic reconstruction from extant parish records in Goa.

SLAVERY AND THE CREATION OF A CATHOLIC EMPIRE

Unlike the European empires that followed in the seventeenth century, the Portuguese entered the Indian Ocean with avowedly religious aims rather than solely commercial ambitions. Bolstered by papal permission to monopolize trade and make conquests, the Portuguese embarked on a project of creating a Catholic empire. This project shaped slavery—its legal justification, the status of converted slaves as religious insiders in Portuguese colonial society, the rights and privileges of slaves, and the religious responsibilities of slaveholders. Yet the process of making a Catholic empire instigated violent antagonisms.

The Portuguese encountered a religiously pluralistic region with a prominent Muslim population. Over the course of the medieval era, Muslim traders had taken their faith into the Indian Ocean, and the early modern era saw the continuation of conversions to Islam. Moreover, at the time of the Portuguese arrival, much Indian Ocean trade was in the hands of Muslim merchants.[55] On the Deccan Plateau of the Indian subcontinent, where the Portuguese would base their empire, state building by Muslim-ruled sultanates flourished. There the Portuguese would encounter the Bahmani Empire's successor states (the Deccan sultanates), including the formidable Ahmadnagar and Bijapur. Moreover, the Mughal Empire had its own state-building agenda on the subcontinent. In addition, non-Muslim polities such as the Marathas would pose a threat to Portuguese imperial pretentions in India.[56] Beyond the subcontinent, Portuguese imperial-religious interests collided with the Ottoman, Safavid Persian, and Omani Empires in addition to Muslim sultanates in Southeast Asia, such as Aceh.[57] These states checked the power of the Portuguese. Moreover, in East Africa the conquered Swahili city-states continued to challenge Portuguese rule through the underlying threat of Muslim populations allying themselves with the Estado's enemies.[58] Critically, even before the Portuguese encountered these states, they conceptualized imperial expansion as a means for religious conversion. In other words, extending Christendom legitimized empire building. Moreover, the requisite warfare of empire building produced legitimate captives.

From the roots of the medieval reconquest of the Iberian Peninsula (the Reconquest, or Reconquista), Portuguese imperial expansion in the Indian Ocean wove together religion and slavery.[59] During the Reconquest, wars to liberate Christians from Muslim rule produced Muslim captives, and both the wars and the ensuing enslavement of Muslims were conceptualized in religious terms.

Some military campaigns in the twelfth and thirteenth centuries were even supported by crusaders, weaving the fight for Iberia into the wider struggle for Christendom.[60] Crucially, Christian theologians and rulers categorized the military conflicts between Christians and Muslims as "just wars" rather than illegitimate conflicts. Muslims, and non-Christians more broadly, qualified as legitimate military targets by impeding the spread of Christianity.[61] Supported by theologians, the Portuguese then extended this application of just-war theory beyond Iberia to their fifteenth-century campaigns in Morocco, making the case that Muslim-ruled Morocco was previously a Christian territory in need of reincorporation into Christendom.[62] The Portuguese likewise exported the concept of just war to the Indian Ocean, just as the Spanish would do in the Philippines.[63]

The concept of just war and the attendant production of legitimate captives encompassed the Indian Ocean even before the Portuguese ships arrived. A succession of fifteenth- and sixteenth-century papal bulls legitimized Portuguese conquest for the expansion of Christendom. Underpinning these decrees was a thirteenth-century belief that the pope had the religious authority as Christ's earthly representative to repossess non-Christians' territory and subsequently transfer it to Christians; such repossession would then bring the territory and its non-Christian inhabitants under rightful Christian rule.[64] By this logic, the Portuguese king Dom Afonso V received permission from Pope Nicholas V to take non-Christians' territory and enslave non-Christians in the 1452 papal bull *Dum diversas.* Building on this bull was *Romanus pontifex,* the 1455 bull in which Nicholas V established the Portuguese right to monopolize "all conquest, navigation, and commerce from the Maghrib to the Indies."[65] This right came with the responsibility to extend Christendom. Pope Calixtus III's 1456 papal bull *Inter caetera* further supported the Portuguese rights and religious responsibilities connected to imperial expansion.[66] In particular, the head of the Order of Christ, a post filled by Portuguese royal family members, inherited spiritual jurisdiction over Portuguese territories.[67]

Backed by *Inter caetera* and the 1514 bull *Praecelsae devotionis,* Portuguese kings who simultaneously occupied the governorship of the Order of Christ patronized the church in their overseas dominions. This royal patronage (*padroado real*), which was further established in the 1551 papal bull *Praeclara charissimi,* made the king responsible for nominating candidates for ecclesiastical offices, collecting tithes to support the church overseas, and constructing churches.[68] Thus, the Portuguese imperial project from its conception and sixteenth-century development was legitimized with religious authority and embodied with religious purpose. This not only shaped the justification of slavery but also the lived experience of slavery.

Enslaved individuals in Portuguese India lived in an increasingly Catholic landscape. Goa, the colonial capital, was a site of missionary expansion to the broader Indian Ocean. The city became the seat of the archbishop and hosted the Goa Tribunal of the Portuguese Inquisition, which was the only overseas tribunal ever established by the Portuguese. Instituted in 1560, it was active until 1812, with a break from 1774 to 1778.[69] The tribunal's establishment coincided with the Catholic Reformation and ensuing intensification of Catholicism in India in the mid-sixteenth century.[70] The provincial councils, ecclesiastical councils created as a result of the Council of Trent, met in Goa from 1567 to 1606 to bring the empire's Christians into orthodoxy.[71] Ecclesiastical and secular decrees authorized the destruction of temples and mosques, removed Hindu "orphans" (creatively defined) from their families, prohibited non-Christian ceremonies, and coercively contributed to an era of mass baptisms.[72]

In this Catholic landscape, enslaved individuals were envisioned as Catholic subjects. Enslaved converts were connected to the Father of Christians (Pai dos Cristãos), who was responsible for the interests of all new converts.[73] Moreover, slaves' conversions placed them under the jurisdiction of the Inquisition (like their free Catholic counterparts). Crown and ecclesiastical decrees targeted enslaved individuals' conversions and mandated their spiritual growth in an attempt to create a Catholic empire. In this context, the owner-slave relationship had a religious and imperial significance. One of the imperial-religious responsibilities of slaveholders was to facilitate their slaves' membership in the empire.[74]

Through baptism, enslaved Catholics were birthed into the wider colonial Catholic society with attendant rights and responsibilities. Belonging to the Catholic community promised access to the protection of the Catholic Church, whose authorities in India mediated and regulated slavery. The church in India crafted decrees on the relationship between enslavers and the enslaved. In this framework, slave ownership included the duty to baptize enslaved dependents. Moreover, Catholic slaves had the right to marry and receive a Catholic burial. In other words, the church decreed that slaves had the right to belong in the Catholic community. This invitation to membership was significant in the Portuguese Empire in India because no one could fully belong—whether enslaved or free—if he or she were not Catholic in the sixteenth and seventeenth centuries.[75] Overall, being a recognized member of the Catholic community gave enslaved Catholics a space for agency and a set of expectations about their lives. Though they were enslaved, the religious rights they attained as Catholics provided them with an opportunity to contest their owners' unchristian actions and claim the religious rights that their enslavers sought to deny.

Belonging did not preclude social stratification, however. This book is not making the case that religious conversion eased the way into equality. There was a tension in membership based on religious identity and the earthly reality of status based on other forms of identity. Membership in the Catholic community was tiered. European Old Christians, who by definition had longer lineages of Christianity, had a higher status. Newer converts possessed newer claims to membership and therefore had a lesser status. Thus, European New Christians whose blood was less "pure" were below in this hierarchy, and examinations of purity of blood helped uphold this social hierarchy. Non-Europeans were lower still because their conversions were usually even newer.[76] Thus, imported Iberian notions of religious genealogical lineage created tiers in membership.[77] Moreover, indigenous caste hierarchies were retained upon conversion, creating yet another form of social stratification within the Catholic community.[78]

RECONSTRUCTING ENSLAVED LIVES

In its exploration of religious conversion, this book contributes to the study of slave voices and individual lives. It is my contention that enslaved individuals had something noteworthy to say about their condition, about their lives, and about their enslavers and the wider society in which they lived. Critiques of the concept of agency notwithstanding, this book also emphasizes the actions of enslaved people.[79] Scholars of Indian Ocean slavery studies have recently turned to the examination of the everyday lived experiences of enslaved individuals in European empires. Such analyses place the enslaved at the center as subjects in their own right, rather than relegating them to the background. Moreover, through the analysis of these individual lives, historians have been able to examine the broader history of slavery.[80]

In Portuguese India, Inquisition records fill an important gap. Following in the footsteps of historians who have used continental tribunals to examine slavery in the Portuguese Atlantic, this book also joins a growing literature using Inquisition records to examine slavery in the Portuguese Indian Ocean.[81] Beyond the recorded actions and words in Inquisition records, slaves' lives as Catholic subjects were also documented in highly underutilized local Goan parish records.[82] The parish records of São Bartolomeu stand out for their relatively rare inclusion of early modern data; later centuries are far better represented across an array of parishes.[83]

The following chapters attempt to reconstruct the lives of the enslaved. Chapter 1, "Slavery and the Household," examines the meaning of slavery and freedom in the Portuguese Indian context. Chapter 2, "Enslavers as Religious Stewards," analyzes the imperial and ecclesiastical project of creating a Catholic empire. This project took place primarily at the household level, where competing claims of authority—the church's claim over the soul and the slaveholder's claim over the body—created tensions as enslaved men and women asserted their agency as Catholics. Chapter 3, "Arming Slaves for the Catholic Empire," delves into the Portuguese imperial desire for an armed Catholic presence in India, leading to its reliance on unfree labor, including the enslaved. Creating Catholic slaves through religious conversion was part of the larger imperial project of sustaining the Portuguese Empire in India, while conversions to Islam were perceived as a security threat. Chapter 4, "Bonds of Conversion," examines the jurisdictional repercussions of slaves' religious conversions. Converting to Catholicism created an indissoluble bond that outlasted manumission, flight, and conversion to Islam; bonds of conversion outlasted bonds of enslavement. Chapter 5, "Choosing

Catholic Community," analyzes the actions of slaves who voluntarily remained in the Catholic community. Their assimilatory acts in favor of Catholicism were just as agentive as flight and conversion to Islam. The book concludes with suggestions for future research and reflections on the significance of religion juxtaposed against the current memory of race-based slavery in the former Portuguese Empire in India.

ONE

Slavery and the Household

IN 1557–59 ISABEL Malavar, an enslaved cook and co-laborer of the aforementioned Ilena Machada, appeared before inquisitorial judges in Goa who were keenly interested in the religious activities of her New Christian owners, Diogo Soares and Leonor Fernandes.[1] The notary recorded her denunciation of Leonor, in which she gave a scathing portrayal of her owners as secret members of the "caste of the Jews."[2] Precious personal information about Isabel's own life also emerged in her sixteenth-century inquisitorial encounter. Isabel was born in Bengal but grew up on the Malabar Coast. She identified herself as "*malavar*" and declared that she knew the language of the area very well.[3] The forty-year-old cook had cost her owners 140 pardaos, which was a large sum.[4] She had served in their household for about six or seven years.[5] Personal details about Isabel's life in the Soares-Fernandes family was not limited to her words alone. Her owners had something to say about her role in the household as well. According to them, she had refused to work and attempted to redeem herself by saving the necessary money. Her owners also brought up her (alleged) sexual activities and the violent punishment they inflicted to correct all her transgressions.[6] Thus, in the multiple narratives recorded in the Inquisition cases, a picture of slavery at the household level emerged.

Probing slavery in Portuguese India necessitates an examination at the household level, as it was the place in which the church and crown intervened to create a Catholic empire. Households were simultaneously collections of connected people but also messy conflations of shared living spaces, locations of violence, and everyday worksites. Households consisted of the people to whom labor was owed and the people from whom protection and patronage were expected. In short, households were the place where daily life occurred. The everyday experience of slavery—the daily struggles, contests over power, griefs, ambitions, tragedies, and triumphs—all transpired within households.

MAKING SLAVES: IMPERIAL GEOGRAPHY AND THE SHAPING OF HOUSEHOLDS

The imperial geography shaped the legal creation of slaves for the household. Regulations on slavery were bound up in the beginnings of imperial expansion, and these regulations included papal bulls, followed by a mixture of both secular and religious laws after the establishment of colonies. These regulations mandated who could be enslaved and who could be an enslaver.

Religious Identity and Enslavement

Ideas about slavery and religious difference in Portugal informed justifications for enslavement in Portuguese India. The Reconquista, the recapturing of Iberia from North African Muslim occupation, produced Muslim captives who labored as slaves. Fifteenth-century wars against Morocco likewise supplied more Muslim slaves on the Iberian Peninsula.[7] Papal bulls, such as *Dum diversas* (1452) and *Romanus pontifex* (1454), extended the concept of enslaving non-Christian enemies through "just wars" to the broader Portuguese Empire.[8] While the gradual immersion of Muslims in Portugal and the development of Atlantic slave trading helped decouple the tight link between enslavement and Muslim identity, Muslims and other non-Christians were targeted as possible slaves in Portuguese India.[9] In 1520 King Manuel's *Ordenações da Índia* legalized the enslavement of any Muslims in the Indian Ocean who traded in particular spices.[10] Moreover, wars against non-Christians in Portuguese India constituted a legally legitimate source of slaves.

In the Portuguese Empire in India, the Catholic Church regulated slavery. Following the Council of Trent, the provincial councils convened in Goa from 1567 to 1606. These ecclesiastical councils' decrees extended to the subject of slavery. Church decrees categorized who was legally eligible for enslavement, distinguishing this population from those who were protected from illegitimate or unjust captivity. In 1567 the First Provincial Council issued guidelines that stated the five categories of permissible enslavement.[11] The decree supported the enslavement of children born to slave mothers.[12] Likewise, captives of just wars against enemies were eligible for enslavement. There were two categories linked to impoverishment: one could sell oneself into slavery, and a father could sell his child into slavery in cases of poverty. The last form of legitimate enslavement was the captivity of people sentenced for committing crimes.

The church in India reiterated its conceptualization of legally permissible enslavement in the seventeenth century. Bemoaning the moral dilemma of unjust enslavement, the Fifth Provincial Council addressed the issue in 1606. The council members called it an embarrassment to people who feared God, proclaiming concern for the heavy sin hanging over the Estado da Índia.[13] Alarmed that the number of unjust captivities had increased, the council designed a decree that finally added the punishment of offenders.[14] When leaving ports often associated with the slave trade, all owners were compelled to have their slaves examined to certify unjust enslavement had not occurred. If this was not possible in a particular port, then owners were required to present the enslaved people to the vicar or deputies in the first port of arrival. Failure to have one's slave examined (with the proof of written certification) triggered the freedom of the enslaved person, a fine of two hundred pardaos, and excommunication.[15] In order to perform these examinations, the council charged the bishops with appointing religious authorities to be stationed at the ports. The Fifth Provincial Council also requested the viceroy to appoint other examiners in addition to the church-appointed deputies.[16] Despite these guidelines, church officials continued to document the presence of illegally acquired slaves, even delaying their freedom instead of immediately releasing them.[17]

Clearly slaves were often acquired in ways that contravened the guidelines of "just" captivity as defined by the provincial councils; however, these guidelines were not irrelevant. These recurring decrees show the endurance of an ideology linking initial enslavement with religious identity, as non-Christian captives taken in just wars continued to count as legitimate slaves. In addition, enslavement spurred by poverty matched ecclesiastical decrees' provisions regarding the sale of oneself and/or one's children in times of impoverishment. During his late sixteenth-century stay in Goa, Jan Huygen van Linschoten witnessed such enslavement. Describing poverty-induced captivity, he wrote,

> Also in time of povertie or dearth the fathers may sell their children, as it happened in my time, that there was such a dearth, and scarsitie of victualls in the firme lande, and countries bordering uppon Goa, that the men of India came to Goa (and other places where the Portingales are resident) to sell there children in great numbers, and for small prices, to buy them victuals. I have seene Boyes of eight or ten yeares, given in exchange for five or sixe measures of Rice, and some for three or foure Ducats the peece, and some came with their wives and children to offer themselves to bee slaves, so that they might have meate and drinke to nourish their bodies.[18]

Thus, in times of famine, the Portuguese acquired slaves from areas surrounding Goa and the territories close to other Portuguese Indian ports and cities.

The Convergence of Religious Identity and Ethnic Protections

Church regulations of legitimate enslavement also took into account ethnicity. Certain ethnic categories gave protections against enslavement. The First Provincial Council in 1567 expressed concern for Christians who had been made captives by "infidels" and then were sold at Portuguese ports to both Christian and non-Christian buyers. Ethnic groups described as Christians included Abyssinians, Armenians, Georgians, and "Charqueses."[19] To remedy the practice of unjust enslavement, the council ordered that the prelates and vicars examine those slaves found within Portuguese territory. Enslaved Christians were to be removed from their owner (regardless of the religious identity of the slaveholder) and restored to freedom.[20] Crucially, while the decree also extended to illegally enslaved Christians of "all nations," the aforementioned ethnic groups were explicitly tied to a Christian identity.[21] In this framework, the named ethnic categories were code words for fellow coreligionists worthy of redemption. Yet other ethnic categorizations conveyed legal protection from enslavement as well. Jesuits attempted to end Portuguese slave trading in Japan and Macau, for example, persuading Goan officials to restrict the slave trade.[22] Regarding Japan, a 1571 decree outlawed the enslavement of Japanese non-Christians.[23] It cited the hindrance to conversion that slave trading created, adding that the Portuguese lacked any justification for enslaving the Japanese.[24] Likewise, slaves from China were prohibited in 1595.[25] However, the trade in enslaved East Asians continued.[26] Thus, legal protection based on ethnic identity was not always effective.

While guidelines regarding ethnicity shaped the legalities of slavery, these ethnic identities were legal categories—not necessarily self-understandings.[27] Moreover, these categories could shift based on geography, and enslaved individuals could cycle through different ethnic categories over a lifetime. Hence, the freed, border-crossing Gabriel described in a 1595 Inquisition case accumulated different categories along his journeys. In the highlands of what is today Ethiopia he was a Jewish Falasha, and in the Deccan Sultanate of Ahmadnagar he became a Sidi, a term emphasizing his African descent.[28] Then in Portuguese India he became an Abyssinian, even documented as a native of "Preste" (Prester John)—despite the fact that Gabriel had stated he was not a native of the Christian kingdom.[29] Similarly, the enslaved Paulo was a "cafre" in Portuguese India, whereas he was categorized as "*preto*" and "*negro mouro*" in Portugal.[30] These shifts in categorization matched the experiences of enslaved people in the Portuguese Atlantic, where they also collected various ethnic labels that changed based on location.[31] While unpacking these categories for ethnic roots and charting the imprecisions are projects beyond the scope of this discussion, the categories that people inhabited had legal repercussions connected to enslavement because legal rights (and the denial of these rights) were attached to the ethnonyms.[32]

GATHERING SLAVES FOR THE HOUSEHOLD: FROM THE INDIAN OCEAN SLAVE TRADE TO THE MARKETPLACE

As discussed in the introduction, the Portuguese in the Indian Ocean engaged in the trade of enslaved Africans and Asians. A recent estimate by Richard Allen approximates a volume of at least 53,875 to 101,750 exported individuals from 1500 to 1834.[33] By at least the late sixteenth century, there was a regular trade in slaves from East Africa and Mozambique to Portuguese India.[34] Precise quantitative data is elusive for the sixteenth and seventeenth centuries, a fact bemoaned by Thomas Vernet, particularly in his discussion of Portuguese slave trading on the Swahili Coast. Focusing on the understudied period of 1500 to 1750, Vernet suggested a volume of "around a few hundred slaves a year."[35] Despite a general lacuna in the scholarship on the Portuguese slave trade for the sixteenth and seventeenth centuries, contemporary references paint a picture of enslaved individuals and the routes they traversed.[36] Jan Huygen van Linschoten, in his sixteenth-century travel account, stated that "great numbers" of men and women were taken to India from Mozambique.[37] According to him, these enslaved people were captives produced by wars between different polities.[38] Moreover, in his description of Daman, the famed chronicler António Bocarro stated that there were voyages between the Portuguese Indian fortress and the coast of Mombasa. The Portuguese exchanged cloths "of every type" for slaves as well as ivory and amber.[39] In addition to Mombasa, the Portuguese bought slaves in Mozambique. From Chaul, ships traveled to Mozambique with cloth to exchange for slaves, gold, and ivory.[40] Containing biographical details, Inquisition records similarly documented the slave trade from the Swahili Coast and farther inland. For example, Antonio, an enslaved Mozambican living in Goa, was prosecuted for divination in 1564, after which he was sold to Portugal.[41] Bearing the same name, the likewise enslaved Antonio from the coast of Malindi lived in Cochin (Kochi) before his 1566 inquisitorial trial that resulted in his sale and shipment to Portugal.[42] In 1581 Jerónimo, a slave from Mombasa living in Goa, was prosecuted for paganism.[43] In 1585 a slave named Diogo, born in the Kingdom of Mutapa and living in Goa, was sentenced by the Goa Tribunal.[44] The presence of these enslaved Africans in Portuguese India is indicative of a slave trade from East and Southern Africa.[45]

Yet the slave trade feeding laborers into Portuguese India was not limited to Africa. According to Teotonio R. de Souza, the Portuguese obtained slaves from Macau, Japan, and Bengal in addition to East Africa.[46] Similarly, Linschoten described the vastness of the slave trade, stating that the Portuguese were avid traders who procured slaves wherever they traded.[47] This trade resulted in slaves from "all countries to be solde, for the Portingales doe make a living by buying and selling [of them] as they doe with other wares."[48] This encompassing feature of the slave trade to Portuguese India matched larger Indian Ocean patterns of slave trading.[49] The outcome of this traffic was the production of households with slaves whose origins spanned continents. In the capital city of Goa, this geographic diversity is evident upon examination of slaveholders' households. For example, in the mid-sixteenth century, Diogo Soares and his extended family owned a labor force comprising Chinese, Bengali, Malabar, Gujarati, Javanese, Abyssinian, East African, Arabian, Burmese, Sinhalese, and *curumbim* (Sudra) slaves.[50] Likewise, in 1611 Garcia de Melo's household included six Chinese slaves, seven East African slaves, three Bengali enslaved eunuchs, and three other Bengali slaves.[51] Outside these households, Inquisition records show that other families in Goa employed slaves of varying ethnicities. Inquisitors prosecuted local slaves residing in Goa.[52] Moreover, Inquisition case summaries record that Japanese, Bengali, East and Southern African, Indonesian, and Malabar slaves worked in Goa from 1561 to 1623.[53]

The Indian Ocean slave trade that supplied slaves to the Portuguese Empire was not unidirectional.[54] Slaves from Portuguese India also were shipped to the metropole. According to K. S. Mathew, over five to six thousand Indians were sold as slaves per year by the latter half of the sixteenth century.[55] Moreover, some slaves within Portuguese India were sold to Portugal after committing inquisitorial crimes. For example, in 1564 a Burmese slave named Bernardim who lived in Goa was sold to Portugal for having converted to Islam.[56] Similarly, four years later a Javanese slave named Joane was sold to Portugal after being sentenced by the Goa Tribunal.[57] In addition, enslaved individuals accompanying their Portuguese owners entered the metropole.[58]

Upon arrival in the empire, slaves were sold in the different ports in Portuguese Asia. Contemporary travelers have described the auction of slaves in Goa. In the capital city, slaves were sold on the street called the Rua Direita (Straight Street).[59] There they were sold with other items at the market, which was convened daily from the morning hours of six or seven until noon.[60] Exceptions were holidays and Sundays, when the market was closed.[61] Enslaved males and females of various ages were purchased at the market; goods such as spices, Arabian horses, and jewels were also available.[62] On exhibit in the midst of hordes of people who had gathered undeterred by rain or heat, enslaved individuals experienced a highly public sale.[63] It was so crowded, the traveler François Pyrard de Laval observed, that people's "large *sombreros* or parasols" touched so that "the whole seems but one covering."[64] Into this crowded affair, sellers brought "great troops" of slaves.[65] In addition, he described the sale of slaves as a joint effort of both enslaved people and their sellers: slaves sought new owners who would treat them better than the last, while the current owners wanted to successfully sell their slaves.[66] Writing of interactions among slaves, buyers, and sellers, he penned the following:

> Then in order to sell them they praise them and put them up, telling all they can do, their craft, strength, and health, while the buyers examine them, question them, and scan them all over with curiosity, both males and females. The slaves themselves, hoping better treatment with a change of masters, show their disposition and praise themselves to take the fancy of the buyers. In buying, however, a certain day is agreed upon beforehand for repudiating or closing the bargain, so that they have time to learn the truth.[67]

Pyrard de Laval was particularly descriptive of the sale of female slaves, who varied in age and came from "all countries of India" in addition to Mozambique and elsewhere in Africa.[68] Most desired were enslaved African females, described as "*negras de Guinea.*"[69] Reporting on prices, Pyrard noted a range of twenty to thirty pardaos per enslaved Indian female—they cost far less than Arabian horses, which often sold for four hundred to five hundred pardaos.[70] Thus, accounts of the slave market show an active and interactive commercial process that pulled enslaved individuals into their eventual households.

LABORING IN HOUSEHOLDS: PRODUCTIVE, SYMBOLIC, AND REPRODUCTIVE

Once in the household, enslaved people performed a variety of types of labor in Portuguese India. They served as markers of status, provided sexual services, and bolstered their owners' income.[71] Travelers in Goa noticed free residents' dependence on slavery. Linschoten remarked that some residents were supported entirely by slave labor.[72] Pyrard de Laval elaborated, "The largest revenues and wealth of those at Goa are from the labour of their slaves, who, every evening, or at the week's end, bring what they are required to produce; others, again, are retained at their houses to wait upon them."[73] One of their functions, critical to city residents, was the procurement and sale of water from a well located approximately a quarter-mile outside the city.[74] Slaves of artisans worked in the shops of their owners; thus, shoemakers, hatters, coopers, and sailmakers all relied on slave labor to run their businesses.[75] Enslaved women prepared sweets and made needlework, and their enslavers made profits by strategically selecting attractive slaves to sell goods in the street.[76] Arrayed in beautiful clothing, they also made money by sex work. Linschoten recorded that the

> fairest and the youngest of them well drest up with their wares about the stréetes to sell the same, that by the neatnes and bewtie of the said women slaves, men might be moved to buy, which happeneth more for the affection they have to the slaves and to fulfill their pleasures with them, then for any desire to the conserves or néedle workes: for these slaves doe never refuse them, but make their daylie living thereby, and with the gaines that they by that meanes bring home, their maisters may well kéepe and maintaine them.[77]

Pyrard de Laval also remarked on the sale of desserts and embroidery by finely appareled enslaved women, some of whom engaged in sex work as well.[78] The income they earned went to their owners, who determined what portion their slaves could keep. However, enslaved women did not always present the full amount of their earnings. They proactively reserved part for their own use instead of solely relying on their enslavers' decisions about the distribution of funds.[79]

In addition to sex work outside the home, female slaves engaged in sexual labor within their enslavers' households. Some had even been particularly purchased by their owners for the purpose of sexual exploitation after enduring humiliating physical examinations in the marketplace, according to Pyrard de Laval.[80] Sexual labor performed for slaveholders also appeared in mid-sixteenth-century Inquisition cases in Goa. Slaves reported the tense household relations that ensued as a result of owners sleeping with them. For example, Alvaro Gomes's slave Madanela told inquisitors that Alvaro's wife, Lianor, had treated her poorly on account of his affair with her. Madanela bore his child and was subjected to harsh treatment that only subsided after her child died.[81] Likewise, Lianor Chingala had a child by her owner, Diogo Soares, before he sold her, allegedly for two reasons: her knowledge of her owners' religious practices and the jealous hatred of Diogo Soares's wife.[82] Seventeenth-century ecclesiastical records also document the prevalence of coerced sexual labor. In 1606 the Fifth Provincial Council tried to eliminate sexual relations between owners and slaves as well as the sale of slave sex. The council placed restrictions on unmarried men, including widowers, by curbing their ownership of enslaved women under the age of fifty.[83] The same council also decreed that female slaves under the age of fifty could not sell food or needlework on the street, likely linking these activities to the sex work described by travelers.[84] Both decrees reveal a logic that a decrease in easy access to enslaved women would lead to a decrease in prohibited sexual interactions within and outside of the household.

Beyond coerced sexual labor, enslaved people performed domestic chores and served as personal attendants. Soldiers, when they could afford it, would share one or two slaves with their nine to eleven housemates. Among other tasks, soldiers' slaves washed their clothes and accompanied them through the streets, holding hats over them as protection from both the rain and sunshine.[85] Yet soldiers could not always afford the luxury of owning an enslaved person; thus, they sometimes hired local Indians to attend them instead.[86] Slaves also attended Portuguese settlers; besides carrying hats to shield their enslavers from experiencing the brunt of intense rain or sunshine, they also carried their owners' swords when they walked through the streets.[87] However, these enslaved individuals were not just carriers of objects but were also living symbols of their owners' status. Describing the Portuguese "men of quality," Pyrard de Laval remarked that when they walked through the streets, "they are followed by pages on foot, lacqueys, and slaves, in great number, bearing arms and dressed in their liveries. They never go forth but they cause to be carried over their heads by one of their slaves a parasol or sunshade, which they call *sombrero,* and those who cannot afford to possess slaves carry these themselves over their heads."[88]

Slaveholding men did not monopolize the symbolic labor of slaves; women relied on enslaved symbolic labor as well. When slaveholding women ventured out of their homes, they were attended by their enslaved dependents.[89] Describing some of the processions that followed rich women to church, Pyrard de Laval commented on the fifteen to twenty enslaved women and servants who took part. He elaborated that members of this well-dressed retinue were "richly attired in silk of all colours, with a large veil of fine crape over all. . . . They also have smocks of exceeding fine silk, called by them *Bajus.* Amongst them you see some very pretty girls, of all the nations of India."[90] They would have appeared in addition to the four enslaved individuals who transported their owner in a palanquin.[91] Among their other duties were carrying items for their mistress's comfort within the church itself: pillows, carpets, mats to cover the carpets, gilt chairs, fans, and "other requisites."[92] In this way, slaveholding women ostentatiously flaunted their wealth and status through the display of their slaves and other servile dependents. Processions of enslaved individuals also followed wedding parties traveling to church.[93] Hence, regardless of gender, slaves functioned as symbols of the wealth and stature of their enslavers, not only providing practical service but also serving as visible signs of social status when their owners encountered the public.

TALKING ABOUT SLAVERY IN HOUSEHOLDS

Both the enslaved and free talked about slavery as it was experienced at the household level. Inquisition records documented life within households, and the next sections of the chapter will examine a body of Inquisition cases in which slaves testified against their New Christian owners. The Inquisition's main target in Goa was initially the New Christian community comprising descendants of Jews forcibly converted to Catholicism in the late fifteenth century on the Iberian Peninsula.[94] In 1536 the first Portuguese tribunal of the Inquisition was established, spurring an increased level of emigration of New Christians to Portuguese India and the Ottoman Empire.[95] However, a couple decades later the Inquisition caught up with them. In 1557 an investigation was launched in Cochin, an important Portuguese port in India and the former administrative center of the Estado da Índia.[96] That inquiry resulted in the prosecution of ten Cochin New Christians.[97] Later that year in Goa, eighteen slaves and the freed Ilena Machada began denouncing their owners.

Out of the Goan investigation, ten complete Inquisition cases resulted. Eight of those cases concerned Diogo Soares and his family.[98] The inquiry that resulted in their arrest was institutionally important because it directly preceded the establishment of the Goa Tribunal of the Inquisition, the Portuguese Empire's only overseas tribunal. As a result of the inquiry, this New Christian family was jailed, interrogated, and embroiled in a trial lasting four years filled with uncertainty, the loss of wealth, and their removal from India. The documentation about their troubles is particularly rich—they filed a petition, attacked the very legitimacy of the inquiry, and claimed the church officials appointed as judges lacked jurisdiction over them. Their lawyers filed for delays and mobilized witnesses, while the family sought to influence their slaves. In the end, members of the family finally confessed to practicing Judaism, denouncing each other in the process. After confessing, they publicly abjured their religious crimes and heard their sentences, which were ultimately commuted. In the turmoil produced by their inquisitorial experience, slaves' everyday stories were documented.

Slave Voices: Inquisitorial Testimonies and Their Controversies

Besides the words of New Christian slaveholders and other free members of society, the words of enslaved individuals were recorded. Thus, this chapter utilizes slave testimonies, which were a controversial feature of the Iberian Inquisitions. In April 1482 Pope Sixtus

IV criticized Spanish inquisitors' acceptance of slave testimony. He considered such testimony invalid and charged that allowing the testimonies of defendants' slaves and enemies made the inquisitorial process illegitimate. Despite the pope's protests, such testimonies continued, as he capitulated under King Ferdinand's pressure.[99] This papal unease about slave testimonies endures in the form of historians also left with the task of interpreting evidence. Renée Levine Melammed discusses slave testimonies taken in fifteenth-century Jaén by the Spanish Inquisition, raising some key points in her objection to the factuality of slave testimony: coercion, bribery, and secrecy were all inducements to falsehoods.[100]

In the Goan cases against New Christian slaveholders surveyed below, these same factors existed. Diogo Soares and his family members charged in a petition that their slaves had been persuaded to testify falsely against them through promises of freedom and their owners' property. On the other hand, slaves who testified in these cases alleged that their owners attempted to bribe them not to testify.[101] If the reports of this attempted bribery were true, then enslaved witnesses were under considerable pressure from both sides and had an incentive not to testify. While having valid concerns about false testimony injurious to slaveholders, Melammed's assessment overlooks the incentives owners themselves potentially provided to dissuade their slaves from testifying injuriously. Moreover, other circumstances suggest that we give serious attention to slaves' denunciations, rather than summarily dismissing them as irrelevant and false. For example, it is worth probing the extent to which it was in slaves' best interest to testify against their owners. Diogo Soares and his family members referred to a sermon that admonished everyone to denounce the activities of heretics.[102] Thus, it is quite possible that slaves as fellow Catholics acted with religious motivations. While these enslaved witnesses did not mention this sermon in particular, they did refer to their fear of God and their desire to do their Christian duty by sharing the knowledge they had of their owners.[103]

Regarding factuality, another question worth pondering is the extent to which enslaved witnesses would have put themselves at risk by testifying falsely. If slaves were encouraged to lie by the inquisitors themselves (which is not evident in the cases), then they would not have risked much by telling untruths. Lying on their own accord, however, would have been taking an enormous risk. Testifying falsely was a crime prosecuted by the Inquisition, as was inducing others to testify falsely. One such example is a Gujarati slave named Antonio, who in 1576 was whipped and sent to the galleys for inducing others to testify falsely. In particular, he persuaded some people to denounce his owner's wife as a Jew.[104] Likewise, in that same year Joane, a "mulatto" slave of partial Abyssinian descent, was whipped for the same crime, persuading the "*negras*" of his owner to swear falsely that they saw their enslaver's wife doing "Jewish things." Joane also was sent to the galleys, sold with his price given to his owner as compensation.[105] In 1618, the enslaved Anna from Ceylon was similarly whipped for testifying falsely; she appeared in her auto-da-fé wearing a *carocha* (a painted cap) and a noose around her neck.[106]

Beyond these examples of enslaved individuals who testified falsely, free persons were also prosecuted. Seventy-four cases out of a sample of 2,254 involved testifying falsely or inducing others to testify falsely.[107] The crime was admittedly a rarity in terms of its prosecution. Yet while it was not an inquisitorial priority, there was a risk of prosecution and punishment. Furthermore, inquisitorial toleration of the crime threatened the integrity of the institution. Inquisitorial visits from Lisbon took pains to ensure that the outlying tribunal operated properly. The 1632 visitation report, for example, detailed irregularities and critiqued the actions of João Delgado Figueira, then an inquisitor. While his inquisitorial career did not end, his tenure in Goa was cut short.[108]

While there was an institutional check on false statements, inquisitors themselves shaped the production of testimonies. The selective inclusion of particular slaves' words was biased to achieve a successful prosecution against Diogo Soares and his fellow New Christians. The inquisitors were content with reusing particular slave witnesses instead of utilizing the entire pool of potential witnesses. Over seventy slaves could have testified against Diogo and his family, with the exception of those who evaded testifying by flight.[109] Yet only nineteen slaves and ex-slaves testified.[110] Each slave testimony generally implicated more than one member of Diogo's extended family. The notaries, who were also the prosecutors, recorded the testimonies and distributed them among the various cases of the defendants. Thus, the inquisitors were content with using a small subset of slaves who could speak about the bulk of the defendants rather than drawing in all enslaved members of the household. What is lost to us in the present day is the possible corpus of testimonies of slaves who had different stories to tell about their owners. Accordingly, we are also deprived of information that would have been revealed about those slaves—their relationships with their enslavers and their names, ages, and family background. In short, we have an incomplete picture of these households.

Along the same lines, male slaves are often missing from these household portraits.[111] Both the inquisitors and owners had more interest in the knowledge of enslaved women. Female slaves, with their familiarity with food preparation, were able to testify about when owners fasted, what they ate, and what they chose not to eat. Domestic service also enabled them to comment on owners' clothing and bathing rituals. Thus, inquisitors would have had an interest in questioning female slaves. In like manner, the counterstatements of the owners overwhelmingly targeted enslaved women.[112] Accordingly, the records present a depiction of discordant household relations in which female slaves predominated. This spotlight on discord, however, does not preclude an analysis of slavery. On the contrary, the areas of discord reveal the violent nature of slavery in households. Moreover, the violence itself reveals what was at stake in the household.

HOUSEHOLDS AS SITES OF VIOLENCE

A household-level analysis of slavery unearths the violence of the relationship between the enslaved and their enslavers in Portuguese India. Household violence repeatedly appeared as a topic discussed in the Inquisition records. Analyzing this violence is important for two reasons. First, there is the empirical question to consider: Was slavery violent in the Portuguese Empire in India? Scholars have debated the level of violence in Portuguese India. Referring to enslaved Africans in particular, Ann Pescatello argues that their domestic roles tended to protect them from ill treatment.[113] Likewise, Gwyn Campbell and Edward Alpers, assessing slavery more broadly in the

Indian Ocean region, assert that slaveholders generally treated their enslaved dependents well.[114] However, Jeanette Pinto more accurately attests that the violence level was high in Portuguese India.[115] Inquisition records as well as ecclesiastical decrees demonstrate the presence of pervasive violence.

In addition to the empirical question of violence, however, is the second query of what provoked household violence. The purpose of this query is not to blame enslaved survivors of violence or create an apologetic defense of their enslavers. On the contrary, this violence was both morally grievous and sadistic. However, probing provocations of violence and slaves' responses is an attempt to understand the past. By examining slaveholders' rationales and application of violence, we can better understand the lived experience of slavery and mastery. Examining violence at the household level enables an analysis of contested power and slave agency. Slaves experienced violent retributions for resisting the conditions of their enslavement as well as slavery itself. Their chosen forms of resistance, particularly those pursued by female slaves, invite further scrutiny of assumptions about slavery and resistance in the wider Indian Ocean world. While the broad contention of a disinterest in "liberty" as an individualistic, Western-conceived breaking of bonds does align with the Portuguese Indian context, the Inquisition cases clarify that women sought manumission while also embracing the strategy of flight.[116]

Presence of Violence

Violence upheld the owner-slave hierarchy in the households of Diogo Soares and his extended family. In their Inquisition cases, they admitted to treating their enslaved dependents harshly. Multiple testimonies acknowledged that Ilena Machada survived various types of abuse at the hands of her owners. Diogo Soares alleged that he had punished his Arab former slave for having "hid men in the house so that she could sleep with them"; therefore, he whipped her and put her in fetters.[117] His wife, Leonor Fernandes, similarly remarked that Ilena was "very bad and perverse," having hid a man at night to sleep with him.[118] In her own case, Branca de Oliveira likewise alleged Ilena hid men in the house at night. Branca also claimed she discovered one of Ilena's lovers once, which resulted in Ilena's punishment of torture with hot oil followed by being shackled for a year until her sale to Francisco Leal.[119] Estevão Lopes claimed that Ilena was "his captive who was so bad and dishonest that she hid men in the house," adding that "for the love of her he had many differences and displeasures with many men."[120] To discipline her, he put an iron ring (*braga*) around her legs and whipped her.[121] Estevão's wife, Guiomar de Oliveira, also described Ilena's punishment.[122]

The violent life of Ilena Machada was not an exceptional tale. According to Diogo Soares and his family, they inflicted a range of physical punishments upon other slaves. For example, Antonia Malavar, Lianor Jaoa, Madanela Bengala, Filipa Corombim, and Joana Malavar all experienced whippings.[123] Assaulting slaves' appearance was another tactic: Lianor Chingala, Maria Guzarata, and Brianda Jaoa all experienced the humiliation of having their hair cut very short or shaved off completely.[124] Like Ilena Machada, Antonia Malavar had hot oil dripped on her, a form of torture also applied in the household of Ana de Oliveira and Alvaro Gomes.[125] This is merely a short sample of some of the violence. In each of the cases, Diogo Soares and his family described the myriad forms of punishment they inflicted on their slaves.[126]

The violence deployed by the defendants in these Inquisition cases was not exceptional in Portuguese India. Corporal punishment as a tool of power was practiced widely. Contemporary ecclesiastical and royal decrees recorded that slaveholders were particularly violent toward their slaves in Portuguese India. In fact, in the years following these Inquisition cases, the level of violence was so high that multiple provincial councils sought to limit owners' power to punish. In 1567 the First Provincial Council outlawed particular forms of punishment because enslaved people were dying from them. Specifically, they prohibited correction with the cane, fire, or "other extraordinary punishments."[127] Moreover, they declared that noncompliant slaveholders should be denounced for not obeying the decree. In 1599 the king of Portugal, Philip I, likewise sought to limit slaveholders' power to punish in Portuguese India. Upon being informed that slaves were dying from their owners' violence followed by clandestine burials in their owners' houses and gardens, the king ordered the viceroy to begin an annual investigation into slave treatment. This annual investigation was to occur in all the Portuguese territories in the Indian Ocean region so that abusive owners could be punished and compelled to sell their slaves to new owners who would treat them well.[128] In addition, owners guilty of killing their enslaved dependents would be treated as though they had killed a free person.[129]

Seven years after the regal decree, the Fifth Provincial Council found it necessary to reiterate its position about slaveholders' violence. The opening of its decree on the topic established the normalcy of this violence as well as the bodily and spiritual repercussions suffered by the enslaved: "In order for this sacred synod to alleviate the great excess and cruelty with which slaves are punished very ordinarily in these parts, many dying in the torments, and others shortly after without any sacrament, and even hopeless, and others becoming lame and sick for their whole lives . . ."[130] Then, the decree threatened excommunication of all enslavers, regardless of whether they were "ecclesiastics, or seculars, men, or women," if they deployed a range of prohibited punishments.[131] A few of the named forms of torture included whipping with a cane, breaking enslaved people's teeth, placing pepper and other foreign substances in their eyes, dripping hot liquids on their skin, and striking them with palmers (a form of violence similarly applied in the Portuguese Atlantic).[132] After detailing the varied methods of violence, the council also warned that anyone who violated this decree directly or was complicit by allowing its violation in their house would pay a fine of fifty pardaos.[133] In sum, multiple sixteenth- and seventeenth-century decrees against violence demonstrate that enslavers habitually physically abused their enslaved dependents in Portuguese India. The violence experienced by Ilena Machada and other enslaved individuals within New Christian households did not deviate from the norms of punishment in other contemporary households.

Contested Power and Slave Agency

The violent picture of slavery emerging from these cases shows a complex story of owners harshly disciplining their slaves and slaves contesting owners' control of their behavior. As heads of households, owners enjoyed the right to punish their slaves, and inquisitors affirmed that right.[134] Yet the very actions for which slaves were allegedly punished demonstrate their efforts to create lives and livelihoods independent of their owners. Theoretically owners were the dominant party in the relationship, and in practice they utilized violence liberally for domination. However, the very need to wield violence suggested that these households were not firmly within their grasp.

In the Inquisition cases of Diogo Soares and his extended family, the defendants prepared counterstatements, which were formal preventive assertions attempting to disqualify the testimony of enemies who could potentially testify falsely. In these counterstatements, it is evident that enslaved individuals carved out spaces of agency for themselves. Particular battles for control mostly centered on ownership: owners and slaves struggled over control over slaves' bodies, extending to sexuality and freedom. In addition, control over goods (nonhuman property) was contested as well. Slaves expressed their agency and asserted power by attempting to free themselves legally, running away and converting to Islam, having unsanctioned sex, marrying without consent, stealing money and goods belonging to their owners, refusing to work, seeking new patrons, and attempting to physically harm their owners. Owners often sought to regain control over their slaves by utilizing corporal punishment.

One of the most frequent ways in which slaves asserted control over their bodies was the selection of sexual partners without the consent of their owners. This act was especially significant given that male owners often purchased female slaves for their own sexual use.[135] In counterstatement after counterstatement, female slaves were punished for allegedly bringing men into the house to sleep with them. The aforementioned Ilena Machada, formerly enslaved by Diogo Soares and Estevão Lopes, was chastised for bringing men into the house.[136] Diogo Soares's slave Violantinha likewise brought men into the house,[137] as did Ana de Oliveira and Alvaro Gomes's slaves Brianda Jaoa,[138] Brianda Guzarata,[139] and Maria Jaoa (the mother of Brianda Jaoa).[140] Maria Jaoa also had the distinction of hiring out her daughter and others for sex.[141] Antonia Malavar and Lianor Jaoa, both enslaved by Diogo Soares and Leonor Fernandes, were labeled "harlots."[142] While framed in moralistic terms that could discredit enslaved women's testimonies, these allegations simultaneously emphasized the sexual agency (and sexual labor) of enslaved women beyond the control of slaveholders.

Other enslaved individuals enhanced their material possessions by stealing from their owners. Antonia Malavar allegedly stole "many things of the house" as well as money; one night she was found with a cloak and a sword.[143] Likewise, Madanela Bengala, enslaved by Branca de Oliveira, was accused of theft. She also ran away with three other slaves to the "land of the Moors" and lived there as a Muslim for three years before being returned.[144] Flight and conversion to Islam were other modes of agency chosen by slaves to assert control.

While Madanela ran away, some slaves sought to free themselves legally through manumission. While the following attempts were unsuccessful, the details about their efforts reveal both an interest in freedom as well as the particular strategies utilized in attempting to secure it. For example, Isabel Malavar's efforts to free herself from Diogo Soares and Leonor Fernandes were mentioned at the opening of this chapter. As an expensively purchased enslaved cook who refused to work and denied her skills, Isabel also asked many people for money and secured loans for the purpose of freeing herself. She also secured the patronage of the Fathers of São Paulo, who became involved in her pursuit of freedom. Despite this public resistance to slavery, her owners were not interested in freeing her.[145] Likewise, Isabel Guzarata attempted unsuccessfully to free herself legally but was obstructed. She was a cook of Cristovão Mendes, Guiomar de Oliveira's son-in-law.[146] Like Isabel Malavar and Isabel Guzarata, Filipa Corombim sought freedom but was hindered by her owner, Ana de Oliveira. She had also been punished for marrying without consent.[147]

Beyond the pursuit of legal freedom, slaves challenged their owners in other ways. Different from the rest, Lianor Jaoa sought another means of asserting agency: sneaky revenge. She allegedly attempted to murder Leonor Fernandes by poisoning her, taking advantage of her enslaver's request for some water to drink.[148] Appealing to members of the enslaver's household was yet another tactic to improve living and working conditions. Antonia Malavar sought the help of a patron within Diogo Soares's extended family. She complained about Clara Lopes to Leonor Fernandes, Lopes's mother-in-law; for this, she was punished.[149] In sum, these incidents suggest households on which enslavers had a tenuous grip, even before the establishment of the Goa Tribunal and its intervention into the households.

A Hierarchy Turned Upside Down: The Inquisition's Amplification of Slave Voices

By intervening in households, the Inquisition amplified slave voices and destabilized the hierarchical owner-slave relationship. The hierarchy enforced by violence suddenly was reconfigured. Slaves, who had already been in the habit of seeking patrons outside the household to improve their status and living conditions when household relationships failed them, discovered new patrons in the inquisitors. On their part, however, Diogo Soares and his family saw this inquisitorial intervention as an opportunity slaves would seize to take revenge. Accordingly, the family alleged their slaves hated them, and they sought to impugn the characters of their slaves, hoping to disqualify any testimonies brought against them. At the same time, Diogo Soares and his family attempted to persuade their slaves to testify favorably.

Knowing that their enslaved dependents had a voice, Diogo Soares and his family attempted to mute it or at least influence it. After the arrest of the Cochin New Christians, mealtime became theater. Beforehand, the family had taken measures to conceal their fasting from their slaves, so as to prove to their slaves that they followed the Catholic ritual calendar rather than the Jewish one.[150] However, after the Cochin inquiry, the family completely changed their eating habits and called slaves to the dinner table so that these potential witnesses could observe and subsequently have something favorable to report regarding their culinary habits.[151] Previously derelict in their religious duties toward their enslaved dependents, the family of Diogo Soares suddenly took an interest in providing religious instruction. A mere eight days before Diogo Soares's arrest, the female slaves received Christian doctrinal instruction.[152] Thus, as slaves became potential witnesses, owners altered their behavior.

Diogo Soares and his family members allegedly pressured their slaves to both avoid the inquisitorial judges and testify favorably by offering bribes and deploying loyal slaves to influence the others. Branca de Oliveira, Guiomar de Oliveira, Ana de Oliveira, and Leonor Fernandes instructed an elderly enslaved Chinese woman named Violante to tell the younger enslaved women not to say anything, according to Madanela Bengala, who was enslaved by Branca de Oliveira. She also reported that the four slave-owning sisters sent Cristovão Mendes's slave, Belchior Pegu, for the same purpose.[153] In addition, Madanela alleged that her owner implored her to negate anything she had said against her, promising her cloths from Pulicat. The cloths were for those who took her side, while those who did not would be treated poorly.[154] Other slaves also reported that their owners attempted to bribe them. According to the testimony of Madanela Bengala, the enslaved Luzia and Filipa, owned by Branca de Oliveira and Alvaro Gomes respectively, said that their enslavers promised them freedom.[155] According to Diogo Soares's slave Isabel Malavar, he promised cloths and clothing for slaves who were on his side.[156] Lianor Jaoa, also enslaved by Diogo Soares, testified that she heard about her owner's promise of cloth.[157] Moreover, Isabel testified that after she had been removed from the household Leonor Fernandes asked five or six times for her to divulge what she had testified.[158] On the day of her arrest, Guiomar de Oliveira allegedly told her slave Briatiz Jaoa to flee so that inquisitors could not question her. While she was eventually apprehended and questioned in February 1558, Briatiz in fact did run away.[159] Her capture was rather unfortunate for Guiomar de Oliveira as Briatiz testified that her mistress attempted to bribe Maria Guzarata and Lianor Corombim: they had been given the same instructions to flee and were promised letters of freedom in return for denying what they knew and had seen.[160]

In addition to bribery and changing doctrinally suspect behaviors, Diogo Soares and his family maligned their slaves' characters. In the counterstatements described previously, they not only attempted to convey reasons why their slaves would hate them (and would testify falsely), but they also simultaneously portrayed deeds that reflected the bad character of their slaves. Stealing, sneaking male lovers into the house, and converting to Islam were hardly the actions of trustworthy witnesses of good repute. In addition to the counterstatements, Diogo Soares and his family filed a petition protesting the whole process of the investigation that had thrown them in jail. The joint petition criticized their slaves, saying that the slaves in Portuguese India were different from slaves elsewhere: they did not fear God, they ran away to the Moors, they killed their owners, and they were unintelligent.[161] In addition to the general censure of slaves in Portuguese India, the petition directed special attention to Ilena Machada, who was unnamed yet described and blamed for sending them to jail. Referring to her as a freed slave who had to be put in chains and scalded with drippings of oil, they claimed that she swore to take revenge on her owners and their family. They complained that because of this woman's words, the family was imprisoned, their goods were sequestered, and their slaves were removed.[162] In short, the inquisitors' amplification of her voice had toppled the family's hierarchical position.

In the same petition, Diogo Soares and his family members complained about the secrecy embedded in the inquisitorial process. They felt it was unjust that they were not given the names of their denunciators.[163] This lack of knowledge, apparent in the petition, also surfaced in Diogo's family's counterstatements. They cited people they thought would testify injuriously against them. The names they chose when compared to the actual informants highlight the vulnerable position of the New Christian family. On the whole, slaves predominated in the counterstatement lists. However, Diogo and his family did not always identify the right slaves who testified against them. Diogo was rather accurate, though he overshot in his list of counterstatements. Some defendants only guessed one or two actual denunciators.[164] This situation of not knowing who would testify, and accordingly what information would be divulged, explains why slaveholders would employ multiple tactics to protect themselves: they defamed a large number of slaves, while also trying to bribe them.

Despite the family's efforts, inquisitors accepted slaves' words. Empowered by inquisitors, slaves propelled their tormentors into a four-year process of jail, interrogation, and removal from India. Of course, slaves' participation in these cases was not entirely voluntary.[165] In fact, some had no interest in testifying against their owners. For example, recall that Briatiz Jaoa first fled after the arrest of her enslaver, only testifying after she was captured. Moreover, it would be mistaken to assume that these slaves gained freedom through the arrest of their enslavers. The cases do not record what became of them after their owners' journey to Lisbon. Moreover, after their owners' initial arrest, slaves were placed in other households and even in jail. Brianda Guzarata, Alvaro Gomes's enslaved housekeeper, was placed in jail.[166] Isabel Malavar was "deposited in the house of the factor."[167] This placement of slaves highlights the lack of control they had over their own lives even after the detainment of their owners. While this particular owner-slave hierarchy was destabilized, inquisitorial intervention did not mean an overhaul of slavery itself.

DOCUMENTING SLAVERY AND FREEDOM: RECORDING STATUS AND HOUSEHOLD TIES

The upheaval these slaves experienced at the household level lends itself to a further consideration of household ties, slave status, and the meaning of freedom. As seen above, enslaved individuals did not become free after the removal of their owners. Instead, they were placed in other households: an unattached slave was unacceptable in society.[168] At the same time, however, freedom itself was attractive. It is significant that both sides of the inquisitorial process—the prosecution and defense—allegedly offered freedom as an enticement. Moreover, we saw that some slaves sought freedom in multiple ways, ranging from self-purchase to flight. Yet both slaves and freed slaves retained ties to the households in which they were enslaved. Even after freedom, these ties sometimes even persisted into death. The persistence of these ties meant that bonds were hard to break: the legal dissolution of bondage through manumission did not mean a severance of the bond itself.[169] Moreover, for those who remained enslaved, both their status and their ties to a household were re-inscribed upon their deaths. The free soul was still memorialized as one housed in an enslaved body. Church officials recorded slave status and the continuation of household ties, distinguishing the enslaved and freed from the larger free population.[170]

Documenting Bonds of the Freed

Church officials documented slave and freed status, besides regulating who could be enslaved. The Father of Christians, for example, recorded manumissions. Entrusted with the duty of protecting all Christian converts, he documented the details of slaves' passage from slavery to freedom. The Father of Christians' records of manumissions from Goa are still available, covering the years 1682 to 1760.[171] The Father of Christians recorded the name of the slave, date of manumission registration, the owner, the owner's residence, age, dependency status, caste, the remaining years of servitude, whether the person was deposited by the Father of Christians, the slave's status as a catechumen, and the price paid for the slave, among other details. These details come from a sample of three hundred ninety-five entries from 1682 to 1707.[172] A range of ambiguous unfree statuses also appeared, including those who legally should not have been enslaved.

Most importantly, all who were documented were confirmed as freed people either immediately or after a fixed period of service. For many in the records, freedom was a process with a fixed period of servitude allotted before the actual granting of freedom, similar to the predicament of conditional freedom found elsewhere in the Iberian world.[173] For example, from 1682 to 1700, slaves might remain in bondage for an additional two to nineteen years.[174] This long range in bondage was even apparent in 1682. For example, the enslaved Aldonça was ordered to labor two more years for Jorge Dias Ribeiro before receiving her freedom, while the eleven-year-old Ilena was stuck laboring nineteen years for Dona Maria de Mello, assuming that the terms of the manumission agreements were respected and the freed slaves did not perish ahead of time.[175] In my sample, one hundred sixty-four slaves had remaining service requirements before acquiring freedom.[176]

Immediate freedom did not necessarily equate to a separation between freed slaves and their former enslavers. Freed slaves spared the burden of additional service requirements often remained in their former owners' households. For example, Clara and Serafina, enslaved by Izabel Parras, were freed in 1682 but lacked service requirements, although they remained in their former owner's household.[177] In same year, the nine-year-old Estevão entered the manumission records, documented as freed but remaining in Pero Ferrão's household without formally owing any labor.[178] In total, 195 freed slaves in the sample fit this description in the manumission records. In other words, involuntary servitude had ended, and they were freed, yet their tie to the household remained.

Documenting Bonds in Death

Slavery followed the memory of the deceased as the stigma of slavery accompanied slaves to the grave. In death their status as a slave was documented. In addition, their ties to an owner were recorded. Thus, ties to the owner's household persisted. Even in freedom, the specter of slavery followed in death. Ex-slaves were explicitly recorded as "freed," separating them from the free population whose deaths lacked any mention of prior enslavement. Thus, their personal history of slavery was not erased but rather memorialized. Moreover, ties with former owners were sometimes recorded, although this pattern was not consistent. The continuation of these bonds reflected the stickiness of slave status in Portuguese India.

Death records documented slavery. Responsible for all parishioners, priests recorded the name of the deceased, date of death, stage of life (adult or child), residence, burial location, payment of funeral expenses, the presence of a testament (including the names of testators), caste and ethnicity, parental information, spousal information, the financial status of the deceased, and slave or freed status when applicable. While not all these details uniformly appeared, they painted a picture of the parish that included the presence and status of the enslaved deceased. One such parish replete with extant records is São Bartolomeu on the island of Chorão in Ilhas, the same district containing the city of Goa. In the 2,453 death entries recorded in this parish from 1682 to 1708, 142 slaves appeared along with 5 freed slaves.[179] The pattern for slave entries distinguished them from the free. At death, the bonded deceased were remembered as slaves, captives, or children of enslaved mothers. Their status was also indicated by "*moço/moça de,*" "*cafre/cafra de,*" or other ethnic descriptors, with the possessive "*de*" linking the enslaved dependent to an owner. Not only were they continuously categorized as unfree, but the agent enforcing their unfreedom was also remembered: the link between the living enslaver and deceased slave was memorialized. Examples from the year 1684 exemplify the persistent tie between owners and slaves at death. That year 169 people died.[180] Of these deaths, there were five slaves and two ex-slaves. In death Andresa was described as the "*cafrinha* slave of Paschoal Pires."[181] As Joana was remembered as the "*cafra* slave of Francisco Pinto," her tie to her enslaver was also simultaneously recognized in death.[182] Bestowed the same surname of his enslaver, Francisco Gomes was remembered as the "creole (*criolo*) of Lourenço Gomes."[183] Both the maternal bond and owner bond were recorded for the young enslaved Lourenço, remembered as the "child of Jacinta the slave of João de Bragança."[184] Similarly, João the young son of Paulinha was also linked to an owner, as Paulinha was described as the "*moça balgaty*' of the house of

Francisco de Bragança."[185] This pattern of documented affiliation persisted throughout the records of deceased slaves.

Sometimes freed slaves lacked a recorded affiliation to their former enslaver. The previously enslaved Francisco was memorialized as the "freed young man [*moço forro*] of Lourenço Fernandez" in 1684.[186] Yet Baptista was only remembered as a "freed young man" upon his death in 1684; his former owner went unrecorded.[187] The other three freed slaves who appeared in the death register also did not follow a set pattern. In death João was tied to Paschoal Pires in 1683, and Francisco was tied to the "house of Antonio Dessa" in 1691; however, in 1696 the freed cafre João was only described as serving "in the house of João Antonio."[188] As freed slaves did not always have to work for their previous owners, we do not know if João Antonio was a former owner or a wholly new employer. Thus, the specter of slavery lingered in the records of both the enslaved and freed, even though ties of affiliation were not always recorded for the freed. This remembrance of past slavery appeared through the act of categorization. The very term "freed" distinguished the previously enslaved from their free counterparts even in death.

* * *

In the Portuguese Indian context, slaves generally experienced their bondage in households. In a paternalistic relationship, they were tied to their patrons, who exercised power through punishment.[189] The authority to punish reflected the hierarchical nature of the relationship between enslavers and the enslaved as the applier of punishment had the socially recognized authority to sanction the lesser party. The form of punishment chosen was often violence, which occurred as an effort to assert control over enslaved bodies and regain the power slaves contested.

Ties between enslaved individuals and their enslavers were memorialized in death and even followed the freed upon manumission. Central to the documentation of status were church officials, who recorded slaves' ties to households. These household ties were at the root of slavery in Portuguese India, where imperial-religious regulations bolstered the relationship between enslaved individuals and their owners. The nature of this relationship and its imperial significance will be explored in the next chapter.

TWO

Enslavers as Religious Stewards

IN A MULTIYEAR saga beginning in 1557, the New Christian Estevão Lopes found himself in the clutches of the Portuguese Inquisition. Along with other members of Diogo Soares's extended family, he and his wife, Guiomar de Oliveira, stood accused of practicing Judaism. The specific charges against him, however, included far more than a simple allegation of departing from the Catholic faith. Among his alleged misdeeds was his failure to be a religious steward to his enslaved dependents. In particular, he "ordered [his slaves] to work on the holidays that the Holy Mother Church command[ed] to observe."[1] Moreover, he neglected to order his slaves to "confess in the time that the Church command[ed]."[2] In other words, the enslaved Catholics for whom he was responsible had missed the Lenten confession due to his dereliction.

These charges regarding his (non)performance of religious stewardship emerged from the content of denunciations, such as the one provided by the enslaved Briatiz Jaoa. Referring to Estevão's wife, she described Guiomar de Oliveira's resistance to her attempts to make the annual confession during Lent. She only confessed twice, and this was gained only by substantial complaining. Moreover, according to Briatiz, her mistress accused her of confessing Guiomar's sins instead of her own. In addition, Briatiz recounted that she only saw one other slave sent to confession: Lianor Corombim, whom she saw go once.[3] She also commented on the lack of Christian instruction provided by her enslavers.[4] While Guiomar de Oliveira featured heavily in this account, ultimately Estevão was blamed in the inquisitorial context. As the head of the household, he bore enough responsibility that the details of his wife's alleged failures were included in his own Inquisition case.

Estevão, however, had a different account of his performance as a religious steward. He insisted in his defense that he was a "very good Christian" as well as a "friend of God."[5] As part of the proof of his status, he made his enslaved dependents work on Saturdays (rather than Sundays) and sent them to confess during Lent.[6] Witnesses appeared on his behalf, answering questions about Estevão's various defense statements and joining the collective conversation about his Christian status. For example, when queried about Estevão's claims about slave work and confession, the witness Lopo Vaz affirmed that enslaved individuals labored on Saturday (the Jewish Sabbath) and were ordered to confess, also noting that he considered Estevão to be a "good Christian and friend of God."[7] Thus, Estevão's performance as a religious steward within the household was observed, debated, and judged. His religious responsibilities were a socially recognized symbol of his status in the colonial Catholic community.

The church molded households into the larger Catholic imperial image by delegating the duties of religious stewardship to enslavers. This ecclesiastical intervention in the household occurred in the larger context of the Catholic Reformation.[8] Committed to creating a thoroughly Christianized population anchored in orthodoxy, both the Inquisition and the provincial councils sought to discipline enslavers to conform to the assigned duties of religious stewardship. Commanded to facilitate conversion and safeguard spiritual growth, slaveholders had the responsibilities of ensuring baptism, giving religious instruction, respecting marital rights, honoring the Sunday Sabbath, allowing mass attendance, promoting the Lenten confession, and providing a burial. From an ecclesiastical perspective, slaveholders' faithful adherence to these duties would create a Catholic empire at the household level and usher enslaved individuals into the larger Christian society; such feats could not be accomplished by the official church apparatus alone. In the Portuguese Indian context, then, church-mandated religious stewardship was a fundamental aspect of the owner-slave relationship. By performing the role of religious stewards, enslavers confirmed their status as good Christians; failure to provide religious stewardship provoked sanctions and inquisitorial discipline. Unsurprisingly, they resisted elements of religious stewardship as these obligations toward their enslaved dependents corroded their ownership rights.

The obligations of religious stewardship mirrored church-backed rights for enslaved Catholics, similarly to the Iberian American colonial context. Examining the impact of the Catholic Church in his classic comparative analysis of slavery in Protestant and Catholic colonies, Frank Tannenbaum remarks on religious stewardship as well as the interconnection between enslavers' religious obligations and the religious rights of enslaved Catholics:

> Whatever the formal relations between slave and master, they must both recognize their relationship to each other as moral human beings and as brothers in Christ. The master had an obligation to protect the spiritual integrity of the slave, to teach him the Christian religion, to help him achieve the privileges of the sacraments, to guide him into living a good life, and to protect him from mortal sin. The slave had a right to become a Christian, to be baptized, and to be considered a member of the Christian community. Baptism was considered his entrance into the community, and until he was sufficiently instructed to be able to receive it, he was looked upon as out of the community and as something less than human.[9]

Tannenbaum's insights about this idealized conceptualization of rights and obligations fit the Portuguese Indian context. Yet slaveholder resistance meant that enslaved Catholics had to push for their rights, as Michelle McKinley emphasizes in her analysis of slavery in colonial Lima, where slaves likewise had religious rights and owners had religious obligations mandated by the Catholic Church.[10] Slave agency was essential. Instead of harmonious households that automatically conformed to the ideals of religious stewardship, struggles between enslavers and their enslaved dependents ensued when slaveholders failed to perform their obligations and slaves asserted their religious rights. Bound up in this struggle over obligations and rights was the extent to which enslaved individuals had the right to belong as full members of colonial Catholic society.

RELIGIOUS STEWARDSHIP AT THE CONCEPTION OF THE OWNER-SLAVE RELATIONSHIP

The church sought to mandate religious stewardship from the beginning of the owner-slave relationship. In order to spur slaves' conversion to Catholicism and their continuation in the Catholic faith, the church restricted who had the legal right to own slaves. Because of the connection between mastery and religious stewardship, only Christians had the right to own slaves. This was an infringement on ownership rights. Non-Christian slaveholders lost their right to own slaves, while Christian owners lost the right to sell their slaves to whomever and wherever they wished. Intervening in the household, the church upheld slavery for the religious patronage the owner-slave relationship provided, exalting religious stewardship above enslavers' economic interests in slavery.

The provincial councils promoted religious stewardship by intervening in the owner-slave relationship at its inception, whether at the time of purchase or the birth of the enslaved person into the owner's household. In 1567 the First Provincial Council wrote decrees removing Christian slaves from non-Christian owners. Upon reaching the age of discretion, slaves of non-Christian owners had recourse to their owners' opposition to conversion to Catholicism. Upon their baptism, they were to be put in the "houses of virtuous, God-fearing people," a rescue from unbelieving slaveholders that was meant to facilitate the Christian instruction of enslaved individuals.[11] The same council also decreed that non-Christian enslavers could not own Christian slaves, promising freedom to Christian slaves owned by non-Christians.[12] This pairing of Christian slaves with Christian owners was reinforced in an undated imperial law following the Third Provincial Council, which convened in 1585. This law outlined categories of unsuitable owners of Christian slaves:

Jews, "pagans," and heretics. The law also mandated freedom for those enslaved Christians. Moreover, if non-Christian slaves of Jews, "pagans," or heretics wished to convert to Catholicism, then such slaves would be freed.[13] The Fourth Provincial Council, held in 1592, continued to pair Christian slaves with Christian owners. Any owner selling an enslaved Christian to a non-Christian faced the prospect of being "rigorously punished," and the enslaved Christian would be freed.[14] In addition, the same decree barred slaveholding Christians from selling their non-Christian slaves to non-Christian owners. Similarly, the Fifth Provincial Council prohibited Muslims and Jews from purchasing "pagan" slaves in 1606.[15] From a religious standpoint, the councils assumed the influence of Christian owners would eventually draw those enslaved dependents into Christendom.

Seventeenth- and eighteenth-century Goan manumission records likewise reflected this ideal of religious stewardship at the conception of the owner-slave relationship. Manumissions were recorded by the Father of Christians, who was responsible for all new converts. As owners brought their slaves to the Father of Christians in order to register their manumission, some even claimed to have purchased slaves for the sake of the ensuing conversions.[16] For example, in 1682 Francisco Ribeiro presented the seven-year-old enslaved Antonio, who was "purchased to make Christian."[17] To ensure the continuation of this religious stewardship, the Father of Christians ordered fourteen more years of bondage before Antonio's eventual freedom.[18] Similarly, in 1682 Luis Carvalho do Rego participated in the rhetoric of religious stewardship. He presented his eleven-year-old slave, also named Luis, who was "purchased to make Christian."[19] The Father of Christians mandated ten more years of servitude, facilitating a continuation of religious stewardship.[20] Such decisions simultaneously prolonged slaveholders' economic advantages accrued by slave labor, creating an instance in which religious stewardship and the financial benefits of ownership converged.

The Father of Christians also used the rhetoric of religious stewardship and upheld the ideal of slavery for the purpose of conversion. In 1682 the enslaved Joana received four years of continued servitude before her manumission "for the benefit of making [her a] Christian" in the household of Domingos Gomes.[21] The enslaved Ursula, Gracia, and Rafael faced similar fates when their manumissions were recorded that year, owing service to Antonio da Silva de Mello for the same "benefit" of conversion to Catholicism expected in their owner's household.[22] Bound up in these manumission records was the connection between conversion and slavery, and this connection was best ensured by the placement of enslaved individuals into Catholic households under the guardianship of religious stewards. As Patrícia Souza de Faria notes, the Father of Christians saw unfree labor as an exchange for the spiritual and material benefits gained in the Catholic household. Religious concerns over the patronage of new converts even overrode the right to freedom, as the Father of Christians endorsed and perpetuated illegal enslavement in order to ensure that Catholic converts were attached to Catholic households.[23] This acquisition of unfree labor for the purpose of religious stewardship had earlier antecedents. In the late sixteenth century, the newly converted Gabriel Abexim found himself placed by Dominican fathers in the household of a Christian Abyssinian woman without any indication of how long this service would persist. He ultimately escaped this religious stewardship, only to regain it through new forms of bondage when sentenced repeatedly by the Inquisition in 1595.[24] In sum, whether or not their claims to unfree labor were legally legitimate, slaveholders received the church-mandated role of religious stewardship from the moment of acquiring slaves.

DEFINING THE DUTIES OF RELIGIOUS STEWARDSHIP

The provincial councils assigned specific duties to enslavers as religious stewards. Upon the birth or purchase of an enslaved person, the first duty of slaveholders as religious stewards was to baptize their enslaved dependent. This was a critical duty because it represented the slave's passage into the Christian community. Upon baptism, the slave's status shifted to Christian, which was a religious, social, and legal category. With this change in status came the conferral of church-mandated rights for slaves, which mirrored owners' obligations. Enslaved Christians had the right to attend mass, observe the Sunday Sabbath and holidays, receive Christian instruction, confess during Lent, marry, and receive a Christian burial. Parish records provide a look at the performance of some of these rights and corresponding duties.

Baptism

The baptism of enslaved dependents constituted an act of religious stewardship that began with birth—either physical birth into an owner's household or social rebirth through the act of a Christian owner's purchase. The Third Provincial Council in 1585 required Christians who purchased slaves to arrange their baptisms. Slaveholders had one month to baptize children under the age of ten and a longer window of six months to baptize adults who would receive Christian instruction during the waiting period. While the decree acknowledged adults should only be baptized within the specified time period if they had an interest, the expectation of religious stewardship was clear. Owners who failed to baptize their enslaved dependents were subject to a fine of ten pardaos. Moreover, the church threatened to fine negligent owners whose slaves died without having received the sacrament of baptism.[25]

Portuguese laws preceded and followed this ecclesiastical expectation of religious stewardship. The 1514 Portuguese law code, the Manueline Ordinances, delegated the responsibility of slaves' baptisms to their enslavers. Depending on the age of their enslaved dependent, owners had between one to three months to ensure the baptism. Failure to perform the religious duty within the mandated period exposed owners to the loss of legal ownership. In this breach of duty, the crown gained the right of ownership, with the exception of cases in which enslaved adults and children over the age of ten rejected baptism. Thus, to a certain extent, there was an acknowledgment of the varied forms of slaves' religious agency: some would enter the Catholic community, whereas others would decline.[26]

The Philippine Ordinances, which replaced the Manueline Ordinances in 1603, again delegated the duty of baptism to slaveholders. The new code specified a six-month period for baptism, which was longer than the Manueline Ordinances' specification yet similar to the Third Provincial Council's baptism window. Moreover, the code disciplined delinquent religious stewards by stripping of them of their ownership rights: a potential owner could file a suit against the current slaveholder and thereby gain ownership of the unbaptized slaves. Thus, enslavers were legally vulnerable to others who presented themselves as worthier religious stewards. Yet the new law code again acknowledged the possibility that some slaves over the age of ten would refuse baptism altogether. In the event of an enslaved person's refusal, however, the duties of religious stewardship were not automatically abrogated. Owners had the responsibility of formally certifying their attempt to discharge their duty of religious stewardship. This action consisted of notifying the curate of the parish, who then heard the enslaved individual's rejection of the sacrament in the presence of witnesses.[27] In this way, both ecclesiastical and imperial laws conceptualized the role of enslavers as religious stewards whose duties included baptism.

Parish records from São Bartolomeu in Goa documented the performance of religious stewardship by recording baptisms. These records included the baptisms of both enslaved and free parishioners, similar to the continental Portuguese inclusion of Catholics inhabiting different statuses together in the records.[28] Among the approximately 1,768 people whose baptisms were recorded from 1685 to 1717, eighty-four concerned slaves ranging from infancy to adulthood.[29] By presenting their enslaved dependents for baptism, owners created connections in the Catholic community that extended beyond the household. The act of baptism created a link between the enslaved individual and the priest, who represented the larger institution of the church. Moreover, the act of baptism created a formal link between the enslaved individual and their godparents, additional patrons usually beyond the household who helped enmesh the slave in the wider Catholic community. In this way, the enslaved Miguel and Domingos, documented as "adults," underwent a change in status on June 23, 1691. On that date, Miguel de Sá, the curate of the church, baptized both and recorded their godfather as João da Costa de Lima.[30] Following the continental Portuguese custom, the overwhelming majority of slaves received at least one if not two godparents; only ten were bereft of a sponsor.[31] These institutionalized ties to godparents included the free, such as the clergyman assigned to Miguel and Domingos above, as well as fellow slaves. For example, in 1694 the enslaved Estevão received a free godfather, Domingos Rois the sacristan, in addition to an enslaved godmother, Isabel; both Estevão and his godmother shared the same owner, Chrisostomo Lobo.[32] Some godparent ties remained entirely within the household. For instance, the enslaved

Martinho's godfather, assigned to him in 1702, was his owner's slave Pedro.[33] Similarly, at the time of his baptism in 1693, both the enslaved João and his godfather were owned by Joseph Vas.[34] In short, when priests baptized slaves, the owner's religious stewardship was recorded in addition to the slave's change in religious status and the formalization of links to other Christians beyond the owner.

Interim Acts of Religious Stewardship

Covering the entire life cycle, the church mandated acts of religious stewardship that encompassed the interim period between birth and death. The Third Provincial Council decreed that slaves should receive Christian instruction, emphasizing this need in the context of a larger societal lack of religious knowledge in the region.[35] Similarly, the church codified its expectation that slaveholders would facilitate their enslaved dependents' observance of the Christian Sabbath and church attendance. The Fifth Provincial Council barred owners from making slaves—both male and female—work on Sundays and holidays; noncompliant owners were threatened with a fine of five pardaos, which would be paid to the accuser. Moreover, slaveholders were prohibited from sending their enslaved dependents to sell merchandise on the streets on Sundays and holidays; the same fine of five pardaos was applied. In addition, slaves and freed slaves who sold merchandise on the street would lose their wares or pay a fine of one tanga.[36] Thus, not only was the enslaved seller culpable of a religious transgression, but the enslaver also faced condemnation as a derelict religious steward.

Religious stewardship extended to the protection of slaves' marriages. This ecclesiastical protection set slave marriage in the early modern Portuguese Indian Ocean apart from the Dutch Indian Ocean, where enslaved individuals lacked access to formal marriage.[37] In 1592 the Fourth Provincial Council threatened owners with excommunication, charging that creating impediments to slave marriage was unacceptable. The council even protected marriages that had not been sanctioned by owners; thus, the church's sanction of the union overrode the enslaver's lack of consent. In addition, once slaves married, owners were to promote the marriage's welfare by keeping the spouses within a reasonable distance of each other so as to facilitate the conjugal "usage of the marriage." Specifically, the council barred the sale of married slaves "out of the land," fining offending owners two hundred xerafins and excommunicating them. Half the fine was reserved for the person accusing the guilty owner.[38] In 1606 the Fifth Provincial Council reiterated the church's support for slave marriage and the expectation that owners would respect the sacrament; again, the council stated that owners were neither to hinder the marriage itself nor obstruct the "usage" of the marriage. The same fine was reiterated along with the half portion devoted to the slaveholder's accuser. In addition, this council protected the marriage of enslaved individuals to freed slaves; owners were responsible for protecting those unions by not selling a married slave out of the area. The council was also more specific as to what constituted a sale too far away from a marriage partner: the enslaved spouse could not be sold "outside the same coast."[39] Thus, the church incrementally extended more protection to slaves' marriages, intervening in the owner-slave relationship while simultaneously recognizing owners as religious stewards and slaves as Catholics with rights.

Burial

Besides charging enslavers to act as religious stewards during the lives of their enslaved dependents, the church expected owners to continue this stewardship through death to assist slaves' souls. The First Provincial Council codified this expectation. The councilmen lamented that some owners had been "careless in helping the souls of their deceased slaves."[40] According to the decree, there were owners who were failing to bury their slaves properly with the required masses for their souls. To prevent this neglect of slaves' souls, the council ordered that every owner ensure three masses for the enslaved dependent. This responsibility also included notifying the curate of the parish to accomplish a proper burial.[41] In this critical spiritual moment, the owner acted as the liaison between the church and the deceased slave. The only owners excused from this duty were the indigent, because they could not afford the expense. Fulfilling this duty of religious stewardship was theologically essential in the Catholic context because of the belief in purgatory. This belief was affirmed in the contemporaneous Tridentine Profession of Faith: "I steadfastly hold that there is a Purgatory, and that the souls detained there are helped by the acts of intercession of the faithful."[42]

Accordingly, the responsibility of potentially shortening slaves' stay in the "purgatorial period of purification" fell under the purview of slaveholders.[43] Hence, the souls of deceased slaves still had socially recognized claims on their enslavers as religious stewards. Death did not sever the religious bonds of the owner-slave relationship.

Religious stewardship's extension to the earthly grave and eternity appeared in both the empire and continental Portugal. Like in Portuguese India, the problem of burial surfaced in sixteenth-century Lisbon. Some slaveholders in the metropole ignored their responsibilities toward slaves, leading to the exposure of the bodies of the enslaved dead. This spurred King Manuel's instructions in 1515 for the creation of a burial pit in the city, which gained yet another in 1594.[44] Despite this continued dishonor for some, apparently "most Christian slaves" in Portugal were dignified with a "full Christian burial."[45] Part of this process of Christian burial was facilitated by slaveholders, who paid the necessary expenses. Through religious stewardship and the backing of the church, enslaved Catholics were buried on church property, including not only churchyards but also within church edifices.[46]

This religious stewardship in Portuguese India was apparent in the death records of São Bartolomeu from 1682 to 1708. As mentioned in chapter 1, 142 slaves appeared in the death records alongside free parishioners, and in these records the owner-slave tie was documented. This documentation of affiliation was a reiteration of the slave status of the deceased. Yet this memorialization of slave status was also accompanied by the memorialization of the enslavers who dutifully performed their religious obligations toward their slaves. Universally lacking testaments and vulnerable after death, deceased slaves in the parish relied on their enslavers to act on their behalf as religious stewards. Approximately seventy-eight distinct slaveholders were documented as they took care of their deceased enslaved dependents.[47]

One of these religious stewards, Chrisostomo Lobo, appeared in the records on behalf of fourteen deceased slaves from 1689 to 1708.[48] This local Goan Christian's acts of religious stewardship included paying a fee for at least five of his enslaved dependents; he paid the *fabrica* for the enslaved Joana and paid six tangas each for the others.[49] It is unknown whether he made a payment to cover the expenses of the remaining nine slaves. Yet this lack of a recorded payment was common. Of all the enslaved individuals recorded, ninety-six had entries lacking payment information.[50] The remaining entries indicated that owners paid six tangas for twenty-two slaves, three tangas for twelve slaves, the fabrica for seven slaves, and half the fabrica for five slaves.[51] Thus, while there was a range of possible payments, the overwhelming majority lacked this information. In the case of Chrisostomo, however, it would be surprising if he did not pay anything for the burials of his enslaved dependents whose payment information was unrecorded. Given his status, he likely would not have met the requirement of poverty to avoid burial expenses. He was a knight of the Order of St. James and held the city of Goa's post of master physician and apothecary, besides having the distinction of being a *desai-mor* (presumably a head councilman) of Bardez.[52] On his land in the parish, he even had his own hermitage.[53] Also, in terms of status, he was a Brahman on whose land other individuals lived.[54]

Just as the burial payments varied in the parish of São Bartolomeu, the particular locations assigned to enslaved individuals varied as well. From 1682 to 1708, deceased slaves were buried inside and outside the parish church. Seventy-five slaves, representing slightly over half the buried enslaved deceased population, possessed the distinction of a burial inside the church, having a documented location of "the body of the church" or "inside the church." Sixty-five enslaved individuals were buried outside, with locations described as the cemetery and the churchyard. The remaining two slaves lacked a recorded burial location.[55] Even at the household level, an assortment of burial locations existed. For example, the priest recorded two different locations for Chrisostomo Lobo's fourteen enslaved dependents in the death records. Nine slaves were buried inside the church, while four had graves outside in the cemetery and another lacked a recorded burial location.[56] Thus, even though they both perished in 1698, had the same documented East African ethnicity, and shared the same owner, the enslaved Joana was buried in the "body of the church," while Matheus was buried outside in the cemetery.[57]

While deceased Christian slaves were buried alongside the free, burial itself did not equate to equal status. The variation in burial locations described among the enslaved was also apparent within the parish's larger Catholic population. Priests who recorded free parishioners as "poor" not only documented their economic status but sometimes blatantly connected their place of burial to their lack of fortune. The vicar Roque Dias recorded Maria Gonçalves's December 1683 death, noting that she was "poor and as such is buried in the cemetery of this church."[58] Similarly the widowed Catarina Rodrigues's burial in the same location was explicitly linked to her poverty after her April 1684 death.[59] Yet impoverishment was not an assured determinant of an outside burial location, as some poor parishioners were buried inside. For instance, Augustinho Gomes was buried in the "body of this church," and the vicar recording the 1683 death linked the burial location to his poverty.[60] In like manner, in 1684 the impoverished Diogo Dias was buried in the "body of this church"; while his poverty was noted, the vicar did not explicitly correlate the location of burial with his economic status.[61] In sum, the sacred space of church property consisted of different burial locations for members of the Catholic community, yet democratized access did not exist.

Judging from the death records, the enslaved deceased did not enjoy access to all the available church burial locations. Unsurprisingly, none of the recorded slaves were afforded the honor of having their own familial perpetual grave. Thus, in death they existed apart from more elite families whose genealogical lineages were celebrated in the solace of a shared grave. Accordingly, no enslaved individual had the comfort of an expected interment next to a relative, unlike someone such as the free Hieronimo da Fonseca Monis, who knew that his own body would rest alongside the corpses of his parents in their perpetual grave.[62] Along the same lines, enslaved dependents were not interred in the perpetual grave of their owners' families, suggesting that hierarchical distinctions within slaveholding households were still preserved at death. Enslaved Catholics were remembered as fellow Christians but not as blood relations. Just as there were tiers of status within the broader Catholic community, there were tiers within the household itself that were spatially reflected through burial sites. Moreover, as mentioned previously, slaves' unfree status was documented in death, distinguishing them from other members of the community. Thus, unequal social status appeared in the act of burial as well as the documentation of burial. Yet above all, notwithstanding this social stratification, enslaved Catholics were recognized in death as members of the local Catholic community. A proper burial acted as a proxy for community recognition.[63] Their burials as fellow Catholics reflected not only their social incorporation but also the broader Portuguese project of making a Catholic empire in the Indian Ocean—a project that extended to slavery.

RELIGIOUS STEWARDSHIP AND SLAVEHOLDER STATUS

Enslavers proved that they were good Christians by fulfilling their role as religious stewards. One forum in which their performance of religious stewardship was judged was the inquisitorial court. Looking to the owner-slave relationship, inquisitors assessed owners' status as good Christians by examining whether they were good religious stewards of their enslaved dependents. Accordingly, on the inquisitorial stage a conversation among owners, slaves, and witnesses ensued about religious stewardship. In the mid-sixteenth-century cases against the aforementioned Estevão Lopes and his extended New Christian family, defendants insisted they had fulfilled the duties of religious stewardship. Defense witnesses then commented on defendants' actions as religious stewards, often commenting favorably about the fulfillment of the duties. Yet enslaved denunciators focused on slaveholders' resistance to religious stewardship, claiming that owners failed to perform their religious obligations. The timing of these cases is significant because they preceded the provincial councils' codification of the duties of religious stewardship. There was already an expectation of religious stewardship in addition to the idea that the performance of religious stewardship was such a proxy for one's own Christian status that it could be judged.

Enslaved denunciators listed specific examples of owners' faulty religious stewardship. The enslaved Antonia Malavar testified that she had not been allowed to go to church or make her annual confession during Lent.[64] And regarding Christian instruction, she claimed that only in the eight days before her enslaver Diogo Soares's arrest was any attempt made to teach the enslaved females.[65] Antonia also mentioned that an enslaved eunuch named Bastião was sold away to Portugal after having critiqued Diogo's failures as a religious steward: he neglected to order his enslaved dependents to make the Lenten confession. Adding to his blistering assessment of Diogo, Bastião also included Leonor Fernandes in his critique by allegedly telling the children that the married slaveholding couple were Jews.[66] Madanela Bengala, who was enslaved by Branca de Oliveira, testified that she had only confessed twice in twenty years, and those confessions were obtained by complaining about being a "Christian servant of a Jew."[67] Likewise, in her denunciation of Branca de Oliveira, Luzia Corombim reported that her enslaver had prevented her from attending church. Moreover, in the two years she had spent in the household, she had not been allowed to confess.[68] Alvaro Gomes's slave, also named Madanela Bengala, remarked about the lack of slave confession broadly before turning to a dramatic failure of religious stewardship in that regard. Three young enslaved females of the house had died without having confessed, even though there had been sufficient time for this spiritual succor: two had suffered from an illness for four to five months, and the other, a fifteen-year-old, had been sick for a year.[69] Maria Jaoa, who was enslaved by Ana de Oliveira, testified about having a work schedule that violated the Christian Sabbath and interfered with observing holidays.[70] The freedwoman Ilena Machada also commented on slaves' work schedule, noting that her former owners had made their slaves work on Sundays and holidays but only when necessary.[71] These collective commentaries on religious stewardship painted a picture of enslavers who had neglected the duties of good Christians.

Contrary to the denunciations of their slaves, the defendants insisted that they were good religious stewards. Claiming to be "good Christians" constituted part of their overall defense against the charge of practicing Judaism. As slaveholders, evidence of being a good Christian included the religious stewardship of their enslaved workforce. Diogo Soares insisted in his own defense that he was a "good Christian," including his wife Leonor's participation in their joint responsibility as religious stewards. Not only were their children ordered to learn Christian doctrine, but their enslaved dependents were also instructed in the faith and made their yearly confession.[72] Leonor herself confirmed that their slaves received Christian instruction. She ended her defense, arguing that she was a "very good Christian [and] friend of God . . . and always instructed her children and slaves."[73] In short, enslavers recognized that their status as good Christians was tied to fulfilling specific obligations as religious stewards of their enslaved dependents. In the making of a Catholic empire, a direct connection between piety and slave ownership existed, and this connection was continuously reinforced.

Witnesses for the defense correlated religious stewardship with social standing as a good Christian. In Branca de Oliveira's case, twelve witnesses commented on the work schedule of her enslaved dependents. Some uncertainty surfaced in the testimonies. However, most defense witnesses confidently affirmed that neither the defendant nor her slaves abstained from labor on Saturdays (the Jewish Sabbath), occasionally adding an explicit statement about the observance of Sundays and Catholic holidays.[74] On the whole, the presence of Saturday slave labor was a proxy for the entire household's celebration of the Sunday Christian Sabbath. Yet in the end inquisitors accepted the enslaved denunciators' claims over the words of the defendants and their supporters. To the inquisitors who accepted the denunciations, slaves' lack of indoctrination, spotty confession record, and nonobservance of the Christian Sabbath symbolized the irreverence of their owners. Slaveholders were presumed to be religious stewards in the owner-slave hierarchy; failure to act as a proper religious steward invited the possibility of social censure and inquisitorial discipline.

ENSLAVER RESISTANCE TO RELIGIOUS STEWARDSHIP

As seen in the Inquisition records, enslavers did not always conform to their role as religious stewards. Instead, some chose to shirk their obligations, denying slaves of their church-granted rights. Moreover, the provincial councils acknowledged slaveholders' resistance by reiterating decrees and adding higher penalties. However, resistance to religious stewardship did not necessarily equate to a wholesale rejection of the ideal. Despite the aforementioned New Christians' (non)performance of their religious obligations, they still spoke the rhetoric of religious stewardship. In addition, enslavers embraced particular duties of religious stewardship while ignoring others. Slaveholders' approach to marriage is a prime example of the selective performance of religious stewardship.

Promoting the sacrament of marriage and protecting conjugal rights were duties of religious stewardship that not only challenged enslavers' ownership rights but also limited their control over the enslaved body in ways unparalleled by other religious obligations. Their other duties were far less expansive in scope and instead chipped away at enslavers' control. For example, allowing slaves to observe the Sunday Sabbath and the many holidays in the Catholic ritual calendar translated to temporary losses of labor. On those days, slaveholders' rights to the enslaved body were curtailed. Similarly, sending slaves to confession was a limited church-supported challenge to owners' control of the enslaved body; the seasonal period of Lent marked a yearly moment in which the mouths of enslaved Catholics had particular power as they spoke with priests. Along the same lines, providing a Christian burial translated to a lack of legally sanctioned power to wantonly dispose of the enslaved body, yet no further labor could be extracted from a deceased slave.

While each obligation constituted a church-backed slave right and thus a loss of complete bodily ownership, marriage infringed more on owners' rights to the enslaved body—how it could be used and where it could be sold. Other than baptism (the gateway to all other rights), it was the most consequential form of religious stewardship in terms of its clash with ownership rights. Moreover, resistance to slave marriage had a gendered significance. As mentioned in chapter 1, slaveholders purchased women for sex, making the enslaved female body a site of contested control. Thus, a cession of conjugal rights was yet another loss of rights to the female enslaved body. Given these ecclesiastical checks on slaveholders' power, it is unsurprising that obstacles to slave marriage occurred in Portuguese India like the hindrances experienced in Portugal and beyond.[75]

Inquisition Records and Resistance to Slave Marriage

Antagonistic to slave marriage, New Christians Ana de Oliveira and her husband Alvaro Gomes took a selective approach to religious stewardship, as evidenced in her sixteenth-century Inquisition case. In her defense she called herself a "very good Christian" and a "friend of God," in the very same paragraph in which she commented on the Christian instruction received by her enslaved workforce as well as their Lenten confessions.[76] Moreover, she later confirmed her defense statements during questioning, again claiming her commitment to her slaves' religious instruction and confessions.[77] By her own account, then, she was a good religious steward because of the fulfillment of these specific religious obligations. Moreover, multiple witnesses for the defense buttressed this favorable representation by commenting about the religious instruction and Lenten confessions of her enslaved dependents.[78]

However, Ana openly acknowledged the limitations of her religious stewardship. In one of her counterstatements meant to disqualify any injurious testimony against her, she claimed that the enslaved Filipa Corombim hated her and elaborated that Filipa had married without her consent. Instead of deferring to her enslaver's authority, Filipa clandestinely seized the opportunity when sent to confess. Retaliating, Ana whipped the enslaved newlywed. Moreover, Ana invited her slave's hatred in response to her refusal to grant Filipa manumission, despite Filipa's labor to free herself.[79] In short, Ana had blocked Filipa's freedom and had violently opposed her enslaved dependent's sacred and socially recognized marital union protected by the Catholic Church. After seeking to disqualify any testimony by Filipa, Ana proceeded in the next counterstatement to attempt to disqualify testimony by Filipa's freed husband, Duarte. Previously enslaved by Ana, he allegedly nurtured "great hatred" because she had refused to free Filipa and had not wanted to free him either.[80]

During the inquiry about Ana's counterstatements, witnesses were summoned to comment on the enslaved Filipa and her husband on December 5, 1559. While the curate had nothing to say, the canon of Goa's cathedral church, Father Pero Diaz, commented on Filipa and Duarte's quest to marry.[81] After listening to the counterstatement concerning Filipa, he responded that "he, the witness, counseled the defendant [Ana] and her husband to consent" to Filipa's marriage because Filipa "was in mortal sin with [Ana's] other slave."[82] Thus, he clarified that this quest for marriage took place while both Filipa and Duarte were still enslaved. Furthermore, he remarked that the two owners had provided consent and that he married the enslaved couple during Lent approximately four or five years prior to his testimony. Yet Filipa and Duarte had a grievance, complaining to him that they were not allowed to live "as God commands."[83] In other words, Ana had blocked their conjugal rights.

Father Pero Diaz also added that Filipa had worked for Duarte's freedom. Despite this struggle over obligations and rights, he took a neutral stance on the couple's feelings toward Ana, declining any knowledge of whether Filipa hated her owner.[84] Thus, in the canon's description of the conflict, he had acted as an intermediary, spurring Ana's reluctant yet incomplete fulfillment of her religious obligation to promote her enslaved dependents' marriage. With ecclesiastical intervention, the marriage had taken place; however, the enslaved couple encountered retaliation and continued resistance to their conjugal rights.

Beyond the experiences of Filipa and Duarte, the Inquisition records indicate other examples of owner resistance to slaves' desire for church-sanctioned, socially recognized marriages in Portuguese India. In Diogo Soares's Inquisition case, a joint petition including Ana de Oliveira pointed toward this resistance and desire. The New Christian petitioners claimed that their enslaved dependents had been bribed to testify against them with promises not only of freedom but also of marriage.[85] Hence, the petition suggests that a church-sanctioned marriage had been an attractive yet unattainable privilege for enslaved members of the household. Moreover, beyond the scope of these cases, remnants of Goa Tribunal trial records of enslaved defendants point to a broader desire for formal marriage by subalterns, whether church-sanctioned or not. The freed Gabriel Abexim, who crossed into Portuguese territory and converted to Catholicism, made his trek with the intention of marrying his female companion; when thwarted, he returned to the "land of the Moors."[86] Similarly, when the fugitive Paulo returned to Portuguese imperial territory and met with one of his former acquaintances, he took the time to communicate that he had established a marriage back in the Mughal Empire.[87] As an enslaved Catholic in Portuguese imperial territory, he had not enjoyed that right.

Parish Records and Resistance to Slave Marriage

Baptism records from the Goan parish of São Bartolomeu reveal a lack of marriages between slaves. The baptism records are also significant because they simultaneously record the action of slaveholders who had embraced the essential part of religious stewardship: baptizing their enslaved dependents. Owners arranged for the baptism of infants at the parish church and even at home, when illness demanded it. Yet this fulfillment of a religious obligation toward infants often did not reflect a holistic approach to the religious stewardship of their parents. Most enslaved infants were born to unmarried women—enslaved mothers who had not participated in the sacrament of marriage. Among the eighty-four baptized slaves recorded from 1686 to 1702, forty concerned the baptism of enslaved infants.[88] Most common were entries such as the 1697 baptism record for Anna and Seraphina, twin sisters born to the enslaved Maria owned by Joseph Vas; the children's father was recorded as unknown.[89] Only one infant was born to married parents. On April 13, 1696, the Reverend Father Salvador de Almeida baptized the anomalous Gonçalo, who was born to Duarte and his wife Magdalena, both of whom were enslaved by the same owner, Balthazar Dias.[90] With the exception of Gonçalo, all baptized enslaved infants were born to unmarried mothers and unknown or unrecorded fathers. Thus, the glaring absence of husbands in the records reflects a selective performance of religious stewardship. Moreover, the omission of documented paternity obfuscated the existence of slaveholders who had fathered children born to enslaved women.

Similarly, the death records reflect the absence of slave marriage. In the households represented, enslavers had invested their time and money in the final act of religious stewardship—the burial of their enslaved dependents. Yet these same owners who were diligent in death were negligent in marriage. Their negligence was recorded in the records in multiple ways. First, none of the forty-five deceased slaves documented as "children" had fathers recorded.[91] Instead, paternity was erased through the common omission of fathers altogether and the occasional documentation of "unknown father." The six enslaved children with documented unknown fathers were recorded with their mother's names.[92] Thus, when the enslaved João died in 1699, he was remembered as a "child by the name of João, the son of an unknown father and Adrianna, the slave of Aleixo do Rego."[93] More common were enslaved children who were missing any indication of paternity, generally appearing simply as the children of enslaved mothers whose own names were sometimes omitted as well. For instance, upon her death in 1683, Maria was remembered as the child of Phelipa, an enslaved woman of East African descent owned by Lios Rodrigues.[94] Similarly, paternal information was altogether missing when the deceased Lucrecia was remembered as the child of an unnamed enslaved woman in the house of Joseph Vas.[95] The absence of paternity distinguished enslaved children from their free deceased counterparts. Entries for free children included the father's name and generally omitted the mother's name. For example, in March 1684 four children were documented with their father's name on one folio of death records: Baltezar was described as "the son of João Rebello," Esperança was recorded as the "child of Antonio Vas," Domingos was memorialized as the "son of Luis Rodrigues," and Paulina was identified as the "child of Diogo Rebello."[96]

Moreover, none of the deceased enslaved women in the parish had husbands listed.[97] The lack of any recorded husbands suggests an omission of marriage and a divergence from the pattern for free women's deaths.[98] A range of possibilities appeared for free women. Some appeared alone even when not explicitly identified as single, while others appeared with their husband's identification. In 1683 Maria Gonçalves appeared without any familial information, while Catarina Gonçalves was recorded as the "wife of Rodrigo Ferreira."[99] Previous marriages were also revealed in the records for free women whose widow status was documented. Upon their deaths in 1684, Catarina Rodrigues was simply described as a widow, while Gracia Fernandes was remembered particularly as Valentim Rodrigues's widow.[100] These variations for free women reflected a range of choices and experiences absent in the lives of enslaved women, who were often denied the option of marriage.

An attempt to compare the records of deceased free and enslaved men is far less straightforward as it is difficult to track marriage patterns among free men. For instance, when Rafael Rangel died in 1698, he was not listed as a widower or husband. His wife's name was unrecorded, and his marital status was altogether omitted, although the names of his three executors appeared.[101] Yet we know from the parish records that he was married at some point. Esperança de Meneses, documented as his wife, appeared as a godmother in a 1696 baptism record for the enslaved Gonçalo.[102] Beyond the omission of wives in free men's entries, the broader patriarchal pattern seems to be that all men's dependents (wives, children, and slaves) were unrecorded. On the other hand, male dependents' links to a patriarch were more likely to be recorded. Thus, there are examples of free unmarried men recorded as sons. In 1685 Joseph Fernandes, Paschoal, and Antonio were documented as single and had their fathers' names recorded.[103] Unsurprisingly, deceased enslaved men lacked recorded wives and the designation of husbands or widowers, while their affiliation with their owners was documented.[104]

Admittedly, this analysis does not take into account enslaved people who were not interested in church-sanctioned unions. We cannot assume that all slaves desired a Christian marriage, and we cannot ignore the presence of coerced sexual unions that produced children.[105] However, given the stated desire of enslaved individuals to marry in the Inquisition records in addition to the rights gained by marriage shown in the provincial council records, it would be naive to assume a universal lack of interest in marriage. Instead, it is more plausible that owners withheld the opportunity for enslaved individuals to participate in the sacrament of marriage. Thus, the baptism and burial records suggest not only a lack of slave marriage but also slaveholders' resistance to slave marriage. Enslaved Catholics' access to marriage was obstructed.

* * *

In the Portuguese Empire in India, the Catholic Church shaped the parameters of the owner-slave relationship by designating slaveholders as religious stewards. From the moment of acquisition, owners were conceptualized as connectors between the church and the enslaved, facilitating the imperial expansion of Christendom at the household level. Along the same lines, enslavers were also conceptualized as connectors between the enslaved individual and the larger Catholic society, easing slaves' integration into the larger community through baptism, the sacrament that opened the doors to documented social membership with its concomitant rights. Expected to perform specific religious duties from birth to burial, slaveholders faced social pressure to conform. Both the free and enslaved observed and commented on enslavers' performance as religious stewards, transforming the household into a public space. Furthermore, church officials disciplined disobedient owners with threats of fines, inquisitorial prosecution, and excommunication, which equated to an ejection from the wider Catholic community. Hence, when they resisted religious stewardship and thus ignored slaves' rights to Catholic membership, owners jeopardized their own membership status in the community. Thus, the stakes of religious stewardship were high for both enslavers as patrons and enslaved individuals as beneficiaries. Yet the selective performance of religious stewardship reflected the harsh realities of household power dynamics. The church could decree and discipline; however, religious stewardship was not automatic, and enslaved Catholics had to press for the fulfillment of obligations in order to protect their church-ordained rights.

THREE

Arming Slaves for the Catholic Empire

IN THE LATE sixteenth century, the enslaved Gonçalo Toscano fled his enslaver's household.[1] He left the Portuguese colonial city of Bassein on the western coast of India, taking up residence in his mother's house in Galiana (Kalyan).[2] Persuaded to return to the religion of his birth, he converted from Catholicism—the religion of his bondage—to Islam.[3] At the end of a two-year sojourn, he contacted his owner back in Bassein and arranged his return to Christendom and servitude.[4] However, three years later (by which time he had been manumitted), Gonçalo again fled Portuguese jurisdiction and reconverted to Islam during a Portuguese war with the Sultanate of Ahmadnagar. In the early 1590s, the sultanate wreaked havoc on the areas surrounding both Bassein and the Portuguese colonial city of Chaul, also on the western coast.[5] Before this reconversion, Gonçalo allegedly profited from the war, acting as a highwayman and carrying tamarind and currency to Portugal's Muslim enemies.[6] An informant, unnamed yet characterized as a "pagan" in Gonçalo's inquisitorial narrative, notified the captain of Bassein, João Gomes de Azevedo, who prepared a warrant for Gonçalo's arrest for these activities.[7] Knowing his arrest was imminent, Gonçalo hid for five or six days in the gardens near Bassein. Then, "tempted by the devil," he crossed over to the Muslim encampment.[8] After crossing over, he ultimately reconverted from Catholicism to Islam and even fought against the Portuguese.[9] When he later recounted his actions before the Goa Tribunal of the Portuguese Inquisition, he seemed to have reconverted solely for strategic means. However, whether he converted interiorly or only exteriorly, Gonçalo's multiple conversions to Islam fit into a larger context of imperial anxieties about slavery, conversion, and military labor.

Early modern European empires in the Indian Ocean relied on unfree labor for their colonial enterprise, and the Portuguese were no exception. Analyzing convict labor, Timothy Coates describes a sophisticated Portuguese exile system that created soldiers and settlers for colonial outposts, and Kerry Ward examines the Dutch use of exile for the "peopling of empire."[10] This chapter extends the discussion of imperial strategies for peopling the empire by examining early modern Portuguese ideas about the relationship between slavery and religious conversion. The often-contested foothold the Portuguese state held on the perimeters of the Indian Ocean depended on loyal slaves. In the colonial imagination, conversion to Islam threatened slaves' perceived military loyalty to a Catholic state surrounded by hostile Muslim neighbors.

While scholars of slavery and the history of the Portuguese Empire have both noted the imperial military reliance on slaves, the religious aspect of arming slaves has been overlooked. Contemporary records reveal interlinked concerns about imperial security and slaves' religious identities. Enslaved individuals who converted to Catholicism helped people the empire in a way that bolstered the Catholic population, thus expanding the potential pool of loyal military laborers. Those who converted to Islam, on the other hand, were a perceived threat. Anxious about conversion to Islam, the Portuguese in India feared that slaves would run away to neighboring sultanates and convert to Islam, subsequently helping those sultanates in wars against the Portuguese like the manumitted Gonçalo Toscano did. To act against the threat of conversion to Islam, the Portuguese criminalized the sale of Catholic slaves to Muslim owners, the transportation of Catholic slaves to Muslim-ruled territories, and slaves' conversions to Islam. These strategies of retaining enslaved Catholic subjects simultaneously reflected the imperial need for loyal military labor and the imperial project of creating a Catholic empire in the Indian Ocean. Thus, rather than examining slavery, imperial security, and religious identity in isolation, this chapter ties the three subjects together. Against the backdrop of an imperial manpower shortage, the Portuguese in India relied upon their enslaved coreligionists to defend the empire.

DEMARCATING A CATHOLIC TERRITORY

For the Portuguese Empire in India, territorial borders and religious boundaries coincided, demarcating neighboring non-Christian territories from Portuguese Catholic territory.[11] This fusion of religious and imperial territory was formed even before the Portuguese had established settlements in India. As mentioned previously, fifteenth-century papal bulls linked imperial expansion with the extension of Christendom. While the Portuguese referred to their territory as the "land of the Christians," the *terra de mouros* ("land of the Moors") constituted Muslim territory. On the Indian subcontinent, the land of the Moors included Muslim-ruled polities such as the Mughal Empire and the Deccan sultanates of Ahmadnagar, Bijapur, Bidar, Berar, and Golconda, although both Muslim and Hindu residents lived in these territories.

The Portuguese imperial project of creating a Christian territory consisted of changing the religious landscape and filling it with Christians. This project intensified in the Catholic Reformation era after an initial period of comparative tolerance. The new landscape saw the construction of churches and the eventual destruction of mosques and temples. A campaign of temple destruction in Goa, the colonial capital, and the surrounding districts of Bardez and Salcete ensued in the 1540s. As a result, hundreds of temples were destroyed.[12] Accompanying the purge of temples in the mid-sixteenth century were policies that coercively produced Christian subjects. Decrees on the seizure and conversion of Hindu orphans as well as preferential employment policies for Christians are just two examples.[13] Moreover, from 1567 to 1606 provincial councils convened in Goa. These ecclesiastical bodies, created after the Council of Trent convened in Rome, promoted religious orthodoxy and the spread of Catholicism in the Estado da Índia. Among the councils' decrees were the destruction of mosques and temples, a policy also backed by secular laws. This policy constituted a wholly different approach to both previous and contemporaneous models of state building on the Indian subcontinent. The sixteenth and seventeenth centuries witnessed wars of expansion by the Deccan sultanates, the vanquishing of the Vijayanagara Kingdom, and the Mughals' steady march from the north. As a result, the political map featured Muslim-ruled states inhabited largely by Hindu populations. However, neighboring Deccan states and the Mughals strategically destroyed or repurposed temples that represented the power of political enemies, while sparing the vast majority of temples that were unconnected to political rivals and conceptualizing mosques as altogether apolitical.[14] The Portuguese project of creating a Catholic empire, however, hinged on religious conversion and the connection between religious identity and religious territory.

In 1567 the First Provincial Council mandated the destruction of mosques and temples.[15] The council also decreed that non-Christians could not convert others because such proselytization hindered the spread of Christianity.[16] In a similar vein, the council broadly prohibited non-Christians from impeding the spread of Christianity.[17] The same council ordered the expulsion of Muslim qadis along with Hindu preachers, yogis, *feiticeiros* (witches), and others who performed non-Christian religious offices.[18] The ecclesiastical authorities present at the council blamed these non-Christian religious leaders for impeding the spread of Christianity. Moreover, a 1567 law instigated by the council authorized the enslavement of Muslim qadis and pagan preachers who did not leave Portuguese territory.[19] This law also mandated that non-Christians who converted others to Islam or paganism would be punished with forced labor for the empire.[20]

The move to destroy temples and mosques continued. In 1585 the Third Provincial Council mandated the destruction of houses of non-Christian religious worship in Diu.[21] Frustrated, the council complained that Muslims were rebuilding their mosques and Hindus were rebuilding their temples. Calling the presence of temples a scandal, the Fifth Provincial Council reiterated in 1606 the decree to tear them down.[22] The recurrence of these decrees on the destruction of non-Christian spaces suggests that the church and state were not strong enough to effectively and consistently enforce their ideas about religious territory.

Despite these laws and decrees attempting to create a uniformly Catholic territory, religious diversity existed on the ground. The provincial councils recognized the presence of non-Christians in Portuguese territory; in 1567 the viceroy, influenced by their suggestions, mandated the residential segregation of non-Christians.[23] In 1606 the Fifth Provincial Council reiterated the need for separate neighborhoods, particularly mentioning "pagan" women and Christian women.[24] Moreover, the traveler Jan Huygen van Linschoten noted that non-Christians lived in Goa and "had freedom of religion" in the 1580s. He commented, "In the towne and Iland of Goa, are resident many Heathens, Moores, (which are Mahometans) Iewes, and all strange nations bordering thereabout, everie one of them using severall customes, and superstitions in Religion. The Moores hold Mahomets law, and the Iewes Moyses law. There are also many Persians, Arabians, and Abexijns, some [of them] Christians, and some [of them] Moores."[25] Thus, there was religious diversity in the "land of the Christians." Furthermore, the very occurrence of Inquisition cases prosecuted against baptized Catholics revealed the religious fluidity within Portuguese Catholic territory.[26]

THE PROBLEM OF PEOPLING A CATHOLIC EMPIRE

Related to the project of creating a Christian territory, the Portuguese state faced the problem of peopling the empire in India and the broader Indian Ocean region from Mozambique to Macau. The empire consisted mainly of coastal port cities and forts, a network designed to control trade and communications in the Indian Ocean. Most of these Portuguese colonial possessions had an urban character with an outward focus on trade, rather than large swaths of territory acquired for the purpose of further inland expansion and the rule of large local populations. Besides the Estado's imperial capital of Goa, some of the empire's most important settlements along the western coast of India included Diu and the Província do Norte (Province of the North), principally comprising Chaul, Bassein, Salsette, and Daman. Beyond their strategic mercantile and military importance, these areas had small yet significant Portuguese settler populations. Overall, the Portuguese had a relatively light presence on the ground on the Indian subcontinent. In 1600 fewer than six thousand Portuguese settlers lived in the entire Estado da Índia.[27] Moreover, many of these settlers were concentrated in Goa. From the mid-sixteenth century through the early seventeenth century, the city's population constituted up to two thousand settlers.[28] Non-Portuguese residents, including local Christians, Hindus, and enslaved individuals, tended to form the bulk of the population of Portuguese-controlled areas.[29]

Intermittently at war with the states neighboring its territories, the Portuguese Empire in the Indian Ocean was vulnerable throughout the sixteenth and seventeenth centuries. On the Indian subcontinent and beyond, the Portuguese faced a host of enemies and shifting alliances. For example, in 1570 the Deccan sultanates of Bijapur and Ahmadnagar allied with the Indonesian sultanate of Aceh and the Hindu zamorin of Calicut, posing an existential threat to the Portuguese territories.[30] Moreover, Mughal expansion and Maratha invasions troubled the Portuguese on the subcontinent.[31] Sixteenth-century warfare with the Ottomans encompassed the broader Indian Ocean, and the growing maritime activity of the Safavid Persians spurred the loss of additional territory.[32] Furthermore, during the Iberian Union of Crowns from 1580 to 1640, Dutch blockades of Goa and attacks on Portuguese settlements in the Indian Ocean and the Atlantic added another level of insecurity; such attacks persisted into the 1660s despite an official end of hostilities.[33] Even the built landscape reflected the ever-present possibility of war; the Portuguese found it necessary to construct fortresses from the beginnings of their colonial endeavors in the Indian Ocean. Siege warfare and invasions, along with their accompanying distress and disease, contributed to a backdrop of uncertainty and danger. By the end of the seventeenth century, the scale of the Portuguese Empire had drastically contracted, with losses on the subcontinent and the broader Indian Ocean world such as Hurmuz, Melaka, Muscat, the Ceylon settlements, Cochin, and Mombasa.

In this context of imperial insecurity, the Portuguese had a severe manpower problem in India. First, they had a small metropolitan population base, which limited the number of colonizers who could be dispatched to the empire.[34] Second, the manpower problem was further exacerbated by the hemorrhaging of soldiers en route to and within India. Sickness depleted the ranks as did poverty. Financial pressures weighed upon soldiers, who were "frequently underpaid, paid late, given promises in lieu of salaries, or simply not paid at all."[35] Responding to such pressures, soldiers escaped military service through a variety of strategies. Marriage turned them into *casados* (settlers), a designation that exempted them from active duty. Soldiers also entered Catholic religious orders to escape the precariousness of Portuguese military service, while others followed a wholly different religious route by becoming renegades and fleeing the empire altogether.[36] As they crossed the border into Muslim-ruled territories and converted to Islam, the Portuguese Empire lost not only military labor but also an imperial presence.

The empire attempted to recover such labor in multiple ways. In the sixteenth and seventeenth centuries, the imperial response to renegades ranged from capture and punishment to the issuance of pardons.[37] Moreover, the Goa Tribunal of the Portuguese Inquisition played an integral role in disciplining and controlling labor as an imperial actor. The institution sought information about renegades in its interrogations of defendants, including the aforementioned Gonçalo Toscano.[38] In addition, the institution prosecuted renegades themselves. For example, in 1565 Antonio Dias was sentenced to the galleys of Portugal for working as an artilleryman for "Moors in the wars that they had against Christians," in addition to converting to Islam.[39] In 1594 Duarte de Meneses was not only charged with converting to Islam but also for helping Muslims in war to the "grand detriment of the Christians."[40] Accordingly, he was sentenced to the galleys for ten years. In the same year, Gaspar Fernandes was likewise sent to the galleys for having helped Muslims militarily against Christians.[41]

While engaged in the project of recovering and disciplining lost subjects, the Portuguese also created colonizers through a sophisticated exile system. Exploring this system in depth throughout the empire, Timothy Coates examines how secular courts and the Inquisition's continental tribunals in Portugal helped ease the manpower shortage through sentences of exile, including galley labor.[42] Yet Goan cases show that the inquisitorial response was not limited to the Lisbon, Coimbra, and Évora Tribunals. The Goa Tribunal participated as well.

The Goa Tribunal supported imperial goals by contributing manpower for the galleys and the gunpowder factory. Galley labor was indispensable, as these coerced laborers enforced the Portuguese trade monopolies by patrolling the coasts of the Indian Ocean.[43] In my sample of 2,254 case summaries from the Goa Tribunal, roughly 10 percent of them contained sentences of galley labor.[44] These sentences of forced labor were generally for fixed periods of time. For example, on the shorter end of the sentencing spectrum, Bras Coelho de Sancoalle, a native Christian living in Salcete, was sentenced in 1607 to the galleys for six months for sodomy; he also was punished for paganism, a religious crime for which he was jailed and ordered to wear a penitential habit forever.[45] On the other hand, sentences of exile "forever" to the galleys were possible, which occurred in the case of Antonio de Matos in 1589 for sodomy.[46] Sentences to the galleys occasionally included enslaved individuals. Out of the sample, only thirteen slaves were sentenced to the galleys.[47] While a less frequently chosen sentence than the galleys, inquisitors sentenced men and women to the gunpowder factory for a variety of offenses.[48]

In addition to these sentences of forced labor, inquisitors in Goa bolstered the population of colonial settlements outside of the capital through sentences of exile to various parts of the Portuguese Empire. The Goa Tribunal frequently assigned Daman and Ceylon as places of exile in Asia.[49] Moreover, Goan inquisitors even exiled some defendants beyond the Indian Ocean to locations such as Angola and Brazil, thereby incorporating the Atlantic.[50] Thus, the Inquisition in Goa provided a practical solution to the problem of peopling the empire. Yet this solution was still inadequate to meet the imperial demand for labor.

SLAVERY AS A SOLUTION TO THE MANPOWER PROBLEM: ARMING SLAVES FOR THE EMPIRE

Enslaved Africans and Asians constituted yet another component of the Portuguese strategy to mitigate the empire's manpower shortage. Purchased for a plethora of occupations in peacetime, they temporarily defended the empire in times of crisis. In the Portuguese imperial context, enslaved artisans, clerks, domestic servants, gardeners, and palanquin carriers could all potentially accompany their enslavers into battle.

Valued as a dual solution for peopling the empire and military protection, armed slaves appear in much of the secondary literature. Historians of the Portuguese Empire as well as the broader early modern Indian Ocean world have long noted the Portuguese reliance on armed slaves.[51] Similarly, scholars of slavery have mentioned this pattern of slave use in Portuguese Asia. In 1977 Ann Pescatello, examining Africans in particular, discussed slave soldiers.[52] In 1985 P. P. Shirodkar referenced military slave use at the turn of the seventeenth century.[53] Likewise, Jeanette Pinto's 1992 monograph included military labor in her description of slaves' occupations in Portuguese India.[54]

More recently, Timothy Walker systematically assessed the Portuguese military use of slaves. He pointed to an early modern empire-wide pattern of relying on enslaved auxiliary soldiers to defend Portuguese settlements ranging from Macau to Brazil.[55] Examining Portuguese military slave use in a comparative context, he argued that the Portuguese pattern differed fundamentally from contemporary South Asian states, such as the Deccan sultanates of Bijapur and Ahmadnagar, which relied on professional slave soldiers to defend rulers from both external and internal threats. The Portuguese, however, relied on slaves to temporarily defend the empire in times of crisis against external threats. His observations about slavery align with Christopher Brown's distinction between arming slaves and the more formal institution of military slavery.[56]

The ethnic component of South Asian military slavery forms another juxtaposition to the Portuguese Empire's reliance on armed slaves. Analyzing military slavery in the Deccan Plateau of India from the mid-fifteenth through mid-seventeenth centuries, Richard Eaton assesses states' reliance on elite African slave soldiers, many of whom arrived from present-day Ethiopia. These enslaved soldiers, known as Sidis, functioned as political elites who often exited slavery upon the death of their owner, married local women, and purchased slaves of their own. Their military presence formed a contrast to the Mughal Empire, which turned to armed peasants for its military labor needs.[57] Like Eaton's exploration of the Deccan sultanates, Helene Basu's analysis of Gujarat examines the role of African soldiers, some of whom were enslaved.[58] In these examples of military slavery, Africans were recruited as enslaved soldiers.

In Portuguese India, however, discussions of arming slaves extended beyond recruiting Africans as slave soldiers. In the context of a manpower shortage, the entirety of the male enslaved labor force was considered. While a dearth of quantitative data challenges a demographic reconstruction of the sixteenth and seventeenth centuries, the diversity of the slave population is apparent. As discussed in chapter 1, the enslaved population included not only Africans but also South Asians, Southeast Asians, East Asians, and Middle Eastern slaves in the sixteenth and seventeenth centuries.

Imperial officials pinned their hopes of imperial security on this multiethnic enslaved population whose origins spanned continents. In fact, slaves were viewed as part of the Portuguese imperial defense system in India. In António Bocarro's 1635 overview of the Indian Ocean empire for Philip III, the chronicler connected slavery and imperial security. When enumerating the population of different Portuguese colonial possessions, Bocarro often included slaves, as shown in table 3.1. Yet his interest in the enslaved population was militaristic. Rather than consistently recording the total number of slaves, he primarily focused on enumerating enslaved individuals who would be available to fight. For example, when describing the fortress of Diu and its population, he included the "fifty-nine slaves [of the Portuguese residents] who can take up arms."[59] When he described the 250 casados residing in the city of Chaul, he noted that they each had one slave who could bear arms.[60] Likewise, in his description of Bardez, he said that each Portuguese casado had three slaves who could fight.[61] For the village of Thana on the island of Salsette, Bocarro likewise concentrated on the number of slaves who would be useful in war. After describing the 180 residents who were all well-armed, he continued with their 150 slaves who "serve in the soldier's war and everything else that is necessary."[62] Similarly, for Cochin, Bocarro informed the king that there were five hundred casados who each had two slaves capable of bearing arms.[63] Moreover, in Daman, two hundred armed slaves were available to defend the empire.[64] In this manner, he covered Portuguese colonial settlements, paying particular attention to the number of slaves each Portuguese possession could depend upon in the event of war.

Table 3.1. Enslaved population of Catholic residents in Portuguese India recorded by António Bocarro

Place	Slave population	Place	Slave population
Agaçaim (Tanadaria de Agaçaim)	2+[a]	Goa (Cidade de Goa)	12,500–13,250[c]
Bardez (Bardes)	?[b]	Karanja (Caranja)	2+[d]
Basrur (Barcelor)	35	Kollam (Coulão)	?[e]
Bassein (Baçaim)	1,800	Mahim (Maim)	200
Chaul (Cidade e Fortaleza de Chaul)	250	Mylapore (São Tomé de Meliapor)	180[f]
Cochin (Cochim)	1,000	Nagapattinam (Negapatão)	1,500[g]
Daman (Damão)	200	Tarapur (Trapor)	100
Diu (Dio)	59	Thana (Tana)	150
		TOTAL	17,978+-18,728+

Source: António Bocarro, *O Livro das Plantas de Todas as Fortalezas, Cidades e Povoações do Estado da Índia Oriental,* ed. Isabel Cid (Lisbon: Imprensa Nacional, 1992), 2:102, 129, 185, 109, 122, 199, 84, 75, 136, 117, 208, 101, 247, 243–44, 100, 115.

Notes: Bocarro generally noted the number of slaves available to fight rather than the total slave population. Some estimates include slaves of non-Portuguese Catholic casados. Enslaved females and children as well as elderly and disabled slaves often went unrecorded. Goa is a notable exception.

[a] The figure for Agaçaim is very conservatively low, coming from Bocarro's ambiguous estimate of "few slaves" (rather than a concrete number). In an alternative reading, it is possible each slaveholder had "few" slaves. Bocarro, 102.

[b] Bardez has a question mark for its slave population as Bocarro recorded three slaves per Portuguese casado without recording the number of casados. Bocarro, 129.

[c] The estimate's lower limit for Goa consists of the 8,000 slaves of Portuguese casados, 1,000 armed slaves of non-Portuguese casados, and 3,500 non-fighting slaves of non-Portuguese casados. The upper limit consists of 8,000 slaves of Portuguese casados, 1,250 armed slaves of non-Portuguese casados, and 4,000 non-fighting slaves of non-Portuguese casados. Calculations of armed slaves of non-Portuguese casados were derived from Bocarro's reference that these slaves numbered half the population of those casados. The calculations varied, as he inconsistently numbered the non-Portuguese casado population at 2,000 and 2,500. Bocarro stated a range of 3,500 to 4,000 non-fighting slaves of non-Portuguese casados. Bocarro, 135–36.

[d] The figure for Karanja is very conservatively low, coming from an ambiguous estimate of "few" slaves (rather than a concrete number). In an alternative reading, it is possible each owner had "few" slaves. Bocarro, 117.

[e] Kollam has a question mark as Bocarro mentioned the existence of enslaved wartime help without providing a number. Bocarro, 208.

[f] This estimate is based on the number of muskets, with one per slave. Mylapore had 500 muskets, 320 of which were used by free Christians. Bocarro, 247.

[g] This estimate is based on the number of muskets, with one per slave. Nagapattinam had 2,000, five hundred of which were used by free Christians. Bocarro, 243–44.

Bocarro's description of the capital city of Goa was somewhat different for its inclusion of slaves who would not be available in the event of war; however, the emphasis on defense remained as Bocarro took the time to distinguish the number of slaves who could fight if needed. He specified that the Portuguese casados altogether owned sixteen hundred slaves, the majority of whom were cafres (East and Southern Africans) and Indians, who could bear arms.[65] On the other hand, the remaining 6,400 slaves of the Portuguese casados could not be depended upon; among those deemed as militarily insufficient were enslaved women and children.[66] Besides the slaves of the Portuguese casados in Goa, Bocarro counted the slaves of the Indian Christian casados. In this category there were between 1,000 and 1,250 available for military service; Bocarro referred to them as "*escravos d'arma*."[67] Additionally, there were between thirty-five hundred and four thousand slaves of the Indian casados who were not capable of performing military service.[68] This focus on the defensive capacity of enslaved people was also emphasized in Bocarro's description of the casados in Goa and the weaponry they had. He noted every casado had "many weapons," proceeding to list several types. Next, he stated that the casados had "superabundant weapons" for both themselves and their slaves, while mentioning a possible lack of adequate gunpowder and munitions.[69]

While enslaved subjects defended the empire during wartime, they also functioned as an armed retinue for private citizens, a pattern also apparent in Brazil.[70] In his travel narrative, Linschoten recounted the actions of such slaves in Portuguese India, who settled feuds on behalf of their enslavers.[71] Likewise, Jean-Baptiste Tavernier, visiting Goa in the mid-seventeenth century, remarked about slaveholders directing their enslaved dependents to commit violent crimes.[72] The traveler François Pyrard de Laval, while not explicitly referencing slavery, described Portuguese noblemen in India who were accompanied by armed "*Cafres* of Mozambique." Six or seven would escort "their masters," and at night they even carried pikes and halberds.[73] This use of armed slaves for private interests meant that enslaved individuals were already trained and familiar with weapons and could fight alongside their owners in battle if needed.[74]

Rather than designating one particular ethnicity as a martial race, Portuguese subjects as well as ecclesiastical councils emphasized religious identity as they affirmed the empire's reliance on armed slaves in India. The Portuguese incorporated the enslaved population through a framework of religious belonging. Through baptism, enslaved individuals became members of the larger Catholic community, although their membership was unequal due to their lower social status. This religious aspect of belonging encompassed all slaves regardless of ethnicity, and their status as religious insiders made them ideal fighters in emergencies. The Portuguese focus on religious-insider status is a juxtaposition to forms of military slavery that emphasized the ethnic-outsider status of enslaved soldiers. In those systems, the ethnicity of the soldier set him apart as a military slave even if he shared the same religion as his enslaver.[75] In Portuguese India, however, baptized enslaved subjects were envisioned as loyal coreligionists ready to defend the empire from the larger non-Christian states that neighbored it.[76] In this conceptualization, slaves' religious conversions to Catholicism created imperial security.

Ecclesiastical councils convening in Goa linked slave ownership to the defense of the empire. In 1567 the First Provincial Council authored a decree banning non-Christian merchants from buying so-called pagan slaves and taking them back to territories outside of Portuguese jurisdiction.[77] The council alleged that these merchants (in particular, Muslims) were buying a "large number of pagan slaves" and these slaves converted to Islam, thereby increasing the Muslim population. They also asserted that this increased Muslim population had the effect of making the Muslims "stronger than the Christians."[78] As a solution, the council barred captains of colonial fortresses from allowing these slaves to leave Portuguese territory, and the council even threatened the captains with excommunication and fines for noncompliance.[79] Almost twenty years later, this movement of "pagan" slaves and their presumed subsequent conversions to Islam still seemed to constitute a threat to Portuguese security; the Third Provincial Council in 1585 reiterated the First Provincial Council's decree.[80]

A similar preoccupation guided Portuguese settlers in Goa in the seventeenth century. In 1603 the Goan municipal council wrote to King Philip II, underscoring contemporary ideas about slaves, security, and religion.[81] Alleging to represent the concerns of the whole state of Portuguese India, the councilmen's letter vehemently protested the viceroy's planned implementation of an old 1570 provision barring the enslavement of Japanese people.[82] Part of the council's argument for a delay centered on imperial security and religious identity. The council argued that when the Japanese became slaves of the Portuguese, these slaves became Christians. Slaves' conversions to Catholicism thereby increased the population of the king's vassals.[83] In other words, through their enslavement and subsequent conversion, the king was provided with an increased number of loyal subjects. Hence, there was a spiritual benefit as well as a tangible military benefit for the king. Along the same lines, the council argued that Japanese slaves who were purchased by Muslim owners became Muslims. According to the councilmen, these conversions to Islam presented a security risk to the Portuguese because this increase in the Muslim population equated to an increase of neighbors who were hostile to the Portuguese Christian state. The councilmen also raised the issue of the small Portuguese population and the challenge of adequately defending Portuguese imperial territory. The council argued that the number of Portuguese could not even defend a small defensive wall of Goa, yet the Japanese were "bellicose," or, rather, fit for fighting in wars. Emphasizing their need for slaves, the council also added that a Portuguese owner with slaves armed with muskets could successfully defend Portuguese territory.[84] Continuing to invoke security concerns, the council argued that if Japanese slaves (and by extension all slaves) were freed, they would rise up and collaborate with the enemy. Then the Portuguese would be obliterated.[85] Thus, while attempting to retain their slaves, the councilmen invoked the role that Catholic slaves played in defending the empire and emphasized the presumed loyalty of such enslaved coreligionists.[86]

COLONIAL CONVERSION POLICIES PREVENTING ISLAM

Desiring a Catholic slave population, ecclesiastical and secular authorities attempted to prevent enslaved people from converting to

Islam and joining the Muslim population of the neighboring states. Christian slaves were to stay in Christian territory under the guardianship of Christian owners. Traders, foreigners, Muslims, Jews, and "pagans" were all liable to lose their slaves upon their captives' conversions to Catholicism. The king of Portugal, Dom Sebastião, in 1559 mandated that any newly converted Catholic slaves belonging to non-Christians had to be sold to Christians and their owners would be reimbursed. The king expressed concern that non-Christian owners would persuade these slaves to leave the Catholic faith. Making a linkage between territory and religious identity, he also decreed that non-Christian owners were not to leave Portuguese cities, forts, or possessions in India without selling their Christian slaves. If these owners did not comply with the law, then they would not only be deprived of their slaves but also would lose the monetary value of their captives.[87] Likewise, in the previous decade, a treaty with the Sultanate of Bijapur established Catholic territory as the rightful place for Catholic slaves. Slaves of Muslim merchants from Bijapur were to be sold upon conversion to Catholicism and their price given to their former enslavers as a reimbursement.[88] Thus, secular law identified non-Christians as unsuitable owners of Christian slaves because of the perceived risk of conversion to Islam.

Church authorities also sought to prevent slaves' conversions to Islam, attempting to pair enslaved individuals with Christian owners. As mentioned in chapter 2, the provincial councils mandated religious stewardship from the conception of the owner-slave relationship in order to facilitate slaves' conversion to Catholicism and their growth in the Catholic faith. To encourage religious stewardship from the point of purchase, the councils decreed that Christian slaves and "pagan" slaves could only be owned by Christian slaveholders; non-Christians, on the other hand, were not to own Christian slaves. The First Provincial Council in 1567 began the mandates, a trend followed by an imperial law instituted after the Third Provincial Council of 1585 and decrees mandated by the Fourth and Fifth Provincial Councils in 1592 and 1606.[89] In 1575 a looser variation of these mandates appeared in the Second Provincial Council, which ordered that slaves who had converted to Catholicism be taken from non-Christian merchants who were not vassals. They were to be sold to either Christians or "infidel vassals" rather than returned to non-Christian territory.[90]

As the ecclesiastical councils tried to pair slaves with Catholic owners, the Inquisition in Goa disciplined those who sold slaves to non-Catholics. For example, in 1586 Gonçalo Vaz Camões was reprimanded and fined one hundred cruzados because he sold his young Christian slave, formerly a Muslim, to another Muslim heading to his own land.[91] Similarly, in 1591 Baltezar Pireira de Castro encountered the Inquisition, receiving a fine and a two-year sentence of exile to Ceylon. One of his transgressions included selling a *cafrinho,* a young male of East or Southern African descent, to Muslims. Making this religious crime even more grievous was the unnamed slave's desire to become a Christian.[92] In 1618 inquisitors sentenced Antonio Lopes Faleiro to the galleys for five years because the soldier had kidnapped a *cafrinho* and sold him to Muslims, who were said to have "made him a Moor."[93]

PROSECUTING CONVERSION TO ISLAM

While ecclesiastical decrees targeted enslavers, the Goa Tribunal of the Portuguese Inquisition targeted the enslaved. During the institution's first six decades, the Goa Tribunal's enslaved defendants tended to be converts from Catholicism to Islam. Since these enslaved defendants were baptized Catholics, the Inquisition had jurisdiction over them, regardless of the circumstances of their initial conversion to Catholicism. The prosecution of enslaved Catholics who deserted the faith reflected larger anxieties. The Portuguese Inquisition was not only a religious institution but also an imperial institution with political, social, and financial concerns.[94] Prosecuting particular doctrinal errors and targeting particular populations were not just religious acts but political acts. Accordingly, the Goa Tribunal's tendency to target religious conversions by slaves can be read as a state interest in the combination of this particular religious crime (conversion to Islam) with a particular population (enslaved Catholics).

This state interest in slaves' conversions is clear upon analysis of João Delgado Figueira's contemporary document, the *Reportorio,* which summarizes the Goa Tribunal's cases from 1561 to 1623.[95] Slaves constituted a small minority of the case summaries, but most of them ran afoul of the Inquisition because of their conversions to Islam. In my sample of 2,254 of these case summaries, 159 enslaved defendants appeared; they constituted only 7 percent of the sample. Yet 70 percent of these slaves prosecuted by the Inquisition in Goa were converts to Islam. Furthermore, the majority of those slaves were males—men who would have been potential auxiliary soldiers during wartime. This is a contrast to the wider sample in which roughly 18 percent, or 410 cases, were prosecutions involving a conversion to Islam as a primary or secondary crime.[96] Thus, inquisitors prosecuted slaves who converted to Islam at a higher rate when compared to the free population prosecuted by the Goa Tribunal for the same crime. There was a much wider range of crimes for which the Inquisition tried non-slave defendants. Enslaved people were prosecuted through the lens of imperial security.

SLAVE FLIGHT AND CONVERSION TO ISLAM

Despite the laws, decrees, and inquisitorial discipline meant to hinder conversion to Islam, enslaved individuals converted and fled across the border to Muslim-ruled territories. These flights were described in various sources. For example, the slaveholding Diogo Soares and his extended family, mentioned in previous chapters, complained about the flight of their slaves to neighboring territories. From 1557 to 1561, the Lisbon Inquisition targeted this New Christian family in Goa for allegedly practicing Judaism. Their Inquisition cases relied on the testimonies of their enslaved dependents. In response to the cases lodged against them, Diogo Soares, Leonor Fernandes, Lopo Soares, Clara Lopes, Estevão Lopes, Guiomar de Oliveira, Ana de Oliveira, and Branca de Oliveira filed a joint petition protesting the denunciations of their slaves against them. They argued not only against their slaves' characters but also alleged that slaves in the area "fled to the Moors every day."[97] While Soares and his family had a vested interest in exaggerating in order to disqualify their slaves' testimonies, other contemporary reports acknowledged the occurrence of slave flights and conversions to Islam.

Church officials recognized the lure of neighboring lands as havens for runaway slaves. In 1606 in Goa, the Fifth Provincial Council discussed slave flight from Portuguese territories, immediately after their decrees about the violent mistreatment of slaves. They were concerned about the religious plight of Christian slaves who had fled from their owners to the "land of the infidels" or, rather, lands outside of Catholic, Portuguese jurisdiction. In those lands, the council alleged, slaves departed from Christianity. Thus, the council arranged for the return of runaway Catholic slaves, seeking to lure them back to Christendom without potential interference from their enslavers. The council ordered the prelates to grant a permit for the slaves' passage to return without notifying their owners. This safeguard would last one month; slaves who wanted to be reunited could be returned to the owner's custody.[98] In addition, the decree took into account slaves who wanted to return to Catholic territory but preferred a new owner; the council requested that the viceroy make a law compelling owners to sell those runaway slaves. In sum, the council explicitly linked flight from Portuguese territory to a departure from Catholicism, and the council tied these flights and even the unjust captivity of slaves to their embrace of non-Christian religions, especially Islam.[99]

The strategy of fleeing slavery was hardly unique to Portuguese India. This public form of resistance occurred elsewhere in European Indian Ocean empires.[100] Moreover, religious conversion accompanied flight for other fugitive slaves.[101] Yet the Portuguese religious-imperial context stands out because of contemporary efforts to suppress the flight of both enslaved and free Christian subjects out of the fear of apostasy. The closest equivalent is the Spanish Philippines, in which the loss of colonial subjects and an ecclesiastical role in retaining them are also apparent.[102] Religious anxieties about apostasy simultaneously merged with imperial security concerns about renegade slaves, whose presence was also documented by the aforementioned António Bocarro. Not only did he record the number of enslaved individuals available to help the Portuguese in wartime, but he also remarked about the vexing problem of runaways who converted to Islam and were provided with weapons.[103]

* * *

Enslaved military labor contributed to sustaining the Portuguese imperial enterprise, a contribution long recognized in the literature: temporarily arming slaves in times of crisis helped fill the need for imperial labor. This pattern of arming slaves set the Portuguese apart from their neighbors on the Indian subcontinent, who turned to other military strategies. For instance, the Deccan sultanates of Bijapur and Ahmadnagar relied on elite African slave soldiers as ethnic outsiders, whereas the Mughals relied on armed peasants. Thus, the Portuguese diverged from the Mughal pattern by incorporating enslaved military labor and diverged from the Deccan sultanates' pattern by incorporating enslaved laborers from areas spanning the Indian Ocean.

Yet only focusing on these particular forms of divergence presents three problems. The first problem is empirical; a focus solely on ethnicity and slave status overlooks the contemporary rhetoric linking slaves' religious identity to imperial security. Second, this focus overlooks the type of empire enslaved people helped defend—an empire with an avowed commitment to extend Christendom in the Indian Ocean world. Within this religious expansionary project was a religious geography separating the Portuguese Empire as the "land of the Christians" (*terra de cristãos*) from the surrounding states alternatively designated as the "land of the infidels" (*terra de infiéis*) and the "land of the Moors" (*terra de mouros*). Enslaved Catholics defended the "land of the Christians." Relatedly, a focus solely on ethnicity and slave status overlooks the role of these armed slaves as religious insiders. Their place in the empire was defined not just by their enslaved status but by their religious status. The imperial project of creating, sustaining, and defending a Catholic state depended on Catholic military labor—both enslaved and free. Baptism bound European soldiers, settlers, and exiles as well as enslaved Africans and Asians into one common colonial endeavor.

In the colonial imagination, Catholic slaves were a bulwark against the strong Muslim-ruled states neighboring the Portuguese on the western coast of India. In a context of intermittent war, reliance on enslaved coreligionists aligned with the "doctrine of necessity," in which slaves were armed because of severe need.[104] The empire faced the challenge of initial recruitment as well as the loss of soldiers through illness, death, marriage, membership in Catholic religious orders, and the exit from empire and Christendom as renegades. Additionally, settlers on whom the empire depended also left the empire, at times crossing the border into Muslim-ruled territories and converting to Islam. While the Portuguese Inquisition provided additional manpower through sentences of exile, the Portuguese in India still lacked sufficient people to adequately sustain the empire. Thus, slaves formed part of the imperial solution of "peopling the empire."

Enslaved Catholic subjects bolstered the empire's population, yet they also made religious choices of their own. Thwarting imperial ambitions, slaves left the empire and converted to Islam. Slaves fled propelled by their relationships with their enslavers, desirous of reunions with family, and seeking a different religious affiliation. Frustrating the imperial project of defending the "land of the Christians," slaves added to the population of the "land of the Moors." Their exit from the empire occurred despite the multiple efforts of the state to retain its enslaved subjects. Laws, decrees, and inquisitorial prosecutions sought to keep Catholic slaves within Catholic territory under the religious stewardship of Catholic owners. However, the colonial imagination was forced to confront the colonial reality. Peopling a Catholic empire and defending it posed a vexing problem. Enslaved subjects, just like their free counterparts, did not always play the imperial role assigned to them.

FOUR

Bonds of Conversion

WHEN THE ENSLAVED and free converted to Catholicism, their religious act placed them under ecclesiastical jurisdiction. Baptism changed one's legal status, conveying rights and privileges that were backed by the church. Conversion created a bond, linking baptized subjects to the church and anchoring them within the larger Portuguese Catholic community. This bond to the church and empire, however, could not be legally severed. The inability to completely dissolve the bonds of conversion shaped the lives of enslaved and freed individuals in the early modern Portuguese Empire in India. They found that while they might shed their bonds of slavery, they could not effectively shed their bonds of conversion while remaining in Portuguese territory. Conversion was meant to be a permanent act, even if baptized subjects wished to change their religious affiliation.

Changes in religious identity invited the response of the Portuguese Inquisition, a disciplinary force that primarily exercised jurisdiction over baptized subjects. While chapter 3 discussed the imperial significance of the Inquisition and the imperial problem of mobile subjects, this chapter will focus on the religious jurisdiction claimed by the institution and take a microlevel approach through the examination of two Inquisition cases. In the 1595 case of Gabriel Abexim, the Abyssinian freedman crossed back and forth over the borders separating Catholicism and Islam, and his mobility provoked the prosecution of the Goa Tribunal. Similarly, the 1689 case of the enslaved Paulo likewise followed the religious journeys of a mobile subject who crossed territorial borders, moving between Islam and Catholicism. Their life stories reveal the bonds created by conversion and the ways in which inquisitorial jurisdiction operated on the ground to keep those bonds intact.

INQUISITORIAL JURISDICTION

The Portuguese Inquisition attempted to exercise perpetual, extraterritorial jurisdiction over baptized subjects. Inquisitorial jurisdiction, as examined in chapter 3, contributed to Portuguese state-building efforts overseas by providing labor for the empire. Beyond its role in state building, however, the Inquisition's jurisdiction helps us understand the stakes of conversion for new converts as well as the automatic repercussions of baptism for the wider Catholic population, including those who were baptized as infants. Baptism created bonds of religious subjecthood to the Catholic Church, which institutionally had ceded the right to prosecute particular religious crimes to inquisitorial tribunals. The perpetual nature of the Inquisition's jurisdiction meant that baptized subjects' religious actions fell under the gaze of the Inquisition for the duration of their lives, even if these subjects turned to other religious practices by supplementing Catholicism with other religious rituals or breaking away from the church altogether. Thus, engaging in Hindu ceremonies, performing sacrifices, embracing Lutheranism, or converting to Islam any time after one's baptism invited the action of the Inquisition—not to mention religious crimes such as bigamy, blasphemy, and beyond. The Inquisition had a right to prosecute such religious transgressions when committed by a baptized subject who was forever bonded to the Catholic community. Non-Christians, on the other hand, were largely outside the purview of the Inquisition, generally appearing as defendants only when they impeded the spread of Christianity, impeded the work of the Inquisition, performed sacrifices or "pagan ceremonies" within Portuguese colonial territories, or transported Christians across territorial borders.[1] In short, they temporarily invited prosecution when they endangered the spiritual health of baptized subjects, whereas baptized subjects perpetually remained under the institution's jurisdiction.

While the Goa Tribunal had a geographical mandate covering the Portuguese Empire in the Indian Ocean, its jurisdiction was not limited to Portuguese imperial territory. Baptized souls housed in mobile bodies exited Portuguese colonial territory. This mobility necessitated a combination of perpetual and extraterritorial jurisdiction. The Inquisition's extraterritorial jurisdiction meant that baptized subjects who left Portuguese territory were still punishable; mobility did not mean full escape. The Inquisition attempted to track down baptized subjects and bring them back into Christendom for the safety of their souls. At the macrolevel, this effort to locate subjects included correspondence between tribunals and within Inquisition networks.[2] At the individual case level, the Goa Tribunal made inquiries regarding the whereabouts of other renegades when questioning a recovered mobile subject, Gabriel, who will be discussed later.[3] Thus, inquisitors used the prosecution of one subject to glean information on others. Yet the perpetual and extraterritorial jurisdiction is especially apparent in the Goa Tribunal's prosecution of baptized subjects in absentia. The Goa Tribunal punished both the temporally absent (the dead) and the geographically absent (living mobile subjects who could not be recovered).

Case summaries show ground-level examples of this jurisdiction in action. The sentences of three absent New Christians prosecuted for Judaism in the auto-da-fé of August 17, 1578, are prime examples of this jurisdiction. Linked by a common fate, they appeared in succession as numbers five, six, and seven on the same folio of João Delgado Figueira's *Reportorio*.[4] Alvaro Gomes, marked as "absent," was delivered to secular justice, the equivalent of being sentenced to death. Similarly notated as "absent," the deceased Antonio Dias's bones and a statue of him were delivered to secular justice. The bones of the deceased Anna Lopez suffered the same treatment. The three shared a common inquisitor, Bertolameu da Fonceca, whose application of extraterritorial perpetual jurisdiction was represented in other case summaries. Of the eighty-two cases delivering the defendant to secular justice in my sample, twenty-nine were either dead or geographically absent.[5] Thus, slightly over one-third of those condemned to death represented those who had temporally or geographically escaped the clutches of the Inquisition but still remained under the institution's jurisdiction.[6] As we will see, this extraterritorial perpetual jurisdiction of the Inquisition especially posed a problem for mobile subjects.

RELIGIOUS IDENTITIES AND THE PROBLEM OF MOBILITY

Mobile subjects encountered the prosecution of the Inquisition because their mobility destabilized their religious identity. As discussed in chapter 3, the exit of colonial subjects from Portuguese territory was problematic for an empire lacking enough labor to sustain and defend itself. Yet a loss of baptized colonial subjects was also a religious problem as movement out of Catholic territory was seen as an endangerment to the soul. Inquisitors endeavored to look after the souls of baptized subjects, and mobility that took Catholics into Muslim-ruled territories threatened the safety of the souls under the church's care. Inquisitors and contemporary missionaries saw the "land of the Moors" as a site of apostasy. Missionaries noted that Christians there forsook their religion on account of being surrounded by non-Christians.[7] Moreover, inquisitors removed Portuguese subjects from India when they deemed it necessary to protect those Christians from leaving the empire (and Christendom).[8]

Through the religious expression of state power, the Goa Tribunal prosecuted Catholic subjects for leaving the bounds of the Portuguese Empire and entering Muslim-ruled territory. Most of the trial records of the Goa Tribunal have been burned; however, João Delgado Figueira's seventeenth-century manuscript contains case summaries, which attest to the prosecution of border crossers. For instance, in 1575 Felipa Mendez was prosecuted for going to the "land of the Moors" and living as a Muslim; the inquisitors ordered that she be given more instruction in the faith.[9] Likewise, in 1576 Francisco Petena was charged with having gone to the "land of the Moors." He was reprimanded with the requirement of instruction.[10] In 1578 João Fernandes was also reprimanded for going to the "land of the Moors" in addition to consuming meat on "prohibited days."[11] While he did not convert to Islam and forsake Catholicism entirely, being in a different territory influenced him enough that he stepped out of the strictures of the Catholic ritual calendar. In 1580 Lianor de Sousa was reprimanded by the Inquisition on account of going to the "land of the Moors," as she did it "without necessity."[12] Christians were not supposed to be in Muslim territories because of the risk that they would convert to Islam. Simply going was suspicious; the area not only was populated by Indian Muslims but also runaway soldiers escaping Portuguese jurisdiction.[13] Religious boundaries were not supposed to be crossed, and inquisitors were eager to know when Portuguese subjects had crossed the line.

Inquisitors also prosecuted non-Christians for taking their Christian family members to the "land of the Moors." For instance, in 1565 a Muslim man named Giraca was charged with having taken his two Christian children to the "land of the Moors," yet he was freed and absolved.[14] Perhaps there was not enough proof against him; the inquisitor did not record why he was let go. In 1617 a man named Bodú appeared before the inquisitors. At the time of his arrest and prosecution, he was described as a "pagan" living on the non-Christian mainland.[15] The inquisitors prosecuted him for having taken his Christian son to the "land of the Moors," the place where he allegedly made that son return to paganism.[16] While the case summary did not provide an update on whether the apostatized son rejoined the Christian faith, the summary did reveal that Bodú made a strategic decision: he converted to Catholicism.[17] Thus, Bodú emerged from his inquisitorial experience pardoned and with a new name, Antonio Rebello; he was now a Christian absolved of all wrongdoing.[18] These cases are illuminating in that the "land of the Moors" was a dangerous territory where Christians were unmade—they succumbed to family pressure and reclaimed their religious heritage.

Besides criminalizing the transportation of family members across religious boundaries, inquisitors prosecuted people for taking nonrelatives to the "land of the Moors." In 1575 Ante Camotim, described as a "pagan," was accused of having taken Christians to the mainland in order for them to become "pagans." Upon his conversion to Catholicism, he was pardoned.[19] Five years later, Luis Barreto, a native Goan, came before the Inquisition for a similar offense. He allegedly transported a person to the non-Christian mainland, resulting in a verbal reprimand accompanied by physical correction: he was struck with a palmer.[20] In 1586 the aforementioned Gonçalo Vaz Camões was reprimanded and fined one hundred cruzados after selling his young Christian slave to a Muslim returning to his own land, which was presumably the "land of the Moors."[21] In 1599 Antonio, a Gujarati slave in Bassein, found himself before the Goa Tribunal not only for converting to Islam but also for taking Christians to the "land of the Moors."[22] Thus, inquisitors prosecuted both the free and the enslaved for transporting others to Muslim territory.

GABRIEL'S CASE

While illuminating, the case summaries only provide a glimpse into inquisitorial jurisdiction and the prosecution of mobility. Case transcripts, however, allow us to probe the operation and impact of inquisitorial jurisdiction in the individual lives of mobile subjects, in addition to the motivations behind individuals' mobility. One such individual was the aforementioned Gabriel, a freed Abyssinian slave who encountered the Goa Tribunal twice in 1595. He had run away from Ahmadnagar, a Deccan sultanate in India, and converted to Catholicism in the Portuguese colonial port city of Chaul. Months later, he returned to Ahmadnagar and resumed life as a Muslim. Yet after the span of about six or seven years, he returned to Chaul to live as a Christian again. Having lived in the so-called land of the Moors, he caught the vicar's interest. After a deposition, the vicar sent Gabriel from Chaul to Goa, the administrative capital of the Estado da Índia. In Goa he was sentenced to servitude in a religious institution by a deputy of the Goa Tribunal in April 1595. For four months, Gabriel worked in the College of St. Thomas in Goa, which was also called a monastery and a convent. Then he ran away, after proclaiming that he was a Muslim and had to return to the "land of the Moors." His flight spurred another trial and a new sentence of exile to the galleys.[23] By December 1597, he was dead, but the inquisitors sent the transcripts of his trial to Lisbon with a plea for advice on how to decide similar cases.[24] The mobility of new converts posed a perplexing problem.

Decades before his encounters with the Goa Tribunal, Gabriel was born in present-day Ethiopia to Jewish Abyssinians called Falasha in the mountains remote from the land of "Prester John" around 1555.[25] According to Gabriel (whose birth name was lost to history), Abyssinian Christians kidnapped him at a very young age. Taken to Arabia, Gabriel was sold multiple times to different Muslim owners. Ultimately an Arabian merchant and teacher of Islamic law named Mulá Mamede purchased Gabriel, and they went first to Chaul de Cima and next to Ahmadnagar.[26]

The slave trade that eventually brought Gabriel to Ahmadnagar enveloped many other Abyssinians.[27] This commerce between Abyssinia and India had begun at least by the thirteenth century, and Ibn Battuta recorded the presence of Abyssinians in India in the fourteenth century.[28] The slave trade intensified during the late fifteenth and early sixteenth centuries, due to political changes in Abyssinia. The newly ascendant Muslim state of Adal in the Horn of Africa raided the interior each year for slaves.[29] Moreover, from 1560 to 1632 there were wars between Jewish polities and the Christian empire in the Ethiopian highlands.[30] It is probable that Gabriel was taken captive in the midst of one of those wars, given that he was captured by Christian Abyssinians.

Gabriel's overseas route as a slave matched other Abyssinians' journeys to India. Abyssinian slaves often stopped first in Arabia and then were taken to India. Their capture frequently spurred their conversion to Islam, which in some cases occurred en route on the ship to Arabia.[31] As a result of this trade, thousands of Abyssinians became slaves serving in the polities of the Deccan Plateau, and among them were those who became soldiers and elite officials.[32] For example, in Bijapur, the sultanate from which the Portuguese wrested Goa, Abyssinians held state offices at least from 1537 to 1558, most of the reign of Ibrahim Adil Shah.[33] Contemporaneous with Abyssinian influence in Bijapur, Abyssinians also played a political role in Ahmadnagar and involved themselves in the late sixteenth-century succession crisis there.[34] One of the most prominent of the Abyssinian slaves in Ahmadnagar's history was Malik Ambar, a regent of the sultan in the seventeenth century who resisted Mughal expansion and conducted diplomatic relations with the Portuguese.[35] Thus, when Gabriel arrived in Ahmadnagar, he was part of a larger Abyssinian diaspora.

Border Crossings and Religious Conversions

For the next couple decades after his capture, Gabriel worked for his enslaver Mulá Mamede in the Sultanate of Ahmadnagar. He remained there until his late twenties to early thirties. Then, he began a relationship with a Muslim woman, Mixa Cobar, and together they fled to the Portuguese colonial port city of Chaul.[36] A composite of his testimonies reveals multiple rationales behind his conversion and flight from the sultanate. He initially stated that he left the sultanate to have a sexual relationship with Mixa Cobar, adding that she had been given to him by his owner for that very purpose.[37] This seems a curious rationale, given his owner's alleged sanctioning of the relationship. Yet the following month, Gabriel complicated the narrative. He later recounted that "after serving [his enslaver] many years, [his enslaver] gave him freedom, telling him to go wherever he wished, and he, the defendant, beginning to have a relationship with the aforementioned Moorish woman . . . fled with her from the aforementioned city of Abdanáguer to the city of Chaul."[38] In this recounting, he pinned the reason for his flight to his enslaver's treatment: "Because the aforementioned Moula Mamede gave him a bad life, he, the defendant, fled with the aforementioned Moorish woman to Chaul with the intention of becoming a Christian."[39] In sum, Gabriel's decision to leave the sultanate suggests he felt a need to go elsewhere to improve his status and his quality of life. Inquisitors later would not dispute the freed status Gabriel claimed in his trial, although the freedom he had gained would prove to be ambiguous.

In Chaul, Gabriel converted to Catholicism. He was catechized and baptized by Dominican fathers, receiving his Christian name and a godfather.[40] However, if his purpose in fleeing Ahmadnagar was to continue his relationship with Mixa Cobar, then his trip to Chaul did not produce the intended results. After converting to Catholicism, the Dominicans placed him in the house of an Abyssinian Christian woman to serve her.[41] Thus, he had been reduced to servitude in his new religious community. Moreover, according to Gabriel, one of his new Abyssinian Christian acquaintances in

Chaul, Sidi Acrodo, prevented his marriage with Mixa Cobar, arguing that she was an unsuitable wife and suggesting that she be sold.[42] In the midst of these circumstances, Gabriel only remained in Chaul two months. He never experienced a Lenten season and was never christened. Not waiting long enough to observe these rituals, he fled Chaul and returned to Ahmadnagar.[43]

According to his trial records, Gabriel remained in Ahmadnagar for about six or seven years.[44] His reintegration into Muslim society was smooth. Such a reentry would have been eased by a reestablished patron-client relationship with his (former) enslaver, if not the resumption of slavery.[45] Whatever his ties to his enslaver may have been, he later implied in his trial that it was rather easy to become known as a Muslim again. He was already circumcised; thus, he could offer physical proof of being a Muslim.[46] Also, he recounted that he did not have to perform any Muslim ceremonies. He simply said to other Muslims that he was a Muslim, and all that was required was the use of his first name, Haliande.[47] This name had not been mentioned in his Chaul deposition. As discussed below, the only two names identifying him in that document had been Gabriel and Sidi Reme.[48] Thus, he acquired a third name, another Muslim appellation. Living in Muslim territory required a Muslim name; it marked or identified him as a Muslim in ways that "Gabriel" did not.

However, in 1595 Gabriel again left Ahmadnagar for Chaul, arriving in the aftermath of the Portuguese Empire's victorious war with the Muslim sultanate. His freedom of movement was short-lived as he entered ecclesiastical custody in March of that year. Gabriel had been apprehended by a soldier of "No Anagra." This soldier was looking for his own slave, who had presumably run away, when he took Gabriel into custody.[49] Chaul, at least by 1635, was known for its small slave population; enslaved individuals frequently ran away from the Portuguese territory to the "land of the Moors."[50] This soldier handed him over to a vicar, launching the inquisitorial process that would hurtle him back into bondage.

Mobility and the Inquisitorial Logic of Territorial Identities

On March 11, 1595, forty-year-old Gabriel Abexim recounted his journeys between the "land of the Moors" and Chaul in the "land of the Christians." His return trip to Muslim territory was of particular interest to Father Manoel Fernandes, the "vicar of the rod," who presided over Gabriel's deposition in Chaul.[51] The vicar emphasized the linkage between religious identity and territory. He wanted to know whether Gabriel became a Muslim with the corresponding conversion ceremonies *before* or *after* leaving Portuguese territory. Gabriel responded that he had not converted to Islam when he returned to the sultanate. The vicar continued to press Gabriel on the issue, asking how many years Gabriel had been a Muslim. In response, Gabriel insisted that he did not convert to Islam after returning to the sultanate, although admitting that he did go to the mosques and prayed Muslim prayers in the company of Muslims. He also added that while there he had forgotten Christ.[52] Thus, to the vicar, going to the "land of the Moors" merited suspicion of conversion, even though Gabriel refused at that particular moment to explicitly acknowledge his conversion.

While Gabriel and his interrogators similarly acknowledged the link between territory and religious identity, elements of his first case along with his subsequent actions revealed fissures in the inquisitorial logic of territorial identities. The idealized vision of binaries was blurred by reality. The March 1595 deposition in Chaul identified Gabriel by two names: a Christian name, Gabriel, and a Muslim name, Sidi Reme.[53] This existence of two different names at first appears to be two distinct identities. Upon conversion, one entered a new community, obtained a new name, and adopted a new form of dress. In inquisitorial logic, one was either Muslim or Christian. Christians practiced Christianity in the "land of the Christians," and Muslims practiced Islam in the "land of the Moors."

In the context of his case, it is evident that Gabriel traveled back and forth between identities. On the surface, it would seem that he switched identities only when switching territories. This would conform to inquisitors' and other religious and political authorities' idealized view of the landscape. Yet in reality Gabriel, the baptized Catholic in Christian territory, was also Sidi Reme, a man whose life history included Muslim rituals, prayers, and past experiences that conversion to Catholicism did not erase. As he would later testify in his second trial, he accessed that subterranean identity in Christian territory. Likewise, an Abyssinian Christian associate of Gabriel's in Chaul had a Christian name, but he was known to Gabriel in Christian territory only as Sidi Acrodo—his Muslim name. Sidi Acrodo's Christian name, Gabriel admitted, was one that he did not know.[54] Thus, Gabriel's baptized Christian friend actively expressed his Muslim identity—or a facet of that identity—by continuing to use a Muslim name in Christian territory.

Gabriel's Reconciliation and Relapse

After his first inquisitorial trial, Gabriel was sentenced to servitude in the new Dominican College of St. Thomas in Goa, which was also called a convent and monastery.[55] This servitude had a particular logic since Gabriel was considered to be in need of Christian instruction. This perceived need was hardly surprising as Gabriel had only lived as a Christian briefly. Thus, the judgment satisfied the labor needs of the convent simultaneously with Gabriel's attainment of religious instruction.[56] Yet labor was not the entire cost of Gabriel's departure from Catholicism. He had to abjure his offense. Thus, he was ordered to appear with a lit candle, bare feet, bareheaded, and in a penitential habit in the Sé Cathedral, renouncing his errors.[57] In attendance at the cathedral were the canons, a bailiff of the Inquisition, the Goa Tribunal's jail guard, and "many other people."[58] Besides enduring this mortification, he was required to pay for the cost of his trial.[59] Thus, he emerged from his inquisitorial experience with a loss of money and the loss of freedom for an undefined amount of time, along with the stigma and embarrassment of the public abjuration. Reconversion had not been kind to Gabriel.

After receiving his sentence to serve in the College of St. Thomas, Gabriel remained in Goa for roughly four months, receiving Christian instruction. Yet, sometime in early or mid-August, Gabriel ran away.[60] His flight, however, was unsuccessful, thwarted by Goa's system of *passos,* fortified checkpoints that regulated entry into and exit from the city. A captain, a garrison, and a scribe surveilled movement, collected tolls, and apprehended fugitive slaves and other runaways. Accordingly, two of the captain's foot soldiers near the Passo da Madre de Deus returned Gabriel to the fathers of the college, who afterward turned him over to the Inquisition.[61] Thus, on August 15, the jailer of the Goa Tribunal imprisoned Gabriel yet again.

Days later, inquisitorial proceedings began. On August 19, three witnesses from the college testified. One was a sixteen-year-old slave, Joané, who made purchases for the fathers of the college.[62] The other two witnesses were freed slaves serving in the college.[63] João Franco, a freed Javanese painter around twenty years of age testified after Joané. Next appeared Domingos, a freed Gujarati acculturated youth only around thirteen or fourteen years old.[64] Their allegations collectively portrayed Gabriel as a Muslim uninterested in learning Christian doctrine, who openly said Muslim prayers. Domingos claimed that Gabriel told him he performed Muslim ceremonies because he was in fact a Muslim.[65] Likewise, Joané saw Gabriel performing certain religious ceremonies and asked Gabriel about them.[66] Specifically, Joané was unfamiliar with his posture of prayer and could not understand the words he spoke. As in his conversation with Domingos, Gabriel told Joané that he was a Muslim and performed Muslim ceremonies.[67] Besides these open statements to his fellow servants, Gabriel was defiantly preserving his Muslim identity in his interactions with his teacher, Paulo, who was attempting to increase Gabriel's knowledge of Christian doctrine.[68]

By the time of his second trial, Gabriel seems to have departed from Christianity. He testified that he initially persisted in the Catholic faith after his previous inquisitorial encounter, but after an unspecified period of time he decided to become a Muslim again. From then on, he was quite open about his Muslim faith. This was not a case of secret observance but defiant devotion. He insisted that he fled the college because of the harsh treatment he received at the hands of other men there. According to Gabriel, they harassed him, calling him a Muslim and "other shameful names," in addition to beating him.[69] Thus, he was verbally and physically abused. In this context, he began practicing his Muslim ceremonies openly and even told a father that he was in fact a Muslim. He also announced that he needed to run away to the non-Christian mainland so that he could practice Islam.[70]

For someone already acquainted with the Inquisition and living in a religious college, Gabriel's actions were seemingly reckless. What spurred him to openly defy the religious norms, fully knowing the possible consequences? It is possible that he decided that ejection from the college would improve his living conditions. In other words, falling into the hands of the inquisitors would be preferable to remaining in his current environment. Whether he hoped to provoke another Inquisition trial or simply flee, it is evident that Gabriel was deeply dissatisfied with life in the college and wanted to leave. Thus, in August 1595, after his pronouncements, he fled from the college. His eventual capture propelled him back to the inquisitorial jail on August 15. At the end of the month and into early September, he was questioned about his actions and rationale for leaving. During his questioning, he initially stated that he fled with the hopes of finding an Abyssinian to house him and help him. This explanation sounded as if it came simply from a man who was ostracized and was looking for someone who would understand him. Moreover, his search for an Abyssinian suggested some level of ethnic consciousness.[71] Only later in his testimony did he confess to converting to Islam.

The inquisitors were baffled by Gabriel. In the third session of his trial, they asked him about his intentions.[72] What did he actually mean when he told others he was a Muslim? What was his intent when he told others he had to flee to the mainland? Gabriel puzzled them so much that they even questioned the interpreters.[73] Antonio Jorge and Antonio da Cunha, who had previously taken oaths to faithfully transmit Gabriel's words, were now transformed into character witnesses. What was their opinion of Gabriel? Was he a "man of understanding?" They testified that he was senseless and that he did not understand what he was saying.[74] The interpreters' analysis of Gabriel's mental state and understanding was accepted by the inquisitor. Ultimately, Marcos da Graça, the deputy, sent Gabriel to the galleys, saying he was not of a sound mind.

Thus abandoned to the galleys for the sake of bolstering an empire, Gabriel's life became enshrined in the folios of inquisitorial documents, interrogating the relationship between territory and religious identity. While he invoked the logic of religious territoriality, he also questioned the need to cling faithfully to one religious identity. When Gabriel was proclaiming that he needed to go to the mainland so he could practice Islam, he also reportedly said that it sufficed to be a Christian in one month and then switch to being a Muslim in another month.[75] Gabriel did not discuss this statement in any of his trial sessions, yet the alleged statement resonates with his actions over the course of his life. He was adept at switching religious categories and taking on different identities. This movement between identities is a constant theme tying his two cases together.

The willingness to oscillate between different religions, while remarkably pronounced in Gabriel's case, was indeed a hallmark of Goan Inquisition cases in general. Inquisitors policed religious boundaries that coincided with Portuguese imperial borders. People were not to go to the "land of the Moors" without a good reason. Those who traveled there without a "good cause" and presumably dared to return were called before the Inquisition. The criminalization of crossing religious spatial boundaries was the very way inquisitors enforced those boundaries. It was an embarrassing, uncomfortable, and potentially financially draining affair to be sentenced by the Inquisition—it was a stigma to be avoided.[76] While inquisitors (and their cadre of employees as well as the watchful eyes of neighbors) were busy policing the boundaries, it is important to note that inquisitors were simultaneously codifying identity. Boundary enforcement and identity codification constituted a dual process. Christians were to behave in an orthodox manner and observe their religion in Christian territory. In sum, the bonds of conversion not only anchored these baptized subjects to a set of religious practices and a religious community but also tied them to a territory. The repercussions of such bonds shaped the life experiences of freed slaves such as Gabriel who fled to Portuguese territory and converted to Catholicism of their own volition. Yet these bonds of conversion would also shape the experiences of captive converts who fled from Portuguese territory, as the case of the enslaved Paulo will demonstrate below. No matter the circumstances surrounding the baptism or the direction of the flight, the bonds were permanent.

PAULO'S CASE

On December 7, 1688, a local fisherman named Francisco Fernandes appeared before a Portuguese inquisitor in Goa in order to denounce his runaway slave, Paulo. Five years earlier, Paulo had allegedly absconded to the so-called land of the infidels, a designation the Portuguese used for Muslim-ruled territory. Now Paulo had brazenly returned to Portuguese colonial territory wearing Muslim articles of dress, and he was staying with an ambassador of the Mughal

Empire. According to Francisco, others in the parish had seen his fugitive slave, and he proceeded to list their names.[77] The inquisitorial machine was thus set in motion.

On December 10, 1688, the inquisitor summoned the three witnesses named by Francisco: Pero Fernandes, Andre de Misquita, and Bernardo de Souza.[78] Each separately testified to have seen Paulo, identifying him as Francisco's captive who had run away and had returned wearing the garb of a Muslim. Just over a month after his owner denounced him, Paulo was arrested and imprisoned by the Goa Tribunal.[79] On January 10, 1689, Paulo appeared before inquisitor Manoel Gonçalves Guião. The notary described the defendant as a twenty-five-year-old married man, who was both a native and resident of the port city of Surat on the western coast of India, where he was known as Sidi Assem Vacanady.[80] The inquisitor asked Paulo if he wished to confess his sins, to which Paulo responded affirmatively and narrated a story of captivity and conversion incorporating the Swahili Coast and western India.[81]

Paulo's Inquisition case highlights the dilemma for slaves whose bonds of conversion were created through the bonds of enslavement. His coerced religious conversion followed his captivity, transforming him into a captive convert. Captive converts circulated in and out of the Portuguese Empire, and the Inquisition enforced their status. Once converted as a captive, one became a subject of the Catholic Church and the Inquisition for life—just like a free convert. Thus, when captive converts attempted to shed their status, they found that they were stuck in their religion of bondage.

Paulo's Capture

Paulo entered Portuguese captivity during an era in which different slave trade routes funneled captives into the Portuguese Empire in India. Different processes transformed captives into the slaves they would later become. For Paulo, war catapulted him into captivity. Before his enslavement, he journeyed from Surat as a young merchant to trade along the Swahili Coast in 1678.[82] However, the Indian Ocean world in which Paulo circulated was beset with rivalries. The Portuguese Empire and the Omani Empire jockeyed over influence on the Swahili Coast from the mid to late seventeenth century. Paulo arrived in Pate, roughly a quarter century after the Swahili city-state rebelled against Portuguese rule and joined forces with the Omanis in 1652.[83] Pate's rebellion (also coinciding with Zanzibar and Pemba's uprising) launched a war between Portugal and Oman, with hostilities between the two powers on the Swahili Coast stretching to the late seventeenth century.[84] Thus, in the context of this conflict, Paulo arrived in Pate and then traveled to Mombasa, which at the time was still under Portuguese rule. As Paulo later recounted before an inquisitorial tribunal, he stayed in the household of some local Muslims. During his sojourn, according to the transcript of his trial, "all of the Christians and native Moors of that land came to take up arms to go to Pate in the company of the [Portuguese] viceroy's *armada,* and because the Moors in whose house he was staying fled, they seized him with four more *cafres,*" as the Portuguese termed East and Southern Africans.[85]

Paulo's capture aligned with Portuguese guidelines for legitimate enslavement, which were partially shaped by religious justifications. As mentioned in chapter 1, in 1567 the First Provincial Council issued guidelines that stated the five categories of permissible enslavement.[86] Most importantly for Paulo's story, one of the categories encompassed captives taken in just wars against Portuguese enemies. As Paulo was a Muslim seized during a "just war," his captivity was recognized as legitimate in the eyes of the Portuguese. Moreover, Paulo also lacked ethnic protection from enslavement. The Catholic Church gave protective status to certain groups, barring their captivity in Portuguese territories. For example, Africans from present-day Ethiopia, who were labeled Abyssinians, were protected by the First Provincial Council from enslavement.[87] Yet Paulo did not fall into a geographic or ethnic category that could protect him from captivity. When probing a witness for information about Paulo, an inquisitor in Goa referred to Paulo as a "cafre."[88] His owner, Francisco Fernandes, and other local South Asian residents also called Paulo a "cafre," bestowing the meta-ethnonym on him.[89] In reality, though, this term might have correlated to his place of capture in East Africa rather than his genealogy. His name in the Mughal Empire, Sidi Assem Vacanady, which designated him as a "Sidi," indicated African descent but did not reveal a more specific place of African origin. Ironically, it is possible that Paulo's ancestors were descendants of Abyssinians who would have had protected status from the Portuguese due to their presumed Christian identity. The slave trade and diaspora linking India and present-day Ethiopia, described above in the analysis of Gabriel's Inquisition case, also impacted Gujarat, the region that encompassed Paulo's birthplace of Surat. However, Paulo seemingly did not contest the "cafre" status assigned to him by the Portuguese. Thus, ultimately, neither his religious background nor ethnicity kept Paulo out of the hands of prospective Portuguese slaveholders.

Conversion and Enslavement

Once captured, Paulo converted to Catholicism, or at least he initially went through the outward steps of converting. According to his first inquisitorial session, he was baptized in the church of Penha da França. This was the parish in which his final enslaver, Francisco Fernandes, resided. Paulo also testified that he received Christian instruction in Francisco's household.[90] However, the details of Paulo's conversion shifted in his second session. The same inquisitor, Manoel Gonçalves Guião, ordered Paulo to appear on January 15, 1689, and asked him for details of his capture—its location, the person/people who effected it, and his place of baptism. In the second rendition of his captivity story, Paulo located his baptism in Mombasa after his capture there, although he remembered neither the cleric who baptized him nor the godfather assigned to him.[91] When the inquisitor pointed out the discrepancy between the two sessions' details about the baptism, Paulo explained that he had been afraid in the first session and misspoke.[92] Regardless of the precise location of his baptism, he became known as a "baptized adult" and a Christian. Thus, for the Portuguese the religious purpose of captivity had been fulfilled: conversion to Catholicism.[93]

As Paulo shared his story of conversion, he also recounted more details about the stages of his captivity.[94] After his capture in Mombasa, Paulo initially entered the custody of the French pilot of a Portuguese ship bound for Goa, afterward becoming the slave of multiple owners. Each transfer created yet another dislocation in an increasingly fragmented and uncertain life. In Goa the French pilot sold Paulo to a Portuguese man named Sebastião Gonçalves. Then, Sebastião sold Paulo to his next owner, a local Goan Christian fisherman by the name of Francisco Fernandes—the owner from whom

Paulo would later abscond in the district of Bardez. Paulo remained in Francisco's custody for five years, and it is possible that Paulo's labor contributed to his owner's work as a fisherman. While Paulo did not discuss the particular work that he performed while in Bardez, those with whom he associated were all fishermen who would later offer witness testimony against him in the Inquisition's court.[95] Whatever his labors may have been, working as the slave of a fisherman would have been an adjustment for a formerly free merchant accustomed to traveling within the wider western Indian Ocean.

Living in Bardez was also likely a shock to him, as it only had about seventy thousand residents in the seventeenth century—quite a contrast to his native city of Surat, the Mughal Empire's second-largest city.[96] Goa and its surroundings experienced population declines because of death and migration. Religious persecution, famines, epidemics, an earthquake, Dutch antagonism, and wars propelled residents into the grave and out of the area.[97] Bardez itself fell into the crosshairs of war multiple times over the course of the seventeenth century. Most importantly for Paulo, the Marathas invaded in 1683.[98] This war presented him with a new opportunity.

The late seventeenth-century Maratha invasion engulfed not only Goa and its neighboring districts but also other parts of the Portuguese Empire in India. In desperation, the Portuguese turned to their neighbors, the Mughal Empire, for assistance. While the Mughal Empire constituted an ever-expanding religious and political enemy, the Marathas were a more immediate threat. A Mughal ambassador sailed southward to Goa and with him came Paulo's brother, whose occupation was described as a "master of a ship."[99] A reunion between the separated brothers ensued, leading to Paulo's decision to run away from his enslaver and return home to Surat.

Life in Surat and Recapture

Having successfully escaped bondage, Paulo resumed his former life in Surat. He returned to practicing Islam and married the woman to whom he had been engaged before his capture in Mombasa. He and his wife had a son, and Paulo worked as a merchant, traveling up and down the coast of western India.[100] Yet in 1688 he accompanied the Mughal ambassador back to Goa.[101] It is likely that he never returned home.

Paulo continued living as a free man when he initially returned to Portuguese colonial territory. Yet this life of liberty was cut short when his former enslaver reasserted his rights of ownership. While Francisco Fernandes did not dare to directly challenge the authority of the Mughal ambassador, under whose protection Paulo had come, the religious court of the Goa Tribunal was a safe forum for reclaiming his lost human property. As a slaveholder, Francisco was a religious steward, one who was expected to ensure that his Christian slave was properly following the tenets of the Catholic faith. Thus, when Francisco appeared before the Goa Tribunal, he was going as a slaveholder with specific spiritual responsibilities. Absconding to the so-called land of the infidels was antithetical to his enslaved dependent's spiritual health. Moreover, failing to report Paulo's return could imperil Francisco's own standing in the Catholic community: as a good Christian he had the religious duty to denounce his returned slave's apostasy so that Paulo could be reconciled and reincorporated into the Catholic community. Moreover, the Goa Tribunal was a safe forum for Francisco's concerns (religious and otherwise) because it had already set a precedent of prosecuting cases of flight. Baptism had bestowed the Catholic Church and Inquisition permanent jurisdiction over Paulo as a baptized subject—no matter if he had decided to change his religious affiliation. Thus, unsurprisingly, when Francisco Fernandes sought an audience with Inquisitor Lopo Alvares de Moura on December 7, 1688, he gave a denunciation that was swiftly pursued by the Goa Tribunal.[102] Days later other witnesses were called.

Inquisitorial Bondage

As a result of the denunciations lodged against him, Paulo entered the Goa Tribunal's jail on January 8, 1689.[103] After two inquisitorial sessions that month, the Goa portion of his trial quickly came to a close. Journeying from Goa to Portugal, he entered the Lisbon Tribunal's jail on October 10, 1689.[104] After inquisitorial sessions and a public auto-da-fé where he renounced his conversion to Islam, he received his sentence of exile to Miranda, a town in northern Portugal.[105]

The entire process of inquisitorial bondage not only reinforced Paulo's (lapsed) Catholic status but also Paulo's slave status. The two were intertwined. For example, by emphasizing Paulo's religious status, Francisco Fernandes reasserted his own status as Paulo's enslaver through the use of the inquisitorial court. Even though Francisco would not regain access to Paulo's labor, the court continued to recognize Francisco's slaveholder status even after Paulo's eventual inquisitorial transfer from Goa to Lisbon.[106] Moreover, the Inquisition reinforced slavery in other ways. Through the acquisition of sinning slaves, the Inquisition became an institutional owner, even occasionally directing their labor to the galleys as a punishment.[107] In addition, the Inquisition sold enslaved individuals to Portugal. For example, an enslaved Mozambican named Antonio was whipped and sent abroad after being prosecuted for divination in 1564. Just two years later, another slave named Antonio but from the "Coast of Malindi" was sold abroad for converting to Islam.[108] These Inquisition cases represented the workings of a relatively new institution in India with the ability to repossess slaves as Catholics and use them for the empire's purposes. On one hand, this was an infringement on owners' control over their slaves, with inquisitors usurping ownership rights as a higher religious authority. Yet, on the other hand, the Inquisition supported the institution of slavery in the Indian Ocean.[109] Thus, when Paulo entered inquisitorial custody, his slave status was reapplied although he had successfully escaped that status through flight. From his incarceration by the Goa Tribunal all the way to his sentencing in Lisbon, Paulo's unfree status was reinscribed over and over. In Goa, he was called a captive.[110] In Lisbon, he was called a slave.[111]

Moreover, Paulo's case demonstrates that whereas one might lose one's captive status by flight or manumission, one could not escape the religious bond that had accompanied captivity. The church exercised eternal extraterritorial claims on the soul that could be enforced in absentia and, most importantly, in person. As Paulo discovered, the Inquisition was able to reassert its religious claims over him when he reentered Portuguese Catholic territory. Upon his return, he discovered the permanence of his "captive convert" status when he was arrested and tried by the Goa Tribunal. Regardless of the previous and future religious decisions of a captive convert, only the conversion to Catholicism was recognized as binding by the Inquisition. Even if one exited captivity, the religious residue of captivity remained. Thus, in the lives of captive converts, the fluid and reversible nature of captivity collided with the eternal permanence of conversion.

* * *

Separated in time by nearly a century, both Paulo and Gabriel grappled with the bonds of conversion. On one hand, their conversion to Catholicism beneficially anchored them to Portuguese colonial society. This bond created a form of social membership that was essential for acceptance and survival when they entered the empire as low-status outsiders. Upon converting to Catholicism after his arrival in Chaul, Gabriel gained a network of support and a place to live. Similarly, Paulo's baptism, though coerced, gave him social ties reaching beyond his enslaver's household. Their liminal status in Portuguese colonial society was ameliorated as they became insiders through religious conversion. Moreover, they came under the jurisdiction of the Catholic Church, an institution committed to protect the rights of Christians, including slaves and the newly converted. Catholic status translated into ecclesiastical protection. On the other hand, the bonds of conversion created a snare because they could not be entirely severed. When Gabriel and Paulo decided to resume living as Muslims and left Catholic territory, they did not escape the jurisdiction of the Catholic Church but rather spurred the disciplinary action of the Inquisition. No matter how Gabriel and Paulo self-identified, they were still Catholics whose souls needed to be reconciled back to the church. Though their religious agency was recognized, it needed to be corrected: actions provoking excommunication needed to be counteracted according to inquisitorial logic. Their reconciliation having been accomplished, Gabriel and Paulo remained firmly bonded to the Catholic community and by default retained their status as imperial subjects. Yet, while they provoked inquisitorial discipline by testing the boundaries of ecclesiastical jurisdiction, it is worth probing the experiences of enslaved individuals who embraced their status as Catholics. That is the topic under exploration in the next chapter.

FIVE

Choosing Catholic Community

INQUISITION CASES SPOTLIGHT unorthodoxies. Accordingly, they are rich records for examining the actions of enslaved Catholics who were nonconformists—those who practiced alternative religions, embraced syncretism, and otherwise broke religious rules. Tracking their religious nonconformity enables an analysis of why enslaved individuals rejected Catholicism in full or in part, which beliefs and practices appealed to them, and whether their actions represented authentic beliefs or survival strategies. Broadly, because the raison d'être of Inquisition records was the documentation of heterodoxy, one can carefully examine the records to ask, What did people actually believe, and what were their religious practices? Many studies on early modern religious beliefs, including those of enslaved people, use the records in this way.[1]

Yet Inquisition records are also documentations of both orthodoxy and Catholic community membership. Denunciators came forward to contrast orthodox and heterodox religious practices. By making distinctions in religious behaviors, they assessed others' religious performance. Witnesses likewise commented on religious practices, discussing not only departures from faith but also religious conformity. They judged some practices as Christian, while judging others as unchristian. Moreover, not all defendants attracted inquisitorial attention for their religious crimes. Rather than being summoned, these defendants voluntarily sought the Inquisition for reconciliation. Acknowledging that they had departed from the Catholic faith, they wished to be restored into membership. All three—denunciators, witnesses, and voluntary defendants—were participating in the inquisitorial process as fellow Catholics seeking to be good Christians.

Like free members of colonial Catholic society, enslaved Catholics exhibited their membership in the Catholic community as denunciators, witnesses, and voluntary defendants in Inquisition cases. Acting in these roles represented an agentive choice of participating in the Catholic community. In the context of conversions shaped by slavery and the broader early modern colonial climate of coercive religious policies, speaking of choice might seem disingenuous. However, the very existence of Inquisition cases showed that both the enslaved and free made religious choices. This chapter focuses on choices made in favor of Catholicism.

Such an examination merits attention for two reasons. First, understanding enslaved people's membership in the Catholic community necessitates an exploration of their own assessments of what constituted acceptable religious behavior, how they conceptualized their own religious identity, and how they assessed the religious practices of others. In short, we are able to see what it meant to be an enslaved Catholic in this time and place by looking at how Catholic status was understood and performed. Second, examining choices enslaved people made in favor of Catholicism enables us to build on broader insights about slavery in the Indian Ocean world. Commenting on the lack of a slave class consciousness and assessing the relationship between the enslaved and their owners, Gwyn Campbell argues that the majority of enslaved people in this part of the world sought to "secure a niche within the dominant society."[2] He also calls attention to religious dynamics, noting that the enslaved "often accepted the religious ideology of slave holders."[3] In the Portuguese Indian Ocean context, this translated to religious assimilation through conversion to Catholicism. By examining assimilatory acts such as voluntary participation in the inquisitorial process, we can suggest a more normative experience of slavery that would be occluded by focusing solely on acts of religious nonconformity as resistance. Thus, the case studies below address assimilated enslaved individuals who desired membership in the Catholic community. The first example follows Antonia Malavar, who appeared in the previously surveyed Inquisition cases against New Christians and denounced her enslavers. The second section of the chapter discusses enslaved witnesses who commented on the religious actions of others. Last, the bulk of the chapter revisits the Inquisition case of the freed Gonçalo Toscano, who chose Catholic community by turning himself over to the Inquisition.

ANTONIA MALAVAR: CHOOSING CATHOLICISM THROUGH DENUNCIATION

In October 1559 the enslaved Antonia Malavar ratified her testimony against her enslavers Diogo Soares and Leonor Fernandes and their extended family, who were suspected of practicing Judaism.[4] This step was hardly surprising; it was customary for the denunciators to ratify their testimonies by hearing and confirming the record of their words. Thus, when she appeared, she took an oath, placing her hand on the Holy Gospels. Afterward, the bishop of Melaka asked her "if she wanted to testify again of what she knew had offended against our holy faith," while also warning her to speak truthfully and not out of hatred or spite.[5] Antonia responded, confirming the purity of her testimony—one neither shaped by coercion nor bribes. Next, she heard the transcript of her denunciations, words that had been recorded not just from one session but over the course of several months. Antonia had been a zealous denunciator. She had not only appeared twice in November 1557 but also the following month and finally in February 1558.[6] These multiple appearances reflected a choice to participate more fully in the inquisitorial process.

Antonia made her first denunciation on November 2, 1557.[7] Born and raised in the house of Diogo Soares, she was described as a nineteen-year-old Christian. Upon taking an oath, she testified about her enslavers' dietary habits. She commented that they ate meat on Fridays and Saturdays, rather than abstaining. Moreover, they used olive oil from Portugal (rather than butter) for their meat, and they did not eat pork, only slaughtering a pig and inviting their enslaved dependents to watch its consumption after the arrest of New Christians suspected of practicing Judaism in the colonial city of Cochin.[8] Proceeding to describe their dress habits, Antonia pointed to an instance in which Diogo Soares, his wife Leonor Fernandes, and his daughter-in-law Clara Lopes wore new clothes on a Friday as well as the "many times" that Leonor washed clothes on Friday to be worn on Saturday.[9] Returning to the theme of food, Antonia mentioned the fasting observed by her enslavers, also remarking that she "never saw them fast any fast of the church."[10] Commenting on her own religious observance, Antonia stated that she was not allowed to go to church or confess, elaborating that "never in all her life had she confessed."[11] After adding an anecdote of her owners' mysterious disappearance one day in August, she concluded her denunciation with an assurance that "she did not wish her masters ill."[12] Due to her illiteracy, her testimony was then signed on her behalf.[13]

The content of Antonia's first denunciation was laden with enough details to point to problematic departures from the Catholic faith. Her enslavers' choice of food, dress, and fasts all ran against Catholic ritual and cultural norms. Moreover, their denial of her right to attend church and confess marked them as poor religious stewards. However condemnatory these details may have been, days later Antonia decided that her first denunciation had been insufficient. When she made her second denunciation, Antonia not only confirmed her judgment of her enslavers' status as bad Christians but also emphasized her own desire to act as a good Christian. Appearing on November 8, 1557, she sought the "discharge of her conscience."[14] Casting herself as someone "new in the matters of the faith" and previously unaware of the extent of her religious obligations during her first denunciation, she had returned determined to withhold nothing.[15] Antonia's new denunciation included details of her enslavers' fasting and dietary habits, fear of prosecution, actions on holidays and Sabbaths, and church attendance, among other details depicting their religious transgressions.

This divulgence of damaging information aided the Inquisition proceedings against Antonia's enslavers. On one level, her denunciations were significant because of their acceptance by inquisitors who confirmed the spiritual and social standing of slaves as fellow

Christians capable of taking oaths and assessing the religious behavior of other members of the Catholic community. Acceptance of her denunciations represented recognition of her Christian status. In this way, inquisitors confirmed slaves' membership in the Catholic community. Yet membership was not only confirmed but was also performed. There was agency exhibited by enslaved Catholics like Antonia who sought to act as good Christians. She voluntarily made assessments of her enslavers' character, and she had done so despite pressure to give a favorable portrayal.

Antonia's second, third, and fourth denunciations emphasized her choice to aid the inquisitorial process. Early in her second denunciation, she made a contrast between her first appearance and her second. The first denunciation occurred when she was brought to testify, similarly to other enslaved people in the household.[16] Like other proceedings, inquisitors gained information by hearing denunciations and confessions from people who came on their own accord as well as people summoned to testify. Antonia's first denunciation was at the behest of the inquisitors; thus, it was made with less choice. At the same time, the content of her first denunciation had been shaped by pressure from another direction—the household itself. According to Antonia, an enslaved disabled Chinese woman coached other slaves on what to say after their enslavers were imprisoned. This unnamed slave instructed them "not to tell the truth of what they knew."[17] In particular, Antonia was coached to say that her enslavers and their family ate pork, did not eat meat with olive oil from Portugal, had butter in their house, and did not eat olive oil from Portugal except with salads, if questioned about these dietary practices.[18] In other words, she was pressured to hide any cultural and religious practices that distinguished her enslavers from the norms of acceptable Catholic practice. Besides further details about her enslavers' religious practices, Antonia's third denunciation likewise revealed pressure within the household not to share any damaging information about her enslavers. She referred to Bastião, Diogo Soares's enslaved eunuch, who had been sold off to Portugal after calling their enslavers Jews and criticizing the lack of slaves' confessions and prayer.[19] Her final denunciation concerned the pressure she had faced personally. She described the efforts of her enslaver's son Manoel Soares and the enslaved Gujarati clerk

Periquo, who sought to intimidate, bribe, and silence her.[20] Thus, Antonia's repeated inquisitorial testimonies represented choices to show religious loyalty rather than fealty to the household in which she had been reared.

Choosing to fully participate in the inquisitorial process, Antonia made multiple denunciations, which were eventually accepted, ratified, and sent along with the rest of her enslavers' files from Goa to Lisbon. Inquisitors depended on denunciators and witnesses like Antonia to share content from which they could devise charges with the ultimate religious goal of bringing the defendant back into reconciliation. While the broader inquisitorial atmosphere was one of compulsion, enslaved participants still had choices on what to say—how much to reveal and how much to conceal. Antonia's denunciations reflected her voluntary participation in the process, without which the Inquisition could not have functioned. Hence, enslaved individuals participated in the surveillance of religious norms as vital members of the Catholic community and contributors to the making of a Portuguese Catholic empire in the Indian Ocean.

THE JUDGMENT OF GABRIEL ABEXIM: ENSLAVED AND FREED CATHOLICS' CENSURE OF THEIR PEERS

Just as enslaved Catholics helped uphold religious norms by commenting on their enslavers, they critiqued the actions of fellow slaves and freed slaves as well. The late sixteenth-century case of Gabriel Abexim, discussed in the previous chapter, exemplified this community policing. After his first Inquisition case, he was placed in the College of St. Thomas as part of his sentence for converting to Islam. As he worked there and received religious instruction, he encountered other workers of servile status. His interactions with these enslaved and freed Catholics would prove to be a snare, trapping him further in the clutches of the Inquisition. Gabriel's second Inquisition trial was precipitated by his flight from the college and subsequent capture; however, the statements of enslaved and freed Catholics shaped the inquisitorial process. Before he appeared for his first session, three witnesses testified. Their testimonies as well as Gabriel's eventual description of their behavior in the college reflected their judgment of his religious behavior.

Ordered to appear before Marcos da Graça, the deputy of the Inquisition, the enslaved Joané was the first to testify about Gabriel on August 19, 1595. He was approximately sixteen years old at the time and made purchases for the fathers of the college. Taking an oath by placing his hand on the Holy Gospels, he "promised to tell the truth and keep it a secret."[21] Then Marcos da Graça queried him about Gabriel, who had been sentenced by the Inquisition to serve in the college in order to "learn all the Christian doctrine and be instructed in the matters of his salvation."[22] Acknowledging their four-month acquaintance in the college, Joané identified Gabriel by name in addition to describing Gabriel's servile status (by calling him a *moço,* which could indicate slave status), his Abyssinian ethnicity or caste, and the reason for his arrival at the college—an inquisitorial sentence.[23] Thus, Gabriel's previous religious transgressions were emphasized; he had arrived at the college with the reputation of an outsider. Immediately following this short yet loaded perception of Gabriel's dubious religious status, Joané commented on their interactions and his own observations about Gabriel's religious behavior. First, he informed the deputy that "many times he heard that [Gabriel] neither wished to know nor learn the Christian doctrine being taught by a *moço* of the aforementioned college named Paulo."[24] Thus, an enslaved teacher was attempting to provide Gabriel with the religious instruction mandated by the Inquisition, and Gabriel was rejecting it.

Continuing his unfavorable portrayal of Gabriel's religious behavior, Joané added that "many times" he had heard Gabriel say he "was a Moor and had to flee to the land of the Moors, and that it was sufficient to him [Gabriel] to be a Christian one month and a Moor another month."[25] Moreover, Joané had seen Gabriel "do certain ceremonies which did not seem good to him."[26] These religious rituals, which he proceeded to describe, were practices that he "had never seen any Christian do."[27] The perplexing particulars included a possible description of the Muslim *salat,* the customary ritual of prayer unnamed explicitly by Joané but suggested by his description of Gabriel's movements as Gabriel spoke "certain words which he, the witness, did not understand."[28] This foreign form of prayer distinguished Gabriel from the familiar religious rituals of the Catholic community, prompting Joané to question Gabriel. In response, according to Joané, Gabriel elucidated that both he and the rituals themselves were Muslim.[29] Wrapping up his commentary on Gabriel, Joané concluded with Gabriel's flight and then proceeded to name some other potential witness under the "obligation of the aforementioned college" who could offer their assessment of Gabriel: João Franco, Hieronimo, and Domingos.[30] By naming these counterparts, Joané aided the inquisitorial process and widened the formal conversation of Gabriel's religious transgressions.

While Hieronimo did not appear, both João Franco and Domingos assessed Gabriel's religious status on August 19.[31] Unlike Joané, the two were categorized as freed slaves in their testimonies. In addition, João Franco was described as an unmarried Javanese painter around the age of twenty, and the younger Domingos was described as acculturated, Gujarati, and approximately thirteen or fourteen years old.[32] Appearing separately after Joané, the two both provided testimonies critiquing Gabriel's disinterest in doctrine. João Franco also commented on Gabriel's desire to flee to the "land of the Moors," while Domingos described Gabriel's prayer habits. Like Joané, he had observed and questioned Gabriel's religious performance. However, his description was more detailed and prompted actions beyond asking questions. Testifying about the prayer, Domingos said that he witnessed Gabriel around noon in the college's garden "with his hands lifted, lowering his head to the ground and lifting it to the heavens, opening his arms now and then, saying certain words between his teeth that he, the witness, did not understand. And, censuring him about the abovementioned ceremonies, the aforementioned Gabriel responded that he did them since he was a Moor."[33] In other words, he had performed the noonday prayer, linking him to the wider Muslim community. Spurred into action, Domingos then informed a teacher.[34] Observing and confronting Gabriel had not been enough. Enforcing the religious norms was a duty.

Collectively, Joané, João Franco, and Domingos participated in the purification project of the Catholic Reformation. They helped officially uphold religious norms of the Catholic community by providing testimony for the Inquisition. Yet, just as important, they observed, commented on, and critiqued religious behaviors before even reaching an inquisitorial court. Not only were they watching and talking, but according to Gabriel they were also socially sanctioning him with their words and actions. In an explanation of his reconversion to Islam, their verbal and physical abuse had propelled his departure from the Catholic faith. By Gabriel's reckoning, they were punishing him for his past—his lack of religious knowledge and his earlier status as a Muslim. Ironically, his inquisitorial sentence to the college was created to bring him back into the Catholic fold, yet his peers within the college reinforced the stigma created by the Inquisition. They rejected the reconciled Catholic as an outsider.[35] Such abuse was absent in the testimonies of Joané, João Franco, and Domingos. However, their testimony alongside Gabriel's defense of himself paints a picture of the informal and formal enforcement of religious normative behavior. The religious college functioned as its own microcosm of the larger colonial Catholic community, and the enslaved and freed played their roles as members.

GONÇALO TOSCANO: CHOOSING CATHOLICISM THROUGH INQUISITORIAL CONFESSION

On May 2, 1597, Gonçalo Toscano voluntarily confessed his religious transgressions to inquisitor Antonio de Barros in Goa.[36] To make this confession he had previously met with the archbishop, surrendering himself to the custody of Capuchin missionaries and ultimately boarding a ship that would take him from Diu to Goa. Upon arrival, he entered the inquisitorial jail and was summoned to give his confession. Emphasizing the voluntary nature of the inquisitorial proceeding, the notary titled the encounter as "Confession and First Session" and initially referred to Gonçalo as the "*confitente*" (denoting that he was making a confession) rather than as a defendant, the label he would later acquire in the case.[37] After being "admonished with words of charity" and urged to make a full confession, Gonçalo proceeded to tell his story of religious journeys between Catholicism and Islam.[38] As the session closed, he called himself "very repentant," an "ignorant young man, weak and miserable sinner, blind and deceived by the devil," and "ready to complete all the penance imposed."[39] Thus presenting himself as a contrite sinner seeking reconciliation, he continued his pursuit of forgiveness over the course of numerous sessions as he and the inquisitors verbally sparred about the nature of his religious choices.

Gonçalo's case, briefly introduced in chapter 3, provides a window into the meaning of religious conversion for the enslaved and freed. For most baptized subjects, Inquisition records documented the process of Catholics' religious and social restoration rather than a permanent estrangement from the Catholic community. The spiritual aim of the Inquisition was to reincorporate Catholic subjects. Thus, after an abjuration of misdeeds, penitents were received back into the Catholic community. This documentation of reincorporation merits special attention for the study of enslaved Catholics, whose initial conversions were often coerced or shaped by religious stewards. On the surface, departing from the religion of bondage would suggest a form of slave resistance and protest. Yet a deeper picture emerges from probing the process of departures and returns to the Catholic faith. An alternative understanding of those religious choices becomes possible. The adversarial yet still dialogic nature of Gonçalo Toscano's inquisitorial proceeding gives us a glimpse of the motives and circumstances behind his multiple conversions.

While no single Inquisition case can explain all the myriad rationales and meanings of religious conversion for enslaved individuals, Gonçalo's case highlights some of them. His conversions seemed to range from authentic changes in belief to conversions of convenience or survival strategies meant to alleviate the pressures he faced as a slave and freed slave. Examining this range in conversions highlights the hardships of slavery and its aftermath, while also acknowledging the multiple forms of religious agency exercised by enslaved people. Moreover, acknowledging the presence of both authentic and strategic conversions allows a flexibility to explore the lives of slaves who were simultaneously spiritual beings who made choices about beliefs and low-status survivors who sought to create lives in a precarious and hierarchical world of limited options. Analyzing Gonçalo's life story, while exceptional in many ways, provides a ground-level exploration of slavery and the manifold meanings of conversion.

Gonçalo Toscano's Enslavement

Born on the Deccan Plateau around 1574, Gonçalo Toscano arrived in Bassein as a four- or five-year-old captive.[40] In Bassein, a principal Portuguese colonial city in the "Province of the North," he was baptized, learning also to read and write. In addition, he learned

Christian doctrine and confessed faithfully every Lenten season.[41] Thus, Gonçalo was an acculturated slave, a young man who was fluent in the Portuguese language, culture, and religion. Yet approximately nine years after his baptism, he was having some troubles with his enslaver, Matteus Carvalho, and decided to run away.[42] Gonçalo did not elaborate further on his relationship with his enslaver, narrating only that he had certain "*desgostos*" with him, vaguely implying displeasures, offenses, or sorrows.[43] While we do not know the particular details behind his discontentment, it is possible that his enslaver was physically abusing him. Contemporary records attest to the violent forms of physical punishment characteristic of slavery in Portuguese India in the sixteenth and seventeenth centuries.[44] Thus, it is possible that physical punishment precipitated his flight. Whatever the precise underlying details, Gonçalo fled to his mother's house in Galiana (Kalyan).[45]

Finding Family and Islam in the "Land of the Moors"

After reaching his mother's home, Gonçalo converted to Islam. He had resolved to become a Muslim beforehand, and his mother paved the way. She advised her son, explaining that "up to that time, he walked in error and outside the path of his salvation by being a Christian, because only the sect of Muhammad was good and true."[46] He was thus fully persuaded. Accordingly, he changed his name, changed his clothing, and was circumcised.[47] Thenceforth, he lived as a Muslim, eating meat indistinctively. This dietary behavior was a marker of identity—an important one because it is explicitly mentioned in his narrative. He effectively stepped outside the Catholic ritual calendar with its proscriptions of meat on certain days. In addition, he celebrated Muslim holidays, fasted for Ramadan, and celebrated the new moon.[48] However, he did not stay with his mother permanently. After two years had passed, he sought to return to Bassein. He contacted his enslaver and secured a safe conduct. Afterward, he told his mother he was going to another village but instead slipped away to Bassein.[49]

Return to Catholicism and Slavery

Around 1590 Gonçalo returned to both Christendom and Catholicism in Bassein.[50] Gonçalo's enslaver, Matteus Carvalho, scrupulously fulfilled the duties of religious stewardship by presenting Gonçalo to an inquisitor who happened to be in Bassein at the time. According to Gonçalo, no confession was taken by the inquisitor. Instead, the inquisitor wrote a note to the rector of São Paulo, and Gonçalo confessed to him. The rector then absolved Gonçalo and gave him penance, which Gonçalo afterward performed.[51] This inquisitorial disinclination to prosecute him for a religious crime was lenient. To an extent, this leniency foreshadowed the eventual Fifth Provincial Council's goal of welcoming runaway slaves back into the Christian fold. Their recovery process explicitly covered Catholic slaves who wished to leave the "land of the infidels" and resume their life in Portuguese Catholic territory, yet Gonçalo's extended stay far exceeded the one-month absence period mandated by the council in 1606.[52] Whatever the inquisitor's motives may have been, Gonçalo lived in Bassein with his enslaver for three years as a Christian after his absolution by the rector. During his time in Bassein, he confessed and received the sacrament of communion, signs that he regularly participated in the Catholic community as an accepted and recognized member.[53]

Wartime Conversion

Despite living three years as a faithful Christian, Gonçalo again fled and returned to Islam. His flight occurred during the early 1590s war between the Portuguese and the Sultanate of Ahmadnagar. During the sultanate's siege of Bassein, Gonçalo faced arrest for operating as a highwayman in addition to carrying money and tamarind to Muslim enemies. With a Portuguese warrant on his head, he initially hid and days later, "tempted by the devil," escaped to the Muslim camp, intending to reconvert to Islam yet again.[54] His flight conformed to patterns of Portuguese renegades, who not only ran away to Muslim states for economic or political gain but also fled Portuguese territory when facing arrest.[55] Moreover, Gonçalo's flight occurred in the midst of other desertions from Bassein. Jesuits noted that Christians in the late sixteenth century were forsaking Catholicism and departing the city for the "land of the Moors."[56]

Arriving in the Muslim camp, he was perceived as a Portuguese Christian, or rather his clothing announced him as such.[57] Yet he assured the captain-major of his religious intentions, which were found credible for a time. He also named his family relations, thus establishing himself as a fellow Muslim.[58] Gonçalo was then given more appropriate clothing, and he dressed himself in the "guise of a Moor."[59] This clothing represented the Muslims' acceptance of him. Moreover, clothing was a powerful symbol that Gonçalo would strategically use as he navigated different communities and crossed borders. In the camp, his clothing as a Muslim symbolized his new allegiance and simultaneously his rejection of the Catholic faith. Merely dressing as a Muslim could instigate inquisitorial prosecution.[60] Clothing was a proxy for identity.

After Gonçalo was received as a Muslim, he was given a horse and was sent out on three campaigns against the Portuguese. Hence, crossing religious lines literally meant changing his military allegiance. He was in the Muslim camp for fifteen days (which included his three battles), before being transferred as a prisoner to the king's headquarters in Ahmadnagar. It is not clear why his new compatriots suddenly distrusted Gonçalo, but he was removed from the camp and stripped of his Muslim garments. As a prisoner, he was put back in Christian dress. In Ahmadnagar, he was presented to the king, Burhan Nizam Shah II, who believed Gonçalo was a spy of the Christians, even after Gonçalo gave him the same account he had given in the Muslim camp.[61] The king delivered Gonçalo to one of his captains, which resulted in Gonçalo's internment in the fortress, where he stayed for three months. During that time he proclaimed to be and was treated as a fellow Muslim. In particular, he prayed Muslim prayers and celebrated the new moon.[62] However, he also looked for a way to escape. During one new moon, the entrance of the fortress was left open. He changed his clothing to appear like a yogi, a Hindu mendicant, and fled.[63]

Travels

For the next three or four months, Gonçalo traveled until he arrived in Diu, a Portuguese fortress on an island near the coast of Gujarat.[64] There he met with some Capuchin friars, telling them about his life. The next day, however, the captain of Diu summoned him. Having heard that Gonçalo had fought in the siege against Christians, he imprisoned him. For the next one and a half years Gonçalo stayed in prison, until an inquisitor passed through Diu. He was presented to this inquisitor, who turned him over to the vicar of the rod.[65] The vicar gave him two options: pay a bond or go back to prison. Tired of prison (and presumably unable or unwilling to pay the bond), Gonçalo schemed to escape. While in the company of a bailiff, he took off running down the street and then hid in the city. The next day after his daring escape, he crossed over to the non-Christian mainland, entering the Mughal Empire.[66]

Gonçalo lived on the mainland "among the Moors" for one and a half years as a Muslim.[67] He wore Muslim clothing, performed Muslim ceremonies, and lived in the company of other Muslims. However, he also communicated with some Portuguese inhabitants, likely renegades. He told them about his experiences, and they told him that in "these parts" there was no solution to his dilemma. He would have to go to Rome, they advised.[68] Hence, Gonçalo clearly told them at least some of his religious transgressions, and we can infer that he was looking for a way back to Christendom—a return to the fold of the church and a return to Portuguese, Catholic territory.

However, after hearing the advice to go to Rome, Gonçalo continued his travels through the Mughal Empire, reaching the land of Cambay. In Cambay he determined that he would go to Mecca. His plan was to embark on a ship that was in the port of Surat. Adept in the art of self-fashioning, he shed his Muslim apparel and again donned the clothing of a yogi.[69] Yet his plans for Mecca changed. A Portuguese armada of Diu arrived, and Gonçalo made contact with some soldiers. He told them about his (previous) plan to go to Rome, and they persuaded him that Rome was not the best place to go for an absolution; instead, he could obtain it from the archbishop who was presently in Daman.[70] Deciding that this was a good option, Gonçalo sent a message to the captain of the armada of Diu, Diogo de Mello. He asked the captain not to hand him over to any other authority of justice except the archbishop. The captain agreed, and Gonçalo embarked on his ship. The armada dropped him off in Diu, entrusting him to the custody of some Capuchin friars. Apparently by this point the archbishop had arrived in Bassein. Accordingly, Gonçalo next embarked from Diu to Bassein and was finally presented to the archbishop. There he gave the archbishop a brief summary of how he became a Muslim, but the archbishop did not have the time for a full account. Accordingly, Gonçalo was put in prison.

The next day, he was sent to Goa by orders of the archbishop in the company of Gonçalo Carvalho.[71] After arriving in Goa, he was placed in the inquisitorial jail on April 1, 1597.[72]

Inquisition

The next month Gonçalo began the first of eight sessions confessing his religious transgressions, reiterating, elaborating, changing, and ratifying their details.[73] At the heart of the sessions were inquisitors' analyses of the timing of his conversions to Islam, his rationale for converting, his knowledge of the gravity of his actions when he converted to Islam, and the sincerity of his confessions. He gave his first confession on May 2, 1597, appearing before the inquisitor Antonio de Barros. The notary recorded that Gonçalo was a native of Balagate of the "Muslim caste," who was also unmarried and a freed young man around the age of twenty-three.[74] Gonçalo took an oath, heard the inquisitor admonish him to give a full account, and then proceeded to describe his travels and multiple conversions. He then ended his account with a plea for mercy.[75] De Barros, however, was not convinced that Gonçalo had divulged everything germane to all those departures from the faith. Accordingly, Gonçalo was sent back to the jail.

Four days later, Gonçalo requested another session with the inquisitor.[76] In this second session, Antonio de Barros asked Gonçalo how long he had been a Muslim. Gonçalo responded that this belief lasted the whole time he was in his mother's house until he returned to Bassein, where he presented himself to an inquisitor.[77] Regarding the other conversions to Islam, however, Gonçalo claimed that he "never in his heart and will stopped being a Christian."[78] Moreover he "entrusted himself to the Virgin our Lady and Saint Francis his advocate to intercede for him to Christ our Lord to forgive his errors and sins."[79] He also added that he "only pretended to be a Muslim in the exterior," claiming that his facade of Muslim belief was a mere charade to enable him to live safely among Muslims.[80] These remarks, however, inflamed De Barros, who said that Gonçalo's statements could not possibly be true. Thus, after further admonishment, Gonçalo returned to his cell.[81]

Five days later, the sessions resumed, and the course of his trial changed; Gonçalo began shifting his statements. In session three held on May 8, 1597, he appeared before two inquisitors, Antonio de Barros and Marcos Gil Frazão.[82] First he told them that he remembered some sins that he had not earlier confessed: he had failed to divulge a pilgrimage he and his mother took to the tomb of a Muslim saint. Moreover, in the Diu prison he had been advised by a "pagan" *feiticeiro* who gave him a silver ring and a small quantity of some sort of root, charms that would free him from his imprisonment, and he had learned a particular Muslim prayer that he said when he went to the mosque.[83] In addition, he disavowed a crucial statement he made in the last session, that his second and third conversions to Islam were mere facades. Instead, he had in fact been a Muslim the entire time he had lived in Muslim territory.[84] He confessed in this session that "he, the defendant, by the deception of the devil in each of the mentioned times, was always a Moor from the heart and will."[85] He proceeded to equate the latter conversions to Islam with his first conversion: all were real. But he also added that when "the memory came to him that he had been a Christian and had lived in the law of Christ our Lord as repentant and stimulated by his own conscience by the error that he had made and committed in leaving our holy faith, he entrusted himself to the Virgin Our Lady and to Saint Francis his advocate to save him and deliver him from that bad tendency, and after that hour by the deception of the devil, he returned another time to the same errors that he had before."[86] After this account, Gonçalo returned to the inquisitorial jail.

In the fourth session on May 12, 1597, the inquisitors probed Gonçalo's rationale for even coming back from the "land of the Moors to the Christians."[87] While the inquisitors did not believe him, he responded that he returned each time because only "the law of Christ" would save him. Skeptically, the inquisitors rejoined that Gonçalo was merely pretending and would return to the Moors if he had a chance; in short, they argued that Gonçalo simply wanted to avoid a heavy punishment.[88] Yet Gonçalo stood firm, answering that if he had not wished for salvation, he would have simply stayed among the Muslims; in that land he was a notary and lacked nothing, adding that many Portuguese people came and resided there.[89] Gonçalo's statements echoed those of João Gomes d'Abreu, a Portuguese soldier prosecuted for "scandalous words." D'Abreu purportedly stated that there was no poverty in the "land of the Moors," if one converted to Islam.[90]

Session five on May 14, 1597, continued the inquisitorial interest in the duration of Gonçalo's Muslim beliefs.[91] Inquisitor Antonio de Barros asked how long Gonçalo believed in the "sect of the Moors." He responded that when he left the fortress of Ahmadnagar dressed as a yogi, he had already intended to journey to the "land of the Christians"; in fact, he was "repentant" and "left the mentioned belief in his heart and will and converted to the aforementioned faith of our Lord Jesus Christ."[92] He continued that while in jail in Diu, he confessed to a Capuchin, who would not absolve him and did not tell him how to become absolved. Yet in jail he was "always a Christian in his heart," entrusting himself to the Virgin Mary and praying the rosary.[93] Fearing more jail time, however, when turned over to the vicar of the rod, he ran away. Moving on to his explanation of the final conversion to Islam, Gonçalo stated that his Muslim beliefs lasted until he asked for a safe conduct.[94] However, the inquisitor disputed Gonçalo's account, insisting the belief in the "sect of the Moors" lasted the whole duration of Gonçalo's travels through the "land of the Moors" to get to Diu in addition to his imprisoned sojourn in Diu until he left again for the "land of the Moors."[95] The inquisitor continued that Gonçalo knew he was an excommunicated man who could only be absolved by the Inquisition yet did not contact the Inquisition. Moreover, Gonçalo had left for the Moors because of "weak" reasons.[96]

To this rejoinder, Gonçalo capitulated. Completely reversing his characterization of his conversions, he now said that he had been "a Moor in his heart" since the second time he "passed to the Moors" until he asked for the safe conduct.[97] Moreover, he stated that he had in fact not been afraid of returning to jail when he ran away from Diu but had crossed over to the Muslims because he was in fact a Muslim. Furthermore, he had only prayed to Mary in Diu in order to "deceive the world so they would consider him a Christian."[98] But now "from his whole heart he was contrite and repentant and he wanted to convert to the faith of Christ our Lord from which he had departed."[99] This departure from the Christian faith, he explained, had occurred because he had been "blinded and deceived by the Devil and had loved the life and liberty and delights of the

Moors."[100] Thus, for a moment, Gonçalo conformed to the inquisitor's views of his conversions to Islam: authentic Islamic beliefs retained in the midst of exterior presentations of Catholic conformity.

Gonçalo would trouble inquisitors' understandings of his conversions, however, in session six on May 22, 1597.[101] In this session Antonio de Barros continued to press Gonçalo on the length of his Muslim beliefs. The inquisitor inquired whether Muslims believed in Mary or other Christian saints, a query to which Gonçalo responded, "No."[102] Next, the inquisitor proceeded to ask whether he had believed in saints and the Virgin Mary when he was a Muslim, querying "if, in the time in which he, the defendant, was a Moor, he believed in Our Lady and entrusted himself to her and called on any saint of Heaven to help and save him?"[103] Frustrating the inquisitor's logic, Gonçalo replied affirmatively. He said that he had appealed to Mary and Saint Francis when he remembered that he had been a Christian and "in the mentioned instant he believed in her as the Christians believe and as he had been taught in St. Paul of Bassein."[104] After this explanation, the inquisitor countered that Gonçalo was contradicting himself and that he could not have been simultaneously Christian and Muslim. Yet, for all of the inquisitor's reasoning, Gonçalo stood firm and insisted that he told the truth. The inquisitor pursued another line of questioning for a moment, yet he returned to a familiar topic, asking how long Gonçalo had remained in the "sect of the Moors in all the times he went to them."[105] Echoing his statements from the latter part of session five, Gonçalo responded that he remained a Muslim the whole time he was in his mother's house and persisted in the belief between his stint in the Muslim campground until his recent request for a safe conduct and return to the "land of the Christians."[106] Despite his concession that he had harbored a belief in the "sect of the Moors" for a longer period than initially confessed, his continued avowal of his belief in Mary and Saint Francis would continue to vex the inquisitors in the following session.

Session seven occurred the following month on June 4, 1597.[107] Gonçalo appeared before Antonio de Barros and Marcos Gil Frazão, and the three continued their tussle over his conversions. Admonishing Gonçalo to tell the truth, the inquisitors insisted that Gonçalo had not really tried to confess and convert back to Catholicism previously. They also seized upon Gonçalo's prior statements about his belief in the Virgin Mary and Saint Francis, contending that it was not true that Gonçalo had entrusted himself to her or any saint when he lived among Muslims. In support, the inquisitors referred to Gonçalo's claim about his time in Diu from the fifth session in which he said that he pretended to pray to Mary when he was among Christians. At this juncture, Gonçalo decided to admit that he had insincerely confessed to the Capuchin as a prisoner in Diu as a deception to appear Christian. However, he refused to back away from his statement that he entrusted himself to "Our Lady as he has said in his confessions" and insisted that he was repentant.[108] The session continued with stern words of warning, as the inquisitors charged that Gonçalo was *still* not a Christian convert. However, it had ended satisfactorily enough to bring the case to a close. Less than a week later, on June 10, a ratification session followed.[109]

Over the course of his several sessions, Gonçalo had shifted his descriptions of conversion under inquisitorial pressure. Initially, he acknowledged one interior conversion to Islam with two subsequent exterior conversions to Islam. Later he claimed three sincere conversions to Islam punctuated by one sincere return to Catholicism as a slave aided by his owner and a completely fake conversion to Catholicism in Diu to fool the world. This supposedly insincere conversion to Catholicism included tricking Portuguese prisoners and even a Capuchin friar. Yet, with all these shifts, he did not seem to relinquish the belief in Mary and Saint Francis, except for a late moment in the fifth session in which he said he pretended to pray to Mary. In the second, third, fifth, sixth, and seventh sessions, he referenced his belief in Catholic saints. However, in the section of the case detailing their decision, inquisitors focused on that one instance in which Gonçalo said he pretended to pray to Mary, claiming that Gonçalo "prayed and entrusted himself exteriorly to Our Lady, it was all feigned and in order for others to consider him a Christian, being a Moor in his heart."[110] This was how they explained Gonçalo's motive for leaving his situation of imprisonment in Diu—a "weak cause" for crossing over to the non-Christian mainland. While inquisitors saw a series of truthful conversions to Islam and deceptive conversions to Catholicism, Gonçalo claimed to have been on a quest to live as a Christian. In the meetings between the defendant and inquisitors, competing narratives collided and eventually converged as the inquisitors' vision of Gonçalo's conversions triumphed and culminated in his abjuration. However, Gonçalo's repeated returns to Catholic territory and repeated claims of belief in Catholic saints across sessions suggest that Gonçalo attributed a different meaning to these conversions than the inquisitors came to accept.

On July 30, 1597, the inquisitors finally decided Gonçalo's sentence.[111] He would be admitted into the reconciliation of the church in the See of Goa with the requirement of wearing the penitential habit at the discretion of the inquisitors.[112] They took into account the fact that he had confessed his offenses, asked to receive mercy and be pardoned, and voluntarily returned from non-Christian territory to present himself to the archbishop in Bassein. Yet they still considered him to be at risk of returning to the Muslims if he remained in India. Thus, they requested the viceroy's permission to send Gonçalo on a ship to Portugal. In the meantime he would stay in prison or some "other safe place" so that he could be "instructed in the matters of faith necessary for the salvation of his soul."[113] Also included in his sentence was the confiscation of all his goods for the benefit of the Portuguese government, namely the royal council and the exchequer.[114] Gonçalo made his abjuration on August 24, 1597, and began his sentence in Goa.[115] By December he had exited India on a ship to Portugal, as the inquisitors had wished.[116]

Interpreting Gonçalo's Conversions: From Cultural Retentions to Authenticity

Just as Gonçalo's conversions and religious convictions raised inquisitorial questions, his religious agency invites analysis of the rationales behind his conversions. Were his conversions evidence of cultural retentions? Were his conversions to Islam authentic or inauthentic, interior or exterior? Questions about a religious core have elicited multiple responses by scholars. Some historians carefully state when their analyzed subject sincerely changed religious affiliations. For example, Eric Dursteler notes that women's strategic border crossings in the Mediterranean world did not equate to merely feigned changes in belief.[117] Taking another approach in his analysis of border crossing and conversions in Germany, Duane Corpis sidesteps the question of authenticity and interior belief, preferring to examine conversions as social acts.[118] However, suggesting a religious core, similar to Natalie Zemon Davis's assessment of the famed sixteenth-century captive Leo Africanus (also known as Yuhanna al-Asad), is analytically useful here.[119] An examination of authenticity provides a pathway forward to understanding Gonçalo's religious journeys more than an assessment through the lens of cultural retentions.

On the surface, Gonçalo's first conversion to Islam after his enslavement resembled the many other conversions by enslaved individuals who were prosecuted by the Goa Tribunal. Ostensibly born to Muslim parents, he was taken captive and then converted to Catholicism, later returning to his Islamic religious roots. Such a narrative would lend itself to the explanatory framework of cultural retentions and survivals, often contrasted with the creolization and assimilation processes other scholars have documented as part of enslaved people's cross-oceanic journeys into unfamiliar settings and new communities.[120] At various times, notaries categorized Gonçalo as "*casta mouro,*" someone of the "Moorish" caste.[121] João Delgado Figueira repeated this designation in his seventeenth-century *Reportorio,* calling Gonçalo "*casta mouro*" and the "*filho de pais mouros*"—that is, the son of "Moorish" parents.[122] Moreover, Gonçalo resumed the use of a "Moorish name," which he had apparently lost upon his enslavement. Interestingly enough, this name was not recorded in his Inquisition case.[123] However, a close reading of Gonçalo's case suggests his religious journey was more complex than a return to Islam. Gonçalo was taken captive around age four or five, but he was not circumcised until he returned to his mother's house several years later. It is highly doubtful that he had a depth of Islamic religious knowledge or strong self-understandings as a Muslim before his enslavement, making his "return" to Islam rather like an entirely new religious conversion.

By taking the risk of assessing the authenticity of Gonçalo's multiple conversions based on his statements and actions, we are able to suggest why he ultimately decided to come back to Catholicism and Catholic territory. While inquisitors insisted that each conversion to Islam was authentic, the circumstances behind each change of religious affiliation suggest otherwise. He converted to Islam after fleeing Bassein as a wanted man, a conversion of convenience that he attempted to undo by voluntarily seeking out Capuchin friars in

Diu after his escape from the fortress in Ahmadnagar. After imprisonment in Diu for one and a half years, he escaped incarceration and again resumed life as a Muslim in the "land of the Moors." This was another conversion of convenience, after which he sought the advice of Portuguese renegades for a pathway back to the Catholic fold. He would later voluntarily, through the mediation of Portuguese soldiers, contact the captain of a Portuguese armada in order to confess his transgressions to an archbishop. Unlike defendants who had been denounced, Gonçalo would request an initial audience with the Inquisition. Such persistence to obtain official readmission to the Catholic Church would suggest that Gonçalo had a Catholic core.

Accepting Gonçalo's distinction between authentic interior conversions and false exterior conversions would place his dissimulations as a yogi on the same plane as his second and third conversions to Islam. Inquisitors neither prosecuted him for paganism nor for the consultation of a *feiticeiro,* although both were inquisitorial crimes for which other contemporaries were punished by the Goa Tribunal.[124] Instead, in Gonçalo's case, these acts seemed to have been recognized as patently inauthentic and merely convenient. Yet inquisitors insisted on seeing all of Gonçalo's conversions to Islam as interior changes in belief because of the "weak" motives that catalyzed them. However, impending arrest, hunger, and fear of endangerment do not appear so "weak," when one views all of Gonçalo's later shifts in affiliations as conversions of convenience. Just as the guise of a yogi conveniently enabled him to move across varying landscapes, living as a Muslim afforded him protection until he was able to resume the life he desired as an absolved Catholic in Portuguese-ruled territory. When presented with the opportunity, he sought to rejoin the Catholic community, which he ultimately achieved by seeking reconciliation through the Inquisition.

* * *

Enslaved and freed Catholics participated in the inquisitorial process in ways that buttressed the institution and confirmed their Catholic identity as a choice. The institution was a secretive yet public forum where Catholics came to discuss their beliefs, words, and actions as well as the religious behaviors of fellow members of the broader Catholic community. Their testimonies informally judged community members across the free-slave divide and created the content for formal inquisitorial judgments. In this way, they claimed membership in the Portuguese Catholic community by making denunciations and giving testimonies. These were actions not unlike those made by their counterparts in Portugal itself.[125] Moreover, they chose to belong to the Catholic community by making confessions in the inquisitorial arena. Thus, Inquisition records not only documented religious heterodoxy but also the orthodoxy of the enslaved. In the religious and political landscape of Portuguese India, both the enslaved and free faced the pressure to conform. In the Portuguese Catholic community, belonging was based on religious identity. Yet this pressure did not erase the agentive acts taken by enslaved individuals to belong. The Inquisition itself was a site not only of pressure but also a recorder of agency. Through the institution's documentation of religious agency, we see how some enslaved and freed Catholics contributed to the project of making an early modern Catholic empire in the Indian Ocean by performing the duties of membership. Sincerely holding beliefs and seeking to discharge their conscience, they chose Catholic community.

Conclusion

IN THE SIXTEENTH and seventeenth centuries, the Catholic Church and the Portuguese crown had a vested interest in enslaved subjects' status as Catholics. The Portuguese imperial project entailed the making of a Catholic empire, and enslaved people were included in the drive to expand Christendom. Accordingly, their conversion was a priority, distinguishing the Portuguese Empire from its early modern European competitors in the Indian Ocean. To facilitate conversions to Catholicism, enslavers were conceptualized as religious stewards responsible for their enslaved dependents' incorporation into the Portuguese Catholic community from the moment of acquisition to beyond their death. Thus, the church and crown intervened at the household level to create a Catholic empire inclusive of enslaved people.

Shaping the religious demography of slavery at the household level not only changed the religious composition of the empire but also enhanced imperial security. Armed slaves defended the Portuguese Empire in India during times of war. In the colonial imagination, the loyalty of these enslaved individuals corresponded to their identity as Catholics. Whether enslaved Catholics themselves made this link between loyalty and religious identity bears more research. However, their status as coreligionists was viewed as a security asset in the context of a consciously post-Reconquest Iberian empire whose power was checked by strong Muslim-ruled states and

Muslim merchant networks in a contested Indian Ocean world. Religious conversion created perpetual and extraterritorial bonds linking enslaved Catholics simultaneously to the Portuguese Empire and the church. Interactions with the Portuguese Inquisition reinforced those bonds, while also shedding light on the relationship between slavery, conversion, and empire.

As fellow Catholics, enslaved individuals appeared before inquisitors in Goa. While in bondage, they testified about their lives, their religious identities, and the religious performance of others. Though they were enslaved, their words had weight. Central to the acceptance of their testimonies and the inquisitorial judgment of their own religious performance was their status as coreligionists. Through their conversion to Catholicism, they became documented members of the Portuguese colonial Catholic community. This membership included both rights and responsibilities. Baptism opened a pathway to participate in church-sanctioned community rituals such as mass attendance, observance of the Sunday Sabbath and Catholic holidays, confession, marriage, and burial. These rituals constituted church-mandated rights for enslaved Catholics. Their rights were reinforced by church-mandated responsibilities bestowed upon their enslavers, who as religious stewards had a duty to encourage and protect enslaved dependents' status as fellow Catholics. Yet the conflicting prerogatives of ownership and duties of religious stewardship led slaveholders to seesaw between blocking and recognizing their enslaved coreligionists' equal spiritual status. Enslavers often privileged religious rights that did not sharply contest their ownership status.

Directives on rights by the church and the Portuguese crown did not automatically guarantee that those rights would actually be enjoyed by enslaved people. Instead, the household was a contested space, where enslaved Catholics struggled for the recognition of their religious rights. At the same time, the household was not only a place where the enslaved contended for their religious rights but also a place where they exercised their own religious responsibilities. They observed and collected information about their enslavers as well as their peers in the quasi-public space of the household. Moreover, they took that information to the more public space of the inquisitorial court. Even in the face of interference, enslaved Catholics acted as agents claiming their status as members of the larger Catholic community.

This religious connection between the empire and household shaped the lived experience of slavery in early modern Portuguese India. Due to the emphasis on religious identity, enslaved Catholics had the right to belong as fellow members of the colonial Catholic community. This religiously defined membership was significant in the context of the empire's denial of rights to non-Catholics. Moreover, this membership was available to both the enslaved and the free. The religious nature of community membership offered enslaved Catholics forms of agency and status that transcended the condition of being an enslaved person. Thus, in a study of slavery in early modern Portuguese India, it is critical that we remember that slave status was not the only determinant of enslaved peoples' experiences. The debilitating category of slave was just one social and legal category of many that enslaved Catholics inhabited, and Catholic status offered a way to resist slavery's attendant dangers, anxieties, and violations. At the same time, Catholic status often came through coercion and exposed the enslaved to the jurisdiction of the Inquisition, creating a different set of dilemmas: the threat of social condemnation, exile, and other sanctions for choosing different religious identities, beliefs, and practices. Yet inquisitorial jurisdiction and community judgment encompassed both enslaved and free people. As fellow members of the Catholic community, all faced the possibility of sanctions as defendants in addition to the possibility of participation in the sanctioning process as witnesses and denunciators. Again, the incorporative nature of Catholic status drew both enslaved and free subjects into one hierarchical yet shared colonial community. Religious incorporation was a defining feature of slavery in early modern Portuguese India. The extent to which the relationship between slavery, religion, and empire constituted a particularly early modern phenomenon remains to be seen, inviting further research on slavery spanning the Portuguese Empire's beginnings in India to slavery's abolition and aftermath in the nineteenth century.

QUESTIONS RAISED FOR FUTURE RESEARCH

While early modern enslaved individuals hailing from multiple continents exercised rights as Catholics, the twenty-first-century popular memory of slavery in the Indian state of Goa is race-based. On

February 11, 2002, a seemingly innocuous set of newspaper articles sparked a local debate on the origins of slavery. Both articles covered the exhibition of a Siddhi dance troupe from Karnataka, a state that neighbors Goa. A reporter for the *Herald* had interviewed Minguel Anton Siddhi, who explained to the reporter that the Siddhis had African origins but considered themselves to be Indians.[1] An anonymous staff reporter for the *Navhind Times* also covered the cultural event, but that article immediately emphasized the Siddhis' slave roots. The reporter began the article with the chronologically erroneous statement, "Nearly 400 years ago, when the British had abolished slavery, the Africans were brought to Goa by the Portuguese for various types of work, but they left Goa and settled at the Yellapur district in Karwar out of sheer fear of tourture [*sic*] from Portuguese [*sic*]."[2] Seven days later, a volley of dueling op-eds and letters to the editor began, lasting until April 19, 2002.[3] At the heart of the debate was Portuguese responsibility for slavery and the slave trade, a conversation that encompassed but also extended beyond the origins of the African-descended community.[4]

While this lively exchange is significant simply for its heated analysis of the legacy of Portuguese colonialism, the debate brings up two interconnected issues related to our discussion of sixteenth- and seventeenth-century slavery in Portuguese India. First is the issue of memory. From these articles, it is clear that slavery in Portuguese India is remembered as an institution whereby African labor was imported from outside the Indian subcontinent. The various participants in the newspaper exchange quibbled over who was responsible for the presence of Africans. This suggests that over time African descent became synonymous with slave status, despite the early modern presence of a multicontinental enslaved population. This local memory of African slavery leads to another point of inquiry. If enslaved people are largely remembered as Africans in the twenty-first century, did the demography of the enslaved population change over time? If so, this would open up a comparative conversation on the transition to race-based slavery, including both the Indian and Atlantic Oceans. Moreover, did a potential shift to race-based slavery make it harder for enslaved people to belong in colonial society? On the other hand, since the local memory of slavery is African, what are the hidden histories of slavery and its aftermath for descendants of non-African slaves in Portugal's former empire in India? Examining these questions would simultaneously enhance the historiography on slavery and memory as well as the literature on African Indians and the African diaspora in the Indian Ocean.[5]

Parish records offer another line of potential research: a deeper examination of South Asian slavery in Portuguese India. Often the study of slavery and the slave trade examines enslaved people who were clearly exported overseas. Yet we know that enslaved South Asians labored in Portuguese India. Some were local to the area in which they lived, while others came from different parts of the Indian subcontinent. The ethnonyms of enslaved South Asians reflected this coerced migration.[6] Just as Paul Tiyambe Zeleza encourages scholars to study "intra-Africa diasporas" (rather than solely focusing on transfers of Africans outside the African continent), it is vital to consider the experiences of enslaved South Asians who never left the Indian subcontinent.[7] Moreover, examining their experiences would allow us to assess the potential connections and distinctions between slavery in Portuguese India and slavery in its neighboring polities.[8] South Asian slaves would have had ideas of their own about slavery that were rooted in their places of origin, whether they were enslaved locally or enslaved in a new destination within the Indian subcontinent. Such an analysis of enslaved South Asians would simultaneously contribute to the histories of slavery in the Portuguese Empire, South Asia, and the Indian Ocean world. As the documented ethnic and caste origins of enslaved individuals indicate, the slave trade funneling laborers to and through Portuguese India was not only oceanic but also subcontinental.

Just as a deeper demographic examination of slavery would present a fuller picture of South Asian slaves, an assessment of the slaveholding population would be instructive. What was the potential impact of slaveholders' ethnic backgrounds on the exercise of mastery, expectations about slave ownership, and the assignment of tasks to enslaved people? While Portuguese slaveholders brought ideas and practices of mastery with them to Portuguese India, South Asian Catholics whose slaveholding rights were preserved through conversion also had their own precolonial histories of slave ownership. Although the names of slaveholding South Asian Catholics in the parish records occluded their indigenous background, the recording of caste revealed it. While the Portuguese used the word *casta* to broadly denote religious heritage (such as "Moor," New Christian, etc.) and ethnicity (such as *cafre* or *china*), they also used the word to denote indigenous South Asian categories of caste. For example, the terms "Brahman" and "Sudra" were recorded in the parish records. Given that South Asian socioreligious categories resonated in the new colonial context even after conversion to Catholicism, it is highly probable that South Asian ideas about slavery and mastery continued to resonate as well. We cannot assume that the Portuguese colonial presence created a complete rupture in the history of slavery in South Asia.[9]

While the above suggestions offer pathways to assess more broadly the subcontinental geography of slavery, revisiting the imperial layer invites yet another route to future research. Goa was distinct as the location of the only overseas tribunal of the Portuguese Inquisition, the seat of the viceroy, the seat of the archbishop, and the center of Indian Ocean Catholic missionary expansion. Proximity to Goa equated to more imperial and ecclesiastical oversight. Similarly, the other port cities examined in this book were of high strategic importance to the empire. To what extent did slavery in Portuguese India differ farther from the center of the empire? Where the geographical reach of the Inquisition and viceroy was weaker, how did the experiences and rights of enslaved people shift? An examination of slavery in the imperial core juxtaposed with its peripheries would be insightful. It is possible enslaved Catholics had less access to church-mandated rights and that their enslavers accordingly ignored church-mandated responsibilities.[10] For example, using the Inquisition as a forum became less likely on the empire's peripheries. While the Goa Tribunal had jurisdiction over the entire Indian Ocean empire, it could only effectively project its power so far. To reach past its center of control, the tribunal employed commissioners and made inquisitorial visits outside of Goa. Yet reliance on these mechanisms was not equivalent to the ease of a resident of Goa approaching the local Goa Tribunal. Thus, the geographical limitations of imperial power likely shaped the experience of slavery. On the other hand, it is possible that the enslaver-slave relationship and its religious overtones were far less important in imperial peripheries, leading enslaved individuals to exercise agency in a wholly different way. For example, on the outskirts of empire we see armed slaves in Mozambique who amassed power, created a new ethnic identity, and held a status not shaped by the church and crown.[11] Thus, assessing this topic would enable us to see differences and similarities within the wider Portuguese Empire in the Indian Ocean. Moreover, it would also offer another opportunity to assess the prevalence of indigenous Indian Ocean patterns of slavery within the empire.

Along the same lines, a critical survey of slavery across the global Portuguese Empire would yield new insights. At its height, the Portuguese Empire included not only locations in the Indian Ocean but also in North Africa, West Africa and on islands off its coast, West Central Africa, and Brazil in addition to its Iberian metropole. A systematic review of Portuguese imperial slavery across the globe has yet to be written.[12] Just as A. R. Disney addresses the need to examine the Portuguese Empire holistically rather than solely focusing on its constituent parts, we could investigate the history of slavery in the Lusophone world by synthesizing the extant rich yet geographically discrete studies of slavery.[13] Such a survey would not only elucidate imperial commonalities and connections but also highlight Indian Ocean (and other regional) particularities.[14] As this study has shown, ideas and mandates about slavery flowed from the metropole to the Portuguese Empire in India. Accordingly, one empire-wide query would be the shared versus distinctive impacts of these metropolitan ideas and mandates across the empire. Yet another way to assess slavery in the empire is to ask what were the potential intellectual and labor connections between different parts of the empire. Rather than a center-periphery analysis connecting Lisbon to India or Lisbon to Brazil, what were the horizontal connections? In other words, if we utilized Kerry Ward's conception of empires as collections of networks, how did ideas about slavery (along with particular slaves and slaveholders) circulate between different nodes of imperial networks?[15] Such an analysis would connect the histories of slavery along imperial peripheries rather than privileging flows of ideas and people from the center.

Thus, with a combination of different geographies and underutilized records, a fuller history of slavery becomes possible. Delving into that history is not only a way to probe slavery in the abstract but also a way to examine the diverse experiences of enslaved individuals in the Indian Ocean and beyond. Such an examination is a project of recovery and memorialization of those who have often been forgotten. In the tradition of recent commemorations of enslaved individuals elsewhere, let us conclude with the names of some who participated in the complex history of empire in the Indian Ocean: Antonia Malavar, Gabriel Abexim, and Gonçalo Toscano.[16] Their stories, and so many untold, await further recognition and remembrance.

Notes

PREFACE

1. Stephanie Hassell, "Inquisition Records from Goa as Sources for the Study of Slavery in the Eastern Domains of the Portuguese Empire," *History in Africa* 42 (2015): 397–418.
2. For an assessment of race and religious identity, see Rudy Bauss, "A Demographic Study of Portuguese India and Macau as well as Comments on Mozambique and Timor, 1750–1850," *Indian Economic and Social History Review* 34, no. 2 (1997): 199–216. Bauss suggests that race was a less important category than religion in Goa until the 1787 Pinto Revolt. Bauss, 205.
3. On currencies, see C. R. Boxer, *The Portuguese Seaborne Empire, 1415–1825* (Middlesex, UK: Penguin Books, 1973), 389, 392–93, and Sanjay Subrahmanyam, *The Portuguese Empire in Asia, 1500–1700: A Political and Economic History,* 2nd ed. (Chichester, UK: John Wiley & Sons, 2012), 297–301. An alternative spelling for *pardao* is *pardau.*

INTRODUCTION

1. Processo de Leonor Fernandes, Arquivo Nacional da Torre do Tombo (ANTT), Inquisição de Lisboa (IL), Processos, No. 7631, fl. 61v. For the digital copy of the case and other ANTT/IL material, see http://digitarq.arquivos.pt/.
2. Processo de Diogo Soares, ANTT, IL, Processos, No. 185, fl. 25/27 (this case has a dual pagination system); Processo de Leonor Fernandes, fl. 21; Processo de Estevão Lopes, ANTT, IL, Processos, No. 360, fl. 16; Processo de Guiomar de Oliveira, ANTT, IL, Processos, No. 11171, fl. 20.
3. Processo de Leonor Fernandes, fl. 21.
4. Descendants of Jews forcibly converted to Catholicism in 1497, New Christians were constantly under the suspicion of continuing

to practice the religion of their ancestors. For New Christians and the Inquisition, see James C. Boyajian, "Goa Inquisition: A New Light on the First 100 Years (1561–1660)," *Purabhilekh-Puratatva* 4, no. 1 (1986): 1–40, and Toby Green, *Inquisition: The Reign of Fear* (New York: Thomas Dunne, 2009).

5. For social death, see Orlando Patterson, *Slavery and Social Death: A Comparative Study* (Cambridge, MA: Harvard University Press, 1982).
6. Michelle A. McKinley, *Fractional Freedoms: Slavery, Intimacy, and Legal Mobilization in Colonial Lima, 1600–1700* (New York: Cambridge University Press, 2016); Michelle McKinley, "Fractional Freedoms: Slavery, Legal Activism, and Ecclesiastical Courts in Colonial Lima, 1593–1689," *Law and History Review* 28, no. 3 (2010): 749–90.
7. Glenn J. Ames, "Serving God, Mammon, or Both? Religious vis-à-vis Economic Priorities in the Portuguese *Estado da India,* c. 1600–1700," *Catholic Historical Review* 86, no. 2 (2000): 193–216.
8. G. V. Scammell, "The Pillars of Empire: Indigenous Assistance and the Survival of the 'Estado da India,' c. 1600–1700," *Modern Asian Studies* 22, no. 3 (1988): 473–89.
9. Patrícia Souza de Faria, "Mais Soldados e Menos Padres: Remédios para a Preservação do Estado da Índia (1629–1636)," *História Unisinos* 16, no. 3 (2012): 357–68.
10. Teotonio R. de Souza, "O Padroado Português do Oriente visto da Índia: Instrumentalização Política da Religião," *Revista Lusófona de Ciência das Religiões* 7, nos. 13–14 (2008): 413–30. For a more recent analysis of missionaries and the relationship between the Portuguese Empire and religion, see Ananya Chakravarti, *The Empire of Apostles: Religion,* Accommodatio, *and the Imagination of Empire in Early Modern Brazil and India* (New Delhi: Oxford University Press, 2018).
11. Ângela Barreto Xavier, *Religion and Empire in Portuguese India: Conversion, Resistance, and the Making of Goa* (Albany: State University of New York Press, 2022).
12. See C. R. Boxer, *The Portuguese Seaborne Empire, 1415–1825* (Middlesex, UK: Penguin Books, 1973); Malyn Newitt, *A History of Portuguese Overseas Expansion, 1400–1668* (London: Routledge, 2005); M. N. Pearson, *The Portuguese in India* (Cambridge: Cambridge University Press, 2006); and Sanjay Subrahmanyam, *The Portuguese Empire in Asia, 1500–1700: A Political and Economic History,* 2nd ed. (Chichester, UK: John Wiley & Sons, 2012).

13. Teotonio R. de Souza, *Medieval Goa: A Socio-Economic History*, 2nd ed. (Saligão, Goa: Goa, 1556, 2009); P. D. Xavier, *Goa, A Social History, 1510–1640* (Panaji, Goa: Rajhauns Vitaran, 1993).
14. Jeanette Pinto, *Slavery in Portuguese India, 1510–1842* (Bombay: Himalaya, 1992).
15. Ann M. Pescatello, "The African Presence in Portuguese India," *Journal of Asian History* 11, no. 1 (1977): 26–48; Timothy Walker, "Slaves or Soldiers? African Conscripts in Portuguese India, 1857–1860," in *Slavery and South Asian History*, ed. Indrani Chatterjee and Richard M. Eaton (Bloomington: Indiana University Press, 2006), 234–61.
16. Rudy Bauss, "A Demographic Study of Portuguese India and Macau as well as Comments on Mozambique and Timor, 1750–1850," *Indian Economic and Social History Review* 34, no. 2 (1997): 199–216; Rudy Bauss, "The Portuguese Slave Trade from Mozambique to Portuguese India and Macau and Comments on Timor, 1750–1850: New Evidence from the Archives," *Camões Center Quarterly* 6/7, nos. 1–2 (Summer/Fall 1997): 21–26; Celsa Pinto, *Trade and Finance in Portuguese India: A Study of the Portuguese Country Trade, 1770–1840* (New Delhi: Concept, 1994); Hugo C. Cardoso, "The African Slave Population of Portuguese India: Demographics and Impact on Indo-Portuguese," *Journal of Pidgin and Creole Languages* 25, no. 1 (2010): 95–119; Andreas Hofbauer, *Diáspora Africana na Índia: Sobre Castas, Raças e Lutas* (São Paulo: Editora Unesp, 2021); Pedro Machado, "A Forgotten Corner of the Indian Ocean: Gujarati Merchants, Portuguese India and the Mozambique Slave-Trade, *c.* 1730–1830," in *The Structure of Slavery in Indian Ocean Africa and Asia*, ed. Gwyn Campbell (London: Frank Cass, 2004), 17–32; Pedro Machado, *Ocean of Trade: South Asian Merchants, Africa and the Indian Ocean, c. 1750–1850* (Cambridge: Cambridge University Press, 2014); Pescatello, "African Presence in Portuguese India," 26–48; and Timothy Walker, "Abolishing the Slave Trade in Portuguese India: Documentary Evidence of Popular and Official Resistance to Crown Policy, 1842–60," *Slavery and Abolition* 25, no. 2 (2004): 63–79. On the slave trade, see also Teotonio R. de Souza, "French Slave-Trading in Portuguese Goa (1773–1791)," in *Essays in Goan History*, ed. Teotonio R. de Souza (New Delhi: Concept, 1989), 119–31.
17. See, for instance, Indrani Chatterjee and Richard M. Eaton, eds., *Slavery and South Asian History* (Bloomington: Indiana University Press, 2006); Emma Kalb, "Slavery in South Asia," in *The*

Palgrave Handbook of Global Slavery throughout History, ed. Damian A. Pargas and Juliane Schiel (Cham, Switzerland: Palgrave Macmillan, 2023), 517–34; and Utsa Patnaik and Manjari Dingwaney, eds., *Chains of Servitude: Bondage and Slavery in India* (Madras: Sangam Books, 1985).

18. Richard M. Eaton, "Introduction," in Chatterjee and Eaton, *Slavery and South Asian History,* 1–16; Indrani Chatterjee, "Renewed and Connected Histories: Slavery and the Historiography of South Asia," in Chatterjee and Eaton, *Slavery and South Asian History,* 17–43.
19. Walker, "Slaves or Soldiers?," 234–61.
20. On the British, see D. R. Banaji, *Slavery in British India,* 2nd ed. (Bombay: D. B. Taraporevala Sons, 1933); Amal Kumar Chattopadhyay, *Slavery in the Bengal Presidency, 1772–1843* (London: Golden Eagle, 1977); Margot Finn, "Slaves out of Context: Domestic Slavery and the Anglo-Indian Family, c. 1780–1830," *Transactions of the Royal Historical Society* 19 (2009): 181–203; and Indrani Chatterjee, *Gender, Slavery and Law in Colonial India* (New Delhi: Oxford University Press, 1999). For the Dutch, see especially the recent works on slavery in Cochin: Matthias van Rossum et al., *Testimonies of Enslavement: Sources on Slavery from the Indian Ocean World* (London: Bloomsbury Academic, 2020), and Alexander Geelen et al., "On the Run: Runaway Slaves and Their Social Networks in Eighteenth-Century Cochin," *Journal of Social History* 54, no. 1 (Fall 2020): 66–87. While we know the French participated in slave trading from India, very little is known about slavery itself in French India. See Richard B. Allen, "Exporting the Unfortunate: The European Slave Trade from India, 1500–1800," *Slavery and Abolition* 43, no. 3 (2022): 533–52, and Marina Carter, "Slavery, Ethnicity, and Identity in the Indian Ocean Colonial World: A Case Study of 'Indian' Slaves on Mauritius," in *Being a Slave: Histories and Legacies of European Slavery in the Indian* Ocean, ed. Alicia Schrikker and Nira Wickramasinghe (Leiden: Leiden University Press, 2020), 43–59. A notable exception is Sue Peabody, *Madeleine's Children: Family, Freedom, Secrets, and Lies in France's Indian Ocean Colonies* (New York: Oxford University Press, 2017), 11–26. The exported Madeleine's enslavement in India is discussed.
21. For an overview, see Richard B. Allen, *European Slave Trading in the Indian Ocean, 1500–1850* (Athens: Ohio University Press, 2014).
22. Richard B. Allen, *Slave, Convict, and Indentured Labor and the Tyranny of the Particular* (Berlin: EB Verlag, 2020).

23. Richard B. Allen, "Merchant Capital and Labor Migration in the Colonial Indian Ocean World," *Historia Crítica,* no. 89 (2023): 136.
24. See table 4 in Allen, "Merchant Capital," 137.
25. Allen, "Exporting the Unfortunate," 533–52.
26. Allen, 536–37; Markus Vink, "'The World's Oldest Trade': Dutch Slavery and Slave Trade in the Indian Ocean in the Seventeenth Century," *Journal of World History* 14, no. 2 (2003): 141–43; and Anthony Reid, "Slavery and Forced Labour in Asia: *Status Quaestionis,*" in *Slavery and Bonded Labor in Asia, 1250–1900,* ed. Richard B. Allen (Leiden: Brill, 2022), 42.
27. Allen, "Exporting the Unfortunate," 539, 541.
28. Richard M. Eaton identified warfare and impoverishment as the key drivers of the production of first-generation slaves in India, yet the internal slave trade itself was not explored in his important coedited volume with Indrani Chatterjee on South Asia. See Eaton, "Introduction," in Chatterjee and Eaton, *Slavery and South Asian History,* 5–6. Similarly, while Amal Chattopadhyay addresses the existence of the internal slave trade and the factors behind Indian enslavement, he does not describe the inner workings of the trade. See Chattopadhyay, *Slavery in the Bengal Presidency,* 11–27. The lack of knowledge on the internal slave trade is also exemplified by Scott C. Levi's examination of the export of Indians to Central Asia; similar factors produced slaves for export and internal South Asian use. However, the functioning of the internal slave trade itself is not described. See Scott C. Levi, "Hindus beyond the Hindu Kush: Indians in the Central Asian Slave Trade," *Journal of the Royal Asiatic Society* 12, no. 3 (2002): 277–88.
29. Gwyn Campbell, "Introduction: Slavery and Other Forms of Unfree Labour in the Indian Ocean World," in *The Structure of Slavery in Indian Ocean Africa and Asia,* ed. Gwyn Campbell (London: Frank Cass, 2004), ix.
30. Souza, *Medieval Goa,* 89; Tatiana Seijas, *Asian Slaves in Colonial Mexico: From Chinos to Indians* (New York: Cambridge University Press, 2014), 49–61; Lúcio de Sousa, *The Portuguese Slave Trade in Early Modern Japan: Merchants, Jesuits and Japanese, Chinese, and Korean Slaves* (Leiden: Brill, 2019).
31. Seijas, *Asian Slaves in Colonial Mexico,* 49–61.
32. K. S. Mathew, *Portuguese Trade with India in the Sixteenth Century* (New Delhi: Manohar, 1983), 137–38; Subrahmanyam, *Portuguese Empire in Asia,* 240. The European continental market for slaves was not limited to Portugal. For the understudied Danish slave trade, see Jorge Simón Izquierdo Díaz, "The Trade in

Domestic Servants (Morianer) from Tranquebar for Upper Class Danish Homes in the First Half of the Seventeenth Century," *Itinerario* 43, no. 2 (2019): 194–217.

33. Portuguese slave trading, in addition to European slave trading more broadly, connected oceans. See Allen, *European Slave Trading,* 21–22. For slavery's connections across oceans, see also Janet J. Ewald, "Crossers of the Sea: Slaves, Freedmen, and Other Migrants in the Northwestern Indian Ocean, c. 1750–1914," *American Historical Review* 105, no. 1 (February 2000): 69–91, and Matthew S. Hopper, *Slaves of One Master: Globalization and Slavery in Arabia in the Age of Empire* (New Haven, CT: Yale University Press, 2015).

34. Titas Chakraborty, "Slave Trading and Slave Resistance in the Indian Ocean World: The Case of Early Eighteenth-Century Bengal," *Slavery and Abolition* 40, no. 4 (2019): 706–26 (Chakraborty examines the Dutch and English); Hans Hägerdal, "The Slaves of Timor: Life and Death on the Fringes of Early Colonial Society," *Itinerario* 34, no. 2 (2010): 19–44; Hans Hägerdal, "Warfare, Bestowal, Purchase: Dutch Acquisition of Slaves in the World of Eastern Indonesia, 1650–1800," *Slavery and Abolition* 43, no. 3 (2022): 553–73; Eric Jones, *Wives, Slaves, and Concubines: A History of the Female Underclass in Dutch Asia* (Ithaca, NY: Cornell University Press, 2011); Linda Mbeki and Matthias van Rossum, "Private Slave Trade in the Dutch Indian Ocean World: A Study into the Networks and Backgrounds of the Slavers and the Enslaved in South Asia and South Africa," *Slavery and Abolition* 38, no. 1 (2017): 95–116; Rik van Welie, "Patterns of Slave Trading and Slavery in the Dutch Colonial World, 1596–1863," in *Dutch Colonialism, Migration and Cultural Heritage,* ed. Gert Oostindie (Leiden: Brill, 2008), 155–259; Rik van Welie, "Slave Trading and Slavery in the Dutch Colonial Empire: A Global Comparison," *New West Indian Guide / Nieuwe West-Indische Gids* 82, nos. 1–2 (2008): 47–96; and Phillip Winn, "Slavery and Cultural Creativity in the Banda Islands," *Journal of Southeast Asian Studies* 41, no. 3 (2010): 365–89.

35. Richard B. Allen, "Slavery in a Remote but Global Place: The British East India Company and Bencoolen, 1685–1825," *Social and Education History* 7, no. 2 (2018): 151–76; Michael D. Bennett, "Slaves, Weavers, and the Peopling of East India Company Colonies, 1660–1730," in Allen, *Slavery and Bonded Labor,* 229–55; Colin Fox, *A Bitter Draught: St. Helena and the Abolition of Slavery, 1792–1840* (Norfolk, UK: Society of Friends of St. Helena,

2017); Shihan de Silva Jayasuriya, "East India Company in Sumatra: Cross-Cultural Interactions," *African and Asian Studies* 8, no. 3 (2009): 204–21; Anna Winterbottom, "From Hold to Foredeck: Slave Professions in the Maritime World of the East India Company, c. 1660–1720," in *Maritime History as Global History*, ed. Maria Fusaro and Amélia Polónia (St. John's, Canada: International Maritime Economic History Association, 2010), 95–124.

36. On the Cape, see John Edwin Mason, *Social Death and Resurrection: Slavery and Emancipation in South Africa* (Charlottesville: University of Virginia Press, 2003); Robert Ross, *Cape of Torments: Slavery and Resistance in South Africa* (London: Routledge & Kegan Paul, 1983); Karel Schoeman, *Early Slavery at the Cape of Good Hope, 1652–1717* (Pretoria: Protea Boekhuis, 2007); Robert C.-H. Shell, *Children of Bondage: A Social History of the Slave Society at the Cape of Good Hope, 1652–1838* (Hanover, NH: Wesleyan University Press, 1994); Robert C.-H. Shell, "The Tower of Babel: The Slave Trade and Creolization at the Cape, 1652–1834," in *Slavery in South Africa: Captive Labor on the Dutch Frontier*, ed. Elizabeth Eldredge and Fred Morton (Boulder, CO: Westview, 1994), 11–39; and Nigel Worden, *Slavery in Dutch South Africa* (Cambridge: Cambridge University Press, 1985). For Mauritius, see Vijaya Teelock, *Bitter Sugar: Sugar and Slavery in 19th Century Mauritius* (Moka, Mauritius: Mahatma Gandhi Institute, 1998); Richard B. Allen, *Slaves, Freedmen, and Indentured Laborers in Colonial Mauritius* (Cambridge: Cambridge University Press, 1999); Megan Vaughan, *Creating the Creole Island: Slavery in Eighteenth-Century Mauritius* (Durham, NC: Duke University Press, 2005); Pier M. Larson, *Ocean of Letters: Language and Creolization in an Indian Ocean Diaspora* (Cambridge: Cambridge University Press, 2009); and Tyler Yank, "Slave Protection and Resistance in Colonial Mauritius, 1829–1830," in *Slaving Zones: Cultural Identities, Ideologies, and Institutions in the Evolution of Global Slavery*, ed. Jeff Fynn-Paul and Damian Alan Pargas (Leiden: Brill, 2018), 224–46.

37. Ethan P. Hawkley, "Reviving the Reconquista in Southeast Asia: Moros and the Making of the Philippines, 1565–1662," *Journal of World History* 25, nos. 2–3 (2014): 285–310; Stephanie Joy Mawson, *Incomplete Conquests: The Limits of Spanish Empire in the Seventeenth-Century Philippines* (Ithaca, NY: Cornell University Press, 2023); Stephanie Mawson, "Slavery, Conflict, and Empire in the Seventeenth-Century Philippines," in Allen, *Slavery and Bonded Labor*, 256–83; William Henry Scott, "Filipino Class

Structure in the Sixteenth Century," *Philippine Studies* 28, no. 2 (1980): 142–75; and William Henry Scott, *Slavery in the Spanish Philippines* (Manila: De La Salle University Press, 1991).

38. Robin Blackburn, *The Making of New World Slavery: From the Baroque to the Modern, 1492–1800* (London: Verso, 1997), 290; Vaughan, *Creating the Creole Island,* 83, 162, 216, 221; and Larson, *Ocean of Letters,* 109–12.
39. Gert Oostindie and Bert Paasman, "Dutch Attitudes towards Colonial Empires, Indigenous Cultures, and Slaves," *Eighteenth-Century Studies* 31, no. 3 (1998): 349–55.
40. For a discussion of this conceptual link in the Atlantic context, see Katharine Gerbner, *Christian Slavery: Conversion and Race in the Protestant Atlantic World* (Philadelphia: University of Pennsylvania Press, 2018).
41. Bennett, "Slaves, Weavers, and the Peopling," 229–55.
42. Bennett, 238–39.
43. For more discussion of conditional freedom, see chapter 1.
44. Matthias van Rossum, Alexander Geelen, and Merve Tosun, "Enslaveability, Slavery and Global Micro Histories: Reflections through the Case of Cali," *Slavery and Abolition* 43, no. 3 (2022): 482–98.
45. On the significance of Portuguese violence, see Michael Pearson, *The Indian Ocean* (London: Routledge, 2003), 123.
46. For overviews of European empires in the context of Indian Ocean history, see Pearson, *Indian Ocean,* and Edward A. Alpers, *The Indian Ocean in World History* (Oxford: Oxford University Press, 2014).
47. For the global rivalry between the Dutch and Portuguese, see A. R. Disney, *The Portuguese Empire,* vol. 2 of *A History of Portugal and the Portuguese Empire: From Beginnings to 1807* (Cambridge: Cambridge University Press, 2009), 61, 73–74, 168–71, 221–31, and Souza, *Medieval Goa,* 4–6. Timor proved an interesting exception to Dutch conquests in the Indian Ocean with the continued presence of both the Portuguese and the Dutch in the seventeenth century. Hans Hägerdal, *Lords of the Land, Lords of the Sea: Conflict and Adaptation in Early Colonial Timor, 1600–1800* (Leiden: Brill, 2012). For a recent analysis of the Dutch Empire in the Indian Ocean, see Kerry Ward, *Networks of Empire: Forced Migration in the Dutch East India Company* (Cambridge: Cambridge University Press, 2009).
48. See chapter 3 for more discussion.
49. Bauss, "Demographic Study," 199–216; Fatima da Silva Gracias, *Health and Hygiene in Colonial Goa (1510–1961)* (New Delhi:

Concept, 1994), 46–63; and Paulo Teodoro de Matos, "The Population of the Portuguese Estado da Índia, 1750–1820: Sources and Demographic Trends," in *The Making of the Luso-Asian World: Intricacies of Engagement,* vol. 1 of *Portuguese and Luso-Asian Legacies in Southeast Asia, 1511–2011,* ed. Laura Jarnagin (Singapore: Institute of Southeast Asian Studies, 2011), 155–77.

50. Cardoso, "African Slave Population," 109.
51. See chapter 3.
52. Bauss, "Demographic Study," 209.
53. Bauss, 209.
54. Matos, "Population of the Portuguese Estado," 170.
55. For overviews of the medieval Indian Ocean and Islam before the Portuguese arrival, see Alpers, *Indian Ocean,* 40–68, and Pearson, *Indian Ocean,* 62–112.
56. For a brief overview of Portuguese India's relations with Indian polities, see Souza, *Medieval Goa,* 6–19. On the Mughals, see John F. Richards, *The Mughal Empire* (Cambridge: Cambridge University Press, 1993).
57. Subrahmanyam, *Portuguese Empire in Asia,* 107–8, 141–45; Disney, *Portuguese Empire,* 135–36, 146, 168–69, 302; and Giancarlo Casale, *The Ottoman Age of Exploration* (Oxford: Oxford University Press, 2010).
58. For instance, the Ottomans found allies among the Swahili. See Casale, *Ottoman Age of Exploration,* 152–79. The 1631 uprising in Mombasa was framed in religious terms with considerations for martyrdom. See G. S. P. Freeman-Grenville, ed. and trans., *The Mombasa Rising against the Portuguese, 1631: From Sworn Evidence* (London: Oxford University Press, 1980). For an overview of the Portuguese on the Swahili Coast, see Michael N. Pearson, *Port Cities and Intruders: The Swahili Coast, India, and Portugal in the Early Modern Era* (Baltimore: Johns Hopkins University Press, 1998).
59. The Reconquest ended in Portugal in the mid-thirteenth century and was complete with the conquest of Granada in 1492, bringing the entire Iberian Peninsula under Christian rule.
60. A. J. R. Russell-Wood, "Iberian Expansion and the Issue of Black Slavery: Changing Portuguese Attitudes, 1440–1770," *American Historical Review* 83, no. 1 (February 1978):17.
61. Russell-Wood, 23–24.
62. Russell-Wood, 24.
63. On just war and the Spanish, see Seijas, *Asian Slaves in Colonial Mexico,* 61–67. For the connection between the Reconquest

and the Philippines, see Hawkley, "Reviving the Reconquista," 285–310.

64. Russell-Wood, "Iberian Expansion," 27.
65. Russell-Wood, 28.
66. Russell-Wood, 28; Boxer, *Portuguese Seaborne Empire,* 230.
67. Boxer, *Portuguese Seaborne Empire,* 231.
68. Boxer, 230–32; C. R. Boxer, *The Church Militant and Iberian Expansion, 1440–1770* (Baltimore: Johns Hopkins University Press, 1978), 78–79.
69. For the Portuguese Inquisition's tribunals in global context, see Francisco Bethencourt, *The Inquisition: A Global History, 1478–1834,* trans. Jean Birrell (Cambridge: Cambridge University Press, 2009). On the Goa Tribunal, see Boyajian, "Goa Inquisition," 1–40; Ana Cannas da Cunha, *A Inquisição no Estado da Índia: Origens (1539–1560)* (Lisbon: Arquivos Nacionais / Torre do Tombo, 1995); Toby Green, "Policing the Empires: A Comparative Perspective on the Institutional Trajectory of the Inquisition in the Portuguese and Spanish Overseas Territories (Sixteenth and Seventeenth Centuries)," *Hispanic Research Journal* 13, no. 1 (2012): 7–25; José Pedro Paiva, "The Inquisition Tribunal in Goa: Why and for What Purpose?," *Journal of Early Modern History* 21, no. 6 (2017): 565–93; Anant Kakba Priolkar, *The Goa Inquisition: Being a Quatercentenary Commemoration Study of the Inquisition in India, with Accounts Given by Dr. Dellon and Dr. Buchanan,* 2nd ed. (Panaji, Goa: Rajhauns Vitaran, 2008); and José Alberto Rodrigues da Silva Tavim, "Um inquisidor inquirido: João Delgado Figueira e o seu Reportorio, no contexto da 'documentação sobre a Inquisição de Goa,'" *Leituras: Revista da Biblioteca Nacional,* no. 1 (Outono 1997): 183–93.
70. On this mid-century intensification, see Pearson, *Portuguese in India,* 116–18.
71. The decrees extended far beyond the capital of Goa. For a discussion of the provincial councils and other religious provisions in East Asia, see Sousa, *Portuguese Slave Trade,* 478–538.
72. Délio de Mendonça, *Conversions and Citizenry: Goa under Portugal, 1510–1610* (New Delhi: Concept, 2002). See also Pearson, *Portuguese in India,* 117–18. Not all children categorized as orphans had actually lost both parents.
73. On the Pai dos Cristãos generally and interactions with enslaved Catholics, see Glenn J. Ames, "Religious Life in the Colonial Trenches: The Role of the *Pai dos Christãos* in Seventeenth Century Portuguese India, c. 1640–1683," *Portuguese Studies Review*

16, no. 2 (2008): 1–23; Patrícia Souza de Faria, "O Pai dos Cristãos e as Populações Escravas de Goa: Zelo e Controle dos Cativos Convertidos (Séculos XVI e XVII)," *História* 39 (2000): 1–30; Teotonio R. de Souza, "Manumission of Slaves in Goa during 1682 to 1760 as Found in Codex 860," in *TADIA, the African Diaspora in Asia: Explorations on a Less Known Fact,* ed. Kiran Kamal Prasad and Jean-Pierre Angenot (Bangalore: Jana Jagrati Prakashana, 2008), 167–81; and José Wicki, ed., *O Livro do 'Pai dos Cristãos'* (Lisbon: Centro de Estudos Históricos Ultramarinos, 1969).

74. See chapter 2 for more discussion.
75. Sanjay Subrahmanyam, *Three Ways to Be Alien: Travails and Encounters in the Early Modern World* (Waltham, MA: Brandeis University Press, 2011); Mendonça, *Conversions and Citizenry.*
76. However, not all non-Europeans in India were new converts to Christianity. The Saint Thomas Christians had long been present when the Portuguese arrived. Pearson, *Indian Ocean,* 59–60.
77. On purity of blood, see Green, *Inquisition,* and Francisco Bethencourt, *Racisms: From the Crusades to the Twentieth Century* (Princeton, NJ: Princeton University Press, 2013). For social hierarchies, see Pearson, *Portuguese in India,* 95–96.
78. The significance of caste was particularly relevant in Goa. Pearson, *Portuguese in India,* 129. Moreover, parish records explored in this book documented caste, attesting to the category's significance in the Catholic community. For broader discussions of caste in India, see Susan Bayly, *Caste, Society and Politics in India from the Eighteenth Century to the Modern Age* (Cambridge: Cambridge University Press, 2001). Bayly's analysis also precedes the eighteenth century. See also Gijs Kruijtzer, *Xenophobia in Seventeenth-Century India* (Leiden: Leiden University Press, 2009).
79. For a critique of slave agency, see Walter Johnson, "On Agency," *Journal of Social History* 37, no. 1 (2003): 113–24.
80. Richard B. Allen, "Marie Rozette and Her World: Class, Ethnicity, Gender, and Race in Late Eighteenth- and Early Nineteenth-Century Mauritius," *Journal of Social History* 45, no. 2 (Winter 2011): 345–65; Peabody, *Madeleine's Children;* Alicia Schrikker and Nira Wickramasinghe, eds., *Being a Slave: Histories and Legacies of European Slavery in the Indian Ocean* (Leiden: Leiden University Press, 2020); van Rossum et al., *Testimonies of Enslavement;* and Nira Wickramasinghe, *Slave in a Palanquin: Colonial Servitude and Resistance in Sri Lanka* (New York: Columbia University Press, 2020).

81. Ananya Chakravarti, "Mapping 'Gabriel': Space, Identity and Slavery in the Late Sixteenth-Century Indian Ocean," *Past and Present* 243, no. 1 (2019): 5–34; Patrícia Souza de Faria, "Cruzando Fronteiras: Conversão e Mobilidades Culturais de Escravos no Império Asiático Português (Séculos XVI e XVII)," *Anais de História de Além-Mar* 17 (2016): 147–78; Stephanie Hassell, "Inquisition Records from Goa as Sources for the Study of Slavery in the Eastern Domains of the Portuguese Empire," *History in Africa* 42 (2015): 397–418; and Matteo Salvadore, "Between the Red Sea Trade and the Goa Inquisition: The Odyssey of Gabriel, a Sixteenth-Century Ethiopian Jew," *Journal of World History* 31, no. 2 (June 2020): 327–60. For slavery and the Inquisition elsewhere in the Lusophone world, see Vanicléia Silva Santos, "Africans, Afro-Brazilians and Afro-Portuguese in the Iberian Inquisition in the Seventeenth and Eighteenth Centuries," *African and Black Diaspora: An International Journal* 5, no. 1 (2012): 49–63; James H. Sweet, *Domingos Álvares, African Healing, and the Intellectual History of the Atlantic World* (Chapel Hill: University of North Carolina Press, 2011); James H. Sweet, *Recreating Africa: Culture, Kinship, and Religion in the African-Portuguese World, 1441–1770* (Chapel Hill: University of North Carolina Press, 2003); and Timothy Walker, "Sorcerers and Folkhealers: Africans and the Inquisition in Portugal (1680–1800)," *Revista Lusófona de Ciência das Religiões* 3, nos. 5–6 (2004): 83–98.

82. Most parish records are indexed separately from the Historical Archives of Goa's main records and have therefore been overlooked. For the use of ecclesiastical records for Goan social history, see Teotonio R. de Souza, "The Voiceless in Goan Historiography: A Case for the Source-Value of Church Records in Goa," in *Indo-Portuguese History: Sources and Problems,* ed. John Correia-Afonso (Bombay: Oxford University Press, 1981), 114–31. For a model of using parish records to study slavery, see Sweet, *Recreating Africa.*

83. São Bartolomeu is located on the island of Chorão and is part of the Ilhas District of Goa. The parish church still stands. For a history of Chorão, see F. X. Gomes Catao, *The Island of Chorao: A Historical Sketch* (Alwaye, India: Mar Louis Memorial Press, 1962).

CHAPTER 1: SLAVERY AND THE HOUSEHOLD

1. She was also known as "Isabel Bengala." For example, Leonor Fernandes refers to her by that name, even though Isabel labeled

herself as "Malavar." Processo de Leonor Fernandes. ANTT, IL, Processos, No. 7631, fls. 21v, 73v.

2. Processo de Leonor Fernandes, fls. 72–73v.
3. Processo de Leonor Fernandes, fl. 73v. Presumably the reference to the Malabar Coast meant she knew the language Malayalam, which predominated. Hugo C. Cardoso, "Convergence in the Malabar: The Case of Indo-Portuguese," *Journal of Pidgin and Creole Languages* 36, no. 2 (2021): 324. However, Malabar as a language could refer to Malayalam or Tamil. Ines G. Zupanov, "Language and Culture of the Jesuit 'Early Modernity' in India during the Sixteenth Century," *Itinerario* 31, no. 2 (2007): 110n41.
4. Processo de Leonor Fernandes, fl. 21v. Pyrard de Laval reported that Indian female slaves sold for twenty to thirty pardaos each at the most in Goa. *The Voyage of François Pyrard of Laval to the East Indies, the Maldives, the Moluccas and Brazil,* ed. Albert Gray (London: Hakluyt Society, 1888), 2, part 1:65–66.
5. Processo de Leonor Fernandes, fl. 72v.
6. Clara Lopes, the daughter-in-law of Leonor Fernandes and Diogo Soares, charged that Isabel slept with her husband, Lopo Soares. She also described Isabel's refusal to work and her pursuit of freedom. Processo de Clara Lopes, ANTT, IL, Processos, No. 7429, fl. 22. Clara Lopes was not alone in her attempt to malign Isabel's character. Diogo Soares, Leonor Fernandes, and Lopo Soares also made statements against her. Processo de Diogo Soares, fl. 25v/27v; Processo de Leonor Fernandes, fl. 21v; Processo de Lopo Soares, ANTT, IL, Processos, No. 2187, fl. 26v.
7. A. J. R. Russell-Wood, "Iberian Expansion and the Issue of Black Slavery: Changing Portuguese Attitudes, 1440–1770," *American Historical Review* 83, no. 1 (February 1978): 16–17.
8. Russell-Wood, 27–28; Jonathan Schorsch, *Jews and Blacks in the Early Modern World* (Cambridge: Cambridge University Press, 2004), 343–44n37.
9. On this decoupling, see Russell-Wood, "Iberian Expansion," 17–18, 25.
10. Carmo D'Souza, "Slavery in Goa: Legal and Historical Perspectives," in *Legacies of Slavery: Comparative Perspectives,* ed. Maria Suzette Fernandes Dias (Newcastle, UK: Cambridge Scholars, 2007), 66–67.
11. J. H. da Cunha Rivara, ed., *Os Concilios de Goa e o Synodo de Diamper,* issue 4 of *Archivo-Portuguez Oriental* (Nova-Goa: Imprensa Nacional, 1862), 53. See Decreto 10.

12. For more discussion of hereditary slavery through the matrilineal line, see Stuart M. McManus, "*Partus Sequitur Ventrem* in Theory and Practice: Slavery and Reproduction in Early Modern Portuguese Asia," *Gender and History* 32, no. 3 (October 2020): 542–61.
13. Rivara, *Concilios,* 267. See Decreto 15.
14. Rivara, 267–68. See Decreto 15.
15. To put this fine in perspective, it greatly exceeded the price of an enslaved Indian woman, which generally reached no more than twenty to thirty pardaos, according to Pyrard de Laval. Pyrard, *Voyage,* 2:65–66.
16. Rivara, *Concilios,* 267–68. See Decreto 15.
17. Patrícia Souza de Faria, "O Pai dos Cristãos e as Populações Escravas de Goa: Zelo e Controle dos Cativos Convertidos (Séculos XVI e XVII)," *História* 39 (2000): 17–18.
18. Jan Huygen van Linschoten, *The Voyage of John Huyghen van Linschoten to the East Indies: From the Old English Translation of 1598, the First Book, Containing His Description of the East,* ed. Arthur Coke Burnell (1885; repr., San Bernardino, CA: Adamant Media, 2005), 1:276.
19. Rivara, *Concilios,* 30. See Decreto 40.
20. Rivara, 30. See Decreto 40.
21. Rivara, 30. See Decreto 40.
22. Teotonio R. de Souza, *Medieval Goa: A Socio-Economic History,* 2nd ed. (Saligão, Goa: Goa, 1556, 2009), 89.
23. *Leis a favor da Cristandade,* HAG, Ms. 7693, fls. 16v–17v.
24. *Leis a favor da Cristandade,* fl. 16v. Thus, the rhetoric of "just enslavement" was invoked.
25. D'Souza, "Slavery in Goa," 71. However, this was not enforced.
26. Geoffrey C. Gunn, *Encountering Macau: A Portuguese City-State on the Periphery of China, 1557–1999* (Boulder, CO: Westview, 1996), 42. The Marquis de Pombal in the eighteenth century again abolished Chinese enslavement. Russell-Wood, "Iberian Expansion," 41. For a detailed analysis of slave trading, see Lúcio de Sousa, *The Portuguese Slave Trade in Early Modern Japan: Merchants, Jesuits and Japanese, Chinese, and Korean Slaves* (Leiden: Brill, 2019).
27. For an insightful discussion on identity and its meanings, see Rogers Brubaker and Frederick Cooper, "Beyond 'Identity,'" *Theory and Society* 29, no. 1 (February 2000): 1–47.
28. On the term "Sidi," see Shihan de Silva Jayasuriya, "Identifying Africans in Asia: What's in a Name?," in *Uncovering the History*

of Africans in Asia, ed. Shihan de Silva Jayasuriya and Jean-Pierre Angenot (Leiden: Brill, 2008), 22–25.

29. For the different ethnonyms in the case records, see Processo de Gabriel, ANTT, IL, Processos, No. 4937, fls. 2, 6v, 7v.
30. Processo de Paulo, ANTT, IL, Processos, No. 3672, fls. 2, 3v, 12v.
31. For example, see James H. Sweet, "Mistaken Identities? Olaudah Equiano, Domingos Álvares, and the Methodological Challenges of Studying the African Diaspora," *American Historical Review* 114, no. 2 (April 2009): 279–306.
32. However, for discussions of ethnic roots and self-understandings in European colonies in the Indian Ocean, see Megan Vaughan, *Creating the Creole Island: Slavery in Eighteenth-Century Mauritius* (Durham, NC: Duke University Press, 2005), and Pier M. Larson, *Ocean of Letters: Language and Creolization in an Indian Ocean Diaspora* (Cambridge: Cambridge University Press, 2009).
33. See table 4 in Richard B. Allen, "Merchant Capital and Labor Migration in the Colonial Indian Ocean World," *Historia Crítica,* no. 89 (2023): 137.
34. As others have noted, the slave trade predated the Portuguese presence. Robert O. Collins, "The African Slave Trade to Asia and the Indian Ocean Islands," in *Uncovering the History of Africans in Asia,* ed. Shihan de Silva Jayasuriya and Jean-Pierre Angenot (Leiden: Brill, 2008), 61, 69–70. For a recent overview of East African slavery and the slave trade in the broader Indian Ocean, see Gwyn Campbell, *Africa and the Indian Ocean World from Early Times to circa 1900* (Cambridge: Cambridge University Press, 2019), 255–79. See also Edward A. Alpers, *Ivory and Slaves: Changing Pattern of International Trade in East Central Africa to the Later Nineteenth Century* (Berkeley: University of California Press, 1975), and Michael N. Pearson, *Port Cities and Intruders: The Swahili Coast, India, and Portugal in the Early Modern Era* (Baltimore: Johns Hopkins University Press, 1998).
35. Thomas Vernet, "Slave Trade and Slavery on the Swahili Coast, 1500–1750," in *Slavery, Islam and Diaspora,* ed. Behnaz A. Mirzai, Ismael Musah Montana, and Paul E. Lovejoy (Trenton, NJ: Africa World, 2009), 50. This discussion of the Portuguese appears in a pathbreaking chapter examining the role of Swahili merchants and the multiple slave trade networks connecting the Swahili Coast to the broader Indian Ocean.
36. Part of the problem of measuring the slave trade is the lack of customs house data for the earlier centuries. Data that would have been housed in the Casa da Índia was destroyed in the 1755

earthquake in Lisbon. The customs house records in the Historical Archives of Goa (HAG), which have import information, are missing for the sixteenth and seventeenth centuries. On the Casa da Índia as an institution, see Ângela Barreto Xavier, "The Casa da Índia and the Emergence of a Science of Administration in the Portuguese Empire," *Journal of Early Modern History* 22, no. 5 (2018): 327–47.

37. Linschoten, *Voyage,* 1:275.
38. Linschoten, 1:275–76.
39. António Bocarro, *O Livro das Plantas de Todas as Fortalezas, Cidades e Povoações do Estado da Índia Oriental,* ed. Isabel Cid (Lisbon: Imprensa Nacional, 1992), 2:97.
40. Bocarro, 2:125.
41. João Delgado Figueira, *Reportorio geral de tres mil oito centos processos, que sam todos os despachados neste sancto Officio de Goa & mais partes da India, do anno de Mil & quinhentos & secenta & hum, que começou o dito sancto Officio até o anno de Mil & seiscentos & vinte & tres, com a lista dos Inquisidores que tem sido nelle, & dos autos publicos da Fee, que se tem celebrado na dita Cidade de Goa,* 1623, Biblioteca Nacional de Portugal (BNP), cód. 203, fl. 96v (4v). António was whipped and sold to Portugal for "divining future things." He had been enslaved by Miguel de Olanda. The *Reportorio* has a dual numbering system.
42. Figueira, *Reportorio,* fl. 98v (6v).
43. Figueira, fl. 396v (597).
44. Figueira, fl. 243 (248). Diogo was prosecuted for converting to Islam and sentenced to incarceration and a penitential habit, a sentence that would end at the discretion of the inquisitors.
45. There are likely other examples in the *Reportorio.* The examples I have provided come from case summaries containing the defendants' place of birth and their place of residency. Other cases include one of the categories rather than both, while still other cases identify the defendant as a cafre, which is suggestive of African origins.
46. Souza, *Medieval Goa,* 89. On the slave trade from East Asia, see also Sousa, *Portuguese Slave Trade.*
47. Linschoten, *Voyage,* 1:276–77.
48. Linschoten, 1:277.
49. For contextualization of this trade, see Richard B. Allen, "Satisfying the 'Want for Labouring People': European Slave Trading in the Indian Ocean, 1500–1850," *Journal of World History* 21, no. 1 (2010): 45–73, and Richard B. Allen, *European Slave*

Trading in the Indian Ocean, 1500–1850 (Athens: Ohio University Press, 2014).

50. For instance, Branca de Oliveira's disabled Chinese slave was mentioned in multiple Inquisition cases. Processo de Ana de Oliveira, ANTT, IL, Processos, No. 6725, fl. 57; Processo de Leonor Fernandes, fl. 63v; Processo de Diogo Soares, fl. 110/123. Branca de Oliveira and her brother-in-law Alvaro Gomes owned Bengali slaves. Processo de Ana de Oliveira, fls. 60, 68. Ana de Oliveira and Diogo Soares owned slaves from Malabar. Processo de Ana de Oliveira, fl. 74v; Processo de Diogo Soares, fl. 108v/121v. Diogo Soares and Alvaro Gomes owned Gujarati slaves. Processo de Leonor Fernandes, fl. 70v; Processo de Diogo Soares, fl. 120/133; Processo de Ana de Oliveira, fls. 63v, 66. Slaves from Java worked for Diogo Soares and his extended family. Processo de Diogo Soares, 118v/131v; Processo de Ana de Oliveira, fls. 71, 72v. Clara Abexim, an Abyssinian enslaved by Diogo Soares, surfaced in Estevão Lopes's Inquisition case. Processo de Estevão Lopes, ANTT, IL, Processos, No. 360, fls. 16v, 50v–51. Guiomar de Oliveira and her husband, Estevão Lopes, owned an East African slave named Filipa. Processo de Guiomar de Oliveira, ANTT, IL, Processos, No. 11171, fl. 20; Processo de Estevão Lopes, fl. 16. Diogo Soares and his family had owned at least one Arabian slave, the eventually freed Ilena Machada. Processo de Diogo Soares, fl. 25/27. Cristovão Mendes owned a *pegu* (Burmese) slave named Belchior. Processo de Diogo Soares, fl. 117v/130v. Diogo Soares had a Sinhalese slave, Lianor Chingala, whom he sold to his relative in Cochin. Processo de Leonor Fernandes, fls. 69v–70, 78. *Curumbim* (also spelled "corombim") referred to the Sudra or agricultural caste, rather than a specific ethnic group. Sebastião Rodolfo Dalgado, *Glossário Luso-Asiático,* 2 vols. (Coimbra: Imprensa da Universidade, 1919–21), s.v. "Curumbim." Diogo Soares's family had multiple slaves described as this category. Processo de Leonor Soares, fl. 77v; Processo de Branca de Oliveira, ANTT, IL, Processos, No. 6569, fl. 61v.
51. Sanjay Subrahmanyam, *The Portuguese Empire in Asia, 1500–1700: A Political and Economic History,* 2nd ed. (Chichester, UK: John Wiley & Sons, 2012), 240.
52. For example, Andre Moreira, a "casta canarim" slave, was prosecuted in 1595 for converting to Islam. Figueira, *Reportorio,* fl. 123 (31).
53. For examples of Japanese slaves, see Constantino Monteiro, who had an Inquisition case in 1592, and Julião Paes, who had an

Inquisition case in 1612. Figueira, *Reportorio,* fls. 220v (193), 421 (648). For examples of Bengali slaves in Goa, see Antonio, who had a case in 1569; Isabel, who had a case in 1565; and Francisco Cordeiro, who had a case in 1623. Figueira, fls. 102 (10), 385v (575), 350 (480). Examples of East and Southern Africans include slaves such as Antonio from Mozambique, who was prosecuted for divination in 1564. Jerónimo, described as "*casta cafre,*" was a slave from Mombasa living in Goa, prosecuted for paganism in 1581. In 1585 a slave named Diogo from the Kingdom of Mutapa was prosecuted for practicing Islam. Figueira, fls. 96v (4v), 396v (597), 243 (248). Inquisitors prosecuted slaves from present-day Indonesia. For example, see Domingos Serrão, for sacrifices in 1601; Francisca, for devil worship in 1574; and Felipe Correa, for a sacrifice in 1609. Figueira, fls. 253v (269), 306v (393), 332v (445). Slaves from Malabar prosecuted by the Inquisition included Britis in 1568, for witchcraft; Antonio in 1596, for Islam; and Jorge in 1570, who also converted to Islam. Figueira, fls. 178v (97), 125 (33), 388v (581).

54. On the multidirectional nature of the Indian Ocean slave trade more broadly, see Gwyn Campbell, "Introduction: Slavery and Other Forms of Unfree Labour in the Indian Ocean World," in *The Structure of Slavery in Indian Ocean Africa and Asia,* ed. Gwyn Campbell (London: Frank Cass, 2004), ix.
55. K. S. Mathew, *Portuguese Trade with India in the Sixteenth Century* (New Delhi: Manohar, 1983), 138.
56. Figueira, *Reportorio,* fl. 177 (94).
57. Figueira, fl. 387 (578).
58. Subrahmanyam, *Portuguese Empire in Asia,* 240.
59. Souza, *Medieval Goa,* 79. The street was also called the *Rua de Leilões,* an appellation referring to the auctions (*leilões*) that occurred there.
60. Pyrard, *Voyage,* 2:64–65.
61. Linschoten, *Voyage,* 1:184.
62. Linschoten, 1:185.
63. Pyrard, *Voyage,* 2:64–65.
64. Pyrard, 2:64.
65. Pyrard, 2:65.
66. Pyrard, 2:65. This dialogic process of sale took place elsewhere in the global experience of slavery. Debra Blumenthal, *Enemies and Familiars: Slavery and Mastery in Fifteenth-Century Valencia* (Ithaca, NY: Cornell University Press, 2009), 46–79. For an illuminating discussion of slave auctions and the ways in which

slaves "shaped" their own sales in the United States, see Walter Johnson, *Soul by Soul: Life Inside the Antebellum Slave Market* (Cambridge, MA: Harvard University Press, 1999), 176–88.

67. Pyrard, *Voyage,* 2:65.
68. Pyrard, 2:65–66.
69. Pyrard, 2:66.
70. Pyrard, 2:65–67, 67n2. The cost of a horse could reach one thousand pardaos. Pyrard's description of slave prices appeared in his commentary on enslaved Indian females; it is possible the prices also applied to enslaved Africans.
71. While not discussed here, enslaved individuals also worked in religious convents and monasteries. Jeanette Pinto, *Slavery in Portuguese India, 1510–1842* (Bombay: Himalaya, 1992), 27.
72. Linschoten, *Voyage,* 1:185–86.
73. Pyrard, *Voyage,* 2:66.
74. Linschoten, *Voyage,* 1:183.
75. Linschoten, 1:187–88.
76. Linschoten, 1:186.
77. Linschoten, 1:186.
78. Pyrard, *Voyage,* 2:66–67.
79. Pyrard, 2:66–67.
80. Pyrard, 2:66.
81. Processo de Ana de Oliveira, fl. 68v.
82. Processo de Leonor Fernandes, fls. 69v–70. Antonia Malavar, another slave of Diogo Soares and Leonor Fernandes, shared this information about Lianor Chingala when she denounced the couple.
83. Rivara, *Concilios,* 263. See Decreto 7.
84. Rivara, 267. See Decreto 14.
85. Linschoten, *Voyage,* 1:199.
86. Linschoten, 1:199
87. Linschoten, 1:193–94, 194n1.
88. Pyrard, *Voyage,* 2:75.
89. Linschoten, *Voyage,* 1:215.
90. Pyrard, *Voyage,* 2:103.
91. Pyrard, 2:75.
92. Pyrard, 2:103–4. Besides this processional, enslaved people arranged stools for their owners at the church. Linschoten, *Voyage,* 1:194.
93. Linschoten, *Voyage,* 1:196.
94. For more on New Christians as a group targeted by the Iberian Inquisitions, see Toby Green, *Inquisition: The Reign of Fear* (New York: Thomas Dunne, 2009). See also James C. Boyajian, "Goa

Inquisition: A New Light on the First 100 Years (1561–1660)," *Purabhilekh-Puratatva* 4, no. 1 (1986): 1–40.

95. Ana Cannas da Cunha, *A Inquisição no Estado da Índia: Origens (1539–1560)* (Lisbon: Arquivos Nacionais / Torre do Tombo, 1995), 19–20. New Christians also emigrated to the Atlantic world. See Peter Mark and José da Silva Horta, *The Forgotten Diaspora: Jewish Communities in West Africa and the Making of the Atlantic World* (Cambridge: Cambridge University Press, 2011).
96. For an overview of the Cochin cases and precursors to the Goa Tribunal's establishment, see Cunha, *Inquisição,* and José Pedro Paiva, "The Inquisition Tribunal in Goa: Why and for What Purpose?," *Journal of Early Modern History* 21, no. 6 (2017): 565–93.
97. Cunha, *Inquisição,* 167.
98. The eight cases against Diogo Soares and his family were Processo de Diogo Soares, Processo de Leonor Fernandes, Processo de Lopo Soares, Processo de Clara Lopes, Processo de Ana de Oliveira, Processo de Branca de Oliveira, Processo de Guiomar de Oliveira, and Processo de Estevão Lopes.
99. Green, *Inquisition,* 39–40.
100. Renée Levine Melammed, "The World of Witnesses and the Holy Tribunal: Fifteenth-Century Trials of Castilian Judaizers," in *Voices from the Bench: The Narratives of Lesser Folk in Medieval Trials,* ed. Michael Goodich (New York: Palgrave Macmillan, 2006), 45.
101. See below for more discussion on bribery.
102. Processo de Diogo Soares, fl. 20/21. This sermon would have been an edict of faith.
103. For example, Antonia Malavar said she testified because of "her conscience." Processo de Leonor Fernandes, fl. 66v.
104. Figueira, *Reportorio,* fl. 106 (14).
105. Figueira, fl. 391 (586).
106. Figueira, fl. 160v (68v). I have assumed that she testified falsely herself, as the summary did not mention that she persuaded others.
107. Figueira, fls. 94 (2)–436 (678). My sample comprises the case summaries contained in these folios. In addition, other specific examples include Bastião Dinis in 1568 (exiled to Ceylon for one year), João de Sousa in 1596 (whipped, heard his sentence in the shameful painted cap [*carocha*], and sent to the galleys for five years), and Antonio D'Abreu in 1612 (whipped, also heard his sentence while wearing a *carocha,* and sent to the galley for six years). Figueira, fls. 178v (97), 407 (618), 153 (61).

108. José Alberto Rodrigues da Silva Tavim, "Um inquisidor inquirido: João Delgado Figueira e o seu Reportorio, no contexto da 'documentação sobre a Inquisição de Goa,'" *Leituras: Revista da Biblioteca Nacional,* no. 1 (Outono 1997): 187–88.

109. In their joint petition, Diogo Soares and the other defendants in his family said that altogether they had over seventy slaves. Processo de Diogo Soares, fl. 20v/21v.

110. In addition to Ilena Machada (freed), the enslaved denunciators included Antonia Malavar, Madanela Bengala (enslaved by Branca de Oliveira), the similarly named Madanela Bengala (enslaved by Alvaro Gomes), Maria Guzarata, Brianda Guzarata, Maria Jaoa, Brianda Jaoa, Joana Malavar, Lianor Jaoa, Isabel Malavar/Bengala, Briatiz Bengala/Guzarata, Pedro/Pero Guzarate, Briatiz Corombim, Violante, Guiomar, Luzia Corombim, Briatiz Jaoa, and Briolania Jaoa. Testimonies of non-slave witnesses implicated Diogo Soares's family as well.

111. Female slaves are in the spotlight in these cases; however, some male slaves are mentioned. Most notably Diogo Soares's slave Pedro Guzarate (also called Pero) denounced his owner in addition to Leonor Fernandes, Estevão Lopes, Clara Lopes, and Lopo Soares. Processo de Diogo Soares, fls. 120/133–123/136; Processo de Leonor Fernandes, fls. 75v–77v; Processo de Estevão Lopes, fls. 60–61; Processo de Clara Lopes, fls. 47/48–48v/49v; Processo de Lopo Soares, fls. 67v–68v. Male (ex)slaves singled out in the counterstatements were generally enslaved by people outside the household, such as the enslaved "cafre" friend of Isabel Guzarata's and the freed Antonio Pachequo. This lack of information means that we do not have a clear picture of what male slaves did in the household, how many male slaves worked for Diogo Soares's extended family, or their origins. For Isabel Guzarata's "cafre" friend enslaved by Mateus da Cunha, see Processo de Diogo Soares, fl. 27/29, and Processo de Estevão Lopes, fl. 16v. For Antonio Pachequo, see Processo de Ana de Oliveira, fl. 22v.

112. A notable exception is Duarte, a previously enslaved male of the household, who was married to Filipa Corombim. Processo de Ana de Oliveira, fl. 22v.

113. Ann M. Pescatello, "The African Presence in Portuguese India," *Journal of Asian History* 11, no. 1 (1977): 48.

114. Campbell, "Introduction," xiv; Gwyn Campbell and Edward A. Alpers, "Introduction: Slavery, Forced Labour and Resistance in Indian Ocean Africa and Asia," in *Slavery and Resistance in Africa*

and Asia, ed. Edward Alpers, Gwyn Campbell, and Michael Salman (London: Routledge, 2005), 3–4.

115. See Pinto, *Slavery in Portuguese India,* 55.

116. For resistance, liberty, and gender in the Indian Ocean, see Campbell and Alpers, "Introduction," 7–9. There is an assumption of women's disinterest in flight, which also appears outside the Indian Ocean literature. For a critique of this assumption in the African context, see Marie Rodet, "Gender, Migration, and the End of Slavery in the Region of Kayes, French Soudan," in *African Voices on Slavery and the Slave Trade: Volume 1, the Sources,* ed. Alice Bellagamba, Sandra E. Greene, and Martin A. Klein (Cambridge: Cambridge University Press, 2013), 319–29. More recently, however, scholars of Indian Ocean history have revisited slave flight. For example, see Alexander Geelen et al., "On the Run: Runaway Slaves and Their Social Networks in Eighteenth-Century Cochin," *Journal of Social History* 54, no. 1 (Fall 2020): 66–87. Their sources include female runaways. On slave resistance in the Indian Ocean more broadly, see Edward Alpers, Gwyn Campbell and Michael Salman, eds., *Slavery and Resistance in Africa and Asia* (London: Routledge, 2005), and Edward A. Alpers, Gwyn Campbell, and Michael Salman, eds., *Resisting Bondage in Indian Ocean Africa and Asia* (London: Routledge, 2007).

117. Processo de Diogo Soares, fl. 25/27.

118. Processo de Leonor Fernandes, fl. 21.

119. Processo de Branca de Oliveira, fl. 21v. A wooden shackle (*cepo*) was used for her restraint.

120. Processo de Estevão Lopes, fl. 16.

121. Processo de Estevão Lopes, fl. 16.

122. Processo de Guiomar de Oliveira, fl. 20.

123. Processo de Leonor Fernandes, fls. 21v–22; Processo de Ana de Oliveira, fls. 22v–23. Madanela Bengala in this instance refers to the woman enslaved by Branca de Oliveira rather than Alvaro Gomes.

124. Processo de Leonor Fernandes, fl. 22v; Processo de Ana de Oliveira, fl. 22.

125. Processo de Leonor Fernandes, fl. 21v; Processo de Clara Lopes, fl. 22; Processo de Ana de Oliveira, fl. 22v. Madanela Bengala, enslaved by Ana de Oliveira and Alvaro Gomes, experienced this torture.

126. These punishments are found in the counterstatement section ("*contraditas*") of each case: Processo de Diogo Soares, fls. 25/27–27v/29v; Processo de Leonor Fernandes, fls. 21–22v; Processo de Lopo Soares, fls. 26–27; Processo de Clara Lopes,

fls. 22–22v; Processo de Ana de Oliveira, fls. 22–23; Processo de Branca de Oliveira, fls. 21–22; Processo de Guiomar de Oliveira, fls. 20–21; Processo de Estevão Lopes, fls. 16–17.

127. Rivara, *Concilios,* 51. I translated "rota" simply as a "cane." According to Anthony Vieyra, the term referred to a type of cane or reed in the Maluku Islands. Anthony Vieyra, *A Dictionary of the Portuguese and English Languages, in Two Parts, Portuguese and English, and English and Portuguese,* 2 vols. (London: J. Nourse, 1773), s.v. "Rota."

128. *Leis a favor da Cristandade,* fls. 53v–54v. This law is also recorded in *Provisões a favor da Cristandade,* HAG, Ms. 9529, fls. 113–14.

129. *Leis a favor da Cristandade,* fl. 54.

130. Rivara, *Concilios,* 269. See Decreto 18.

131. Rivara, 269.

132. Rivara, 269–70. Enslavers used palmers, which were paddles containing holes, to strike enslaved people's hands and other body parts. Used also in Luanda and Rio de Janeiro, the instruments caused swelling and wounds. Vieyra, *Dictionary,* s.vv. "Palmatoada," "Palmatoreada," and "Palmatoria." Mary C. Karasch, *Slave Life in Rio de Janeiro, 1808–1850* (Princeton, NJ: Princeton University Press, 1987), 114.

133. Rivara, *Concilios,* 270.

134. Processo de Leonor Fernandes, fl. 90v.

135. Pyrard, *Voyage,* 2:66.

136. All eight members of the family accused her of sneaking men into the house. Processo de Diogo Soares, fl. 25/27; Processo de Leonor Fernandes, fl. 21; Processo de Lopo Soares, fls. 26–26v; Processo de Clara Lopes, fl. 22; Processo de Ana de Oliveira, fl. 22; Processo de Branca de Oliveira, fl. 21v; Processo de Guiomar de Oliveira, fl. 20; Processo de Estevão Lopes, fl. 16.

137. Processo de Diogo Soares, fl. 25v/27v.

138. Processo de Diogo Soares, fl. 26/28; Processo de Leonor Fernandes, fl. 22; Processo de Lopo Soares, fl. 26v; Processo de Clara Lopes, fl. 22v; Processo de Ana de Oliveira, fl. 22; Processo de Branca de Oliveira, fls. 21v–22; Processo de Guiomar de Oliveira, fl. 20v; Processo de Estevão Lopes, fl. 16v.

139. Processo de Lopo Soares, fl. 26v; Processo de Clara Lopes, fl. 22v; Processo de Branca de Oliveira, fls. 21v–22; Processo de Guiomar de Oliveira, fl. 20v; Processo de Estevão Lopes, fl. 16v.

140. Processo de Lopo Soares, fl. 26v; Processo de Clara Lopes, fl. 22v; Processo de Guiomar de Oliveira, fl. 20v. Processo de Estevão Lopes, fl. 16v.

141. Processo de Ana de Oliveira, fl. 23.
142. Processo de Diogo Soares, fls. 25/27–25v/27v.
143. Processo de Diogo Soares, fl. 25/27; Processo de Leonor Fernandes, fls. 21–21v; Processo de Lopo Soares, fl. 26v; Processo de Clara Lopes, fls. 22–22v.
144. Processo de Diogo Soares, fl. 25v/27v; Processo de Leonor Fernandes, fl. 22; Processo de Lopo Soares, fl. 26v; Processo de Clara Lopes, fl. 22v; Processo de Branca de Oliveira, fl. 21; Processo de Guiomar de Oliveira, fl. 20v; Processo de Estevão Lopes, fl. 16v.
145. Processo de Diogo Soares, fl. 25v/27v; Processo de Leonor Fernandes, fl. 21v; Processo de Lopo Soares, fl. 26v; Processo de Clara Lopes, fl. 22.
146. The family opposed her freedom. Processo de Diogo Soares, fl. 27/29; Processo de Lopo Soares, fl. 27; Processo de Clara Lopes, fl. 22v; Processo de Branca de Oliveira, fls. 21–21v; Processo de Guiomar de Oliveira, fl. 20v; Processo de Estevão Lopes, fl. 16v.
147. Processo de Ana de Oliveira, fl. 22v. See chapter 2 for more discussion.
148. Processo de Leonor Fernandes, fl. 21v; Processo de Diogo Soares, fl. 25v/27v.
149. Processo de Clara Lopes, fls. 22–22v.
150. One of Branca de Oliveira's slaves, Madanela Bengala, recounted the measures the family took to conceal their fasting. Processo de Branca de Oliveira, fl. 55.
151. Antonia Malavar recounted that her enslaver's family had a pig slaughtered, and the slaves were ordered to come to the table, which had never been done. Processo de Diogo Soares, fls. 109/122–109v/122v, 111/124–111v/124v.
152. Antonia Malavar made this allegation. Processo de Diogo Soares, fl. 112v/125v.
153. Processo de Diogo Soares, fl. 117v/130v. By the time Belchior Pegu was sent, Branca de Oliveira, Guiomar de Oliveira, Ana de Oliveira, and Leonor Fernandes were in jail.
154. Processo de Branca de Oliveira, fl. 57.
155. Processo de Branca de Oliveira, fl. 57.
156. Processo de Leonor Fernandes, fl. 73.
157. Processo de Diogo Soares, fl. 120/133.
158. Processo de Leonor Fernandes, fl. 73.
159. Processo de Estevão Lopes, fl. 66.
160. Processo de Estevão Lopes, fl. 66.
161. Processo de Diogo Soares, fl. 20v/21v.

162. Processo de Diogo Soares, fls. 20/21–20v/21v. Ilena Machada was unnamed, yet the family's description of her overlapped with material in the counterstatements against her. For instance, see Processo de Leonor Fernandes, fl. 21.
163. Processo de Diogo Soares, fl. 20/21.
164. In his counterstatements, Diogo Soares identified three of his six enslaved denunciators in addition to the freed Ilena Machada. At the same time, he listed nine other slaves in his counterstatements, who did not denounce him. Processo de Diogo Soares, fls. 25/27–27/29, 105v/118v–123/136. Leonor Fernandes correctly identified four enslaved denunciators by name in her counterstatements (besides Ilena Machada), while casting a broad net by naming three other enslaved women in addition to an unspecified number of unnamed women enslaved by Ana de Oliveira. Processo de Leonor Fernandes, fls. 21–22v, 59–74. On the other hand, Lopo Soares managed to identify only Antonia Malavar and the freed Ilena Machada; the seven additional enslaved women in his counterstatements had not denounced him. Processo de Lopo Soares, fl. 26–27, 61v–70v.
165. Processo de Diogo Soares, fl. 20v/21v. The defendants' slaves were rounded up, after the family's arrest.
166. Processo de Ana de Oliveira, fl. 67.
167. Processo de Leonor Fernandes, fl. 73. The decision to deposit Isabel in the factor's house raises questions about her eventual fate after the Goan portion of the trial. On the one hand, the removal of enslaved witnesses facilitated the collection of testimonies by attempting to decrease the level of potential slaveholder interference. Given the factor's official duties in the imperial trading network, however, was Isabel more likely to have been sold off afterward to benefit either himself or even the state? Regardless, enslaved people's potential status as confiscated "goods" seized by the Inquisition merits further exploration.
168. A similar social unease about unattached slaves also appeared in Portugal. Timothy Walker, "Sorcerers and Folkhealers: Africans and the Inquisition in Portugal (1680–1800)," *Revista Lusófona de Ciência das Religiões* 3, nos. 5–6 (2004): 83–98.
169. This was not a phenomenon limited to the Portuguese. For a Dutch Indian Ocean example, see Kate Ekama, "Precarious Freedom: Manumission in Eighteenth-Century Colombo," *Journal of Social History* 54, no. 1 (Fall 2020): 88–108. Another intriguing comparison is the Islamic concept of *wala,* whereby ties of "fictitious kinship" endured between the manumitted and their former enslavers. These patron-client relationships included rights and

obligations. Bernard K. Freamon, *Possessed by the Right Hand: The Problem of Slavery in Islamic Law and Muslim Cultures* (Leiden: Brill, 2019), 61–63, 224–26.

170. These records were not always straightforward, however. For an interesting discussion of the role of church officials as recorders of slave status as well as the potential problems arising with church records, see the debate on Olaudah Equiano's origins: Vincent Carretta, *Equiano, the African: Biography of a Self-Made Man* (New York: Penguin Books, 2006); Paul E. Lovejoy, "Autobiography and Memory: Gustavus Vassa, alias Olaudah Equiano, the African," *Slavery and Abolition* 27, no. 3 (2006): 317–47; Vincent Carretta, "Response to Paul Lovejoy's 'Autobiography and Memory: Gustavus Vassa, alias Olaudah Equiano, the African,'" *Slavery and Abolition* 28, no. 1 (April 2007): 115–19; Sweet, "Mistaken Identities?," 279–306; Vin Carretta, "Communications," *American Historical Review* 114, no. 3 (June 2009): 886–87; and James H. Sweet, "Communications," *American Historical Review* 114, no. 3 (June 2009): 887–88.

171. *Cartas de Alforria aos Escravos, 1682–1759,* HAG, Ms. 860. Despite the title's date range, the document includes 1760. For an analysis of all entries from 1682 to 1700, see Faria, "O Pai dos Cristãos," 1–30. For an analysis of the document as a whole, see Teotonio R. de Souza, "Manumission of Slaves in Goa during 1682 to 1760 as Found in Codex 860," in *TADIA, the African Diaspora in Asia: Explorations on a Less Known Fact,* ed. Kiran Kamal Prasad and Jean-Pierre Angenot (Bangalore: Jana Jagrati Prakashana, 2008), 167–81.

172. See *Cartas de Alforria,* fls. 5v–8, 9v–10v, 11v–12, 17v–25, 30v–34, 35–36, 42v–44, 46v–47, 48v–50, 55v–61. Three hundred ninety-four enslaved people were recorded, including two entries for Constançia, also recorded as Constasçia, in 1705 and 1706. *Cartas de Alforria,* fls. 59v, 60v.

173. See Michelle A. McKinley, *Fractional Freedoms: Slavery, Intimacy, and Legal Mobilization in Colonial Lima, 1600–1700* (New York: Cambridge University Press, 2016) for her discussion of conditional freedom. Also, see Michelle McKinley, "Fractional Freedoms: Slavery, Legal Activism, and Ecclesiastical Courts in Colonial Lima, 1593–1689," *Law and History Review* 28, no. 3 (2010): 749–90.

174. Faria, "O Pai dos Cristãos," 18.

175. For Aldonça, see *Cartas de Alforria,* fl. 10v. For Ilena, see *Cartas de Alforria,* fl. 44.

176. Constançia, also recorded as Constasçia, appeared twice in the records, in 1705 and 1706. *Cartas de Alforria,* fls. 59v, 60v.
177. *Cartas de Alforria,* fl. 36.
178. *Cartas de Alforria,* fl. 43v.
179. *Óbitos,* São Bartolomeu, 1682–1708, HAG, Sr. No. 147, fls.1–173v. There were also possibly nine other slaves recorded whose status was ambiguous.
180. *Óbitos,* São Bartolomeu, Sr. No. 147, fls. 9–19, 21–22.
181. *Óbitos,* São Bartolomeu, Sr. No. 147, fl.11v.
182. *Óbitos,* São Bartolomeu, Sr. No. 147, fl. 12.
183. *Óbitos,* São Bartolomeu, Sr. No. 147, fl. 10. The record entry also had the owner's name mistakenly recorded in the margin in lieu of Francisco Gomes. I am following the wording within the body of the entry to identify the name of the deceased slave.
184. *Óbitos,* São Bartolomeu, Sr. No. 147, fl. 13v.
185. *Óbitos,* São Bartolomeu, Sr. No. 147, fl. 13v. "Balgaty'" referred to her caste.
186. *Óbitos,* São Bartolomeu, Sr. No. 147, fl. 11v.
187. *Óbitos,* São Bartolomeu, Sr. No. 147, fl. 15.
188. *Óbitos,* São Bartolomeu, Sr. No. 147, fls. 7v–8, 54, 75v.
189. Drawing from Eugene Genovese's insights on paternalism and violence, Patrícia Souza de Faria also examined the paternalistic nature of slavery in Portuguese India. Faria, "O Pai dos Cristãos," 19–22; Eugene D. Genovese, *Roll, Jordan, Roll: The World the Slaves Made* (New York: Vintage Books, 1976).

CHAPTER 2: ENSLAVERS AS RELIGIOUS STEWARDS

1. Processo de Estevão Lopes, ANTT, IL, Processos, No. 360, fl. 2.
2. Processo de Estevão Lopes, fl. 2.
3. Processo de Estevão Lopes, fls. 67v–68.
4. Processo de Estevão Lopes, fl. 67v.
5. Processo de Estevão Lopes, fl. 5.
6. Processo de Estevão Lopes, fls. 5–5v.
7. Process de Estevão Lopes, fls. 28–28v.
8. For discussion of the Catholic Reformation (also called the Counter-Reformation), see Michael A. Mullett, *The Catholic Reformation* (London: Routledge, 1999), and Merry E. Wiesner-Hanks, *Early Modern Europe, 1450–1789,* 2nd ed. (Cambridge: Cambridge University Press, 2013), 186–92.
9. Frank Tannenbaum, *Slave and Citizen* (Boston: Beacon, 1992), 63. Also commenting comparatively, Katharine Gerbner distinguished the Catholic approach to converting enslaved people from

the "anticonversion sentiment" prevalent in Protestant colonies in the Atlantic. Katharine Gerbner, *Christian Slavery: Conversion and Race in the Protestant Atlantic World* (Philadelphia: University of Pennsylvania Press, 2018), 2.

10. Michelle A. McKinley, *Fractional Freedoms: Slavery, Intimacy, and Legal Mobilization in Colonial Lima, 1600–1700* (New York: Cambridge University Press, 2016); Michelle McKinley, "Fractional Freedoms: Slavery, Legal Activism, and Ecclesiastical Courts in Colonial Lima, 1593–1689," *Law and History Review* 28, no. 3 (2010): 749–90.
11. J. H. da Cunha Rivara, ed., *Os Concilios de Goa e o Synodo de Diamper,* issue 4 of *Archivo-Portuguez Oriental* (Nova-Goa: Imprensa Nacional, 1862), 9. The decree clarified that reaching the age of discretion meant that one had the capability to sin. Yet, if there were questions about whether a child had attained that age, baptism was the mandated course of action.
12. Rivara, 17–18.
13. Rivara, 183.
14. Rivara, 186.
15. Rivara, 215–16.
16. Besides explicitly invoking the rhetoric of religious stewardship, another inducement for purchasing "pagan" slaves may have been owners' interest in receiving an indulgence or jubilee for their own spiritual benefit. On indulgences, see Jeanette Pinto, *Slavery in Portuguese India, 1510–1842* (Bombay: Himalaya, 1992), 71.
17. *Cartas de Alforria aos Escravos, 1682–1759,* HAG, Ms. 860, fl. 5v.
18. *Cartas de Alforria,* fl. 5v.
19. *Cartas de Alforria,* fl. 6v.
20. *Cartas de Alforria,* fl. 6v.
21. *Cartas de Alforria,* fl. 24v.
22. *Cartas de Alforria,* fl. 23.
23. Patrícia Souza de Faria, "O Pai dos Cristãos e as Populações Escravas de Goa: Zelo e Controle dos Cativos Convertidos (Séculos XVI e XVII)," *História* 39 (2000): 17–18.
24. Processo de Gabriel, ANTT, IL, Processos, No. 4937, fls. 4v–5. For more discussion of his case, see chapter 4.
25. Rivara, *Concilios,* 142–43.
26. Didier Lahon, "Black African Slaves and Freedmen in Portugal during the Renaissance: Creating a New Pattern of Reality," in *Black Africans in Renaissance Europe,* ed. T. F. Earle and K. J. P. Lowe (Cambridge: Cambridge University Press, 2005), 272–73. Rejecting baptism as a form of slave religious agency was contested

in Portugal by the archbishop of Lisbon in 1568. This friction between the Portuguese law code and ecclesiastical authority in Lisbon opens up a pathway for future comparative research on the extent to which the crown and the church potentially clashed on slaves' religious rights and owners' religious duties.

27. Carmo D'Souza, "Slavery in Goa: Legal and Historical Perspectives," in *Legacies of Slavery: Comparative Perspectives,* ed. Maria Suzette Fernandes Dias (Newcastle, UK: Cambridge Scholars, 2007), 66.
28. A. C. de C. M. Saunders, *A Social History of Black Slaves and Freedmen in Portugal, 1441–1555* (Cambridge: Cambridge University Press, 1982), 90.
29. *Baptismos,* São Bartolomeu, 1690–1702, HAG, Sr. No. 169, fls. 1–170v. While the title indicates 1690, the earliest year recorded is 1685. Both infants and older slaves were baptized. While 1702 is listed in the title, ten entries from 1717 appeared and were likely incorrectly included in the document. There were 1,759 total baptismal entries, and some of these entries recorded multiple individuals. Folio 121v, which was deteriorated, possibly included two individuals in one of the entries, leading to an approximate figure of 1,768 baptized people in the document. Non-baptismal material from the 1730s also appears. The total number of enslaved baptismal candidates excludes two entries of interest. Benedicta, who was likely a free infant, was documented with her enslaved father's information while her mother was unrecorded. Also excluded is an illegible entry concerning a "*cafra*" slave, who either appeared as a godparent or baptismal candidate. *Baptismos,* São Bartolomeu, Sr. No. 169, fls. 121, 159v.
30. *Baptismos,* São Bartolomeu, Sr. No. 169, fl. 9.
31. See Cizilia, Pedro, João, Magdanela (also called Magdalena), João, Alberto, Ventura, Lourenço, Ambrosio, and Matheus; six of them were baptized at home and one on a ship rather than the usual location of the church. *Baptismos,* São Bartolomeu, Sr. No. 169, fls. 2v, 12v, 48v (second folio), 100v, 114, 130v–131, 131v (first folio), 140v, 153v, 159. Some folios had duplicate numbers with different baptisms recorded, hence the distinction between first and second folio. For the Portuguese norm of designating godparents for baptized enslaved individuals, see Saunders, *Social History of Black Slaves,* 90.
32. *Baptismos,* São Bartolomeu, Sr. No. 169, fl. 79v.
33. *Baptismos,* São Bartolomeu, Sr. No. 169, fl. 169.
34. *Baptismos,* São Bartolomeu, Sr. No. 169, fl. 21v.

35. Rivara, *Concilios,* 157.
36. Rivara, 275.
37. Kate Ekama, "Connected Lives: Experiences of Slavery in VOC Colombo," in *Being a Slave: Histories and Legacies of European Slavery in the Indian Ocean,* ed. Alicia Schrikker and Nira Wickramasinghe (Leiden: Leiden University Press, 2020), 108.
38. Rivara, *Concilios,* 196.
39. Rivara, 247.
40. Rivara, 46.
41. Rivara, 46–47.
42. John W. O'Malley, *Trent: What Happened at the Council* (Cambridge, MA: Belknap Press of Harvard University Press, 2013), 284.
43. For this description of purgatory and the impact of prayer and masses, see Lawrence S. Cunningham, *An Introduction to Catholicism* (Cambridge: Cambridge University Press, 2009), 81.
44. Saunders, *Social History of Black Slaves,* 110.
45. Saunders, 110.
46. Saunders, 110.
47. To arrive at this number, I made the following assumptions: In unlisted and Querem residences, Antonio Bragança corresponded to Antonio de Bragança; Bertolameu Dias was also Padre Bertolameu Dias, with unlisted residences; Irmão Jozeph Vaz was also Jozeph Vaz, with unlisted and Querem residences; Jose Madeira was also Jozeph Madeira in Pandivaddo; and Mathias de Sousa of Carebatta was also Mathias de Souza, with an unlisted residence. Rafael Rangel of Carebatta was possibly also Raphael Rangel of Querem. Because of the difference in residence, I counted them separately. *Óbitos,* São Bartolomeu, 1682–1708, HAG, Sr. No. 147, fls. 1–173v.
48. *Óbitos,* São Bartolomeu, Sr. No. 147, fls. 45v, 52v, 66, 68, 74v, 76, 89v, 93v, 106, 124v, 141v, 144v, 173v.
49. Burial entries recording monetary payments as the *fabrica* likely referred to a burial fee designated for the church's building repairs and upkeep. Anthony Vieyra, *A Dictionary of the Portuguese and English Languages, in Two Parts, Portuguese and English, and English and Portuguese,* 2 vols. (London: J. Nourse, 1773), s.v. "Fabrica." See especially the subentry, "fabrica da igreja, ou renda para os reparos della." Elsewhere in the Iberian colonial world, burial fees contributed to church repair funds. See Adriaan C. van Oss, *Catholic Colonialism: A Parish History of Guatemala, 1524–1821* (Cambridge: Cambridge University Press, 1986), xviii, 120.

50. *Óbitos,* São Bartolomeu, Sr. No. 147, fls. 1–173v.
51. *Óbitos,* São Bartolomeu, Sr. No. 147, fls. 1–173v.
52. F. X. Gomes Catao, *The Island of Chorao: A Historical Sketch* (Alwaye, India: Mar Louis Memorial Press, 1962), 88–89. Customarily, *desais* were hereditary holders of a precolonial position in which they represented the chief villages in the *desa*'s council. (Desas were precolonial administrative units.) It is possible that the title *desai-mor* corresponded to the title *sar-dessai,* or "chief of the desais." However, the title of *desai* eventually became an honorific retained within some Goan families without any corresponding representative duties. Sebastião Rodolfo Dalgado, *Glossário Luso-Asiático,* 2 vols. (Coimbra: Imprensa da Universidade, 1919–21), s.v. "Dessai"; and Teotonio R. de Souza, *Medieval Goa: A Socio-Economic History,* 2nd ed. (Saligão, Goa: Goa, 1556, 2009), 32–33.
53. Catao, *Island of Chorao,* 88–89.
54. Among other records, his caste is documented in the baptism entries for his daughter Maria in 1687 and son Manoel likely in 1694. *Baptismos,* São Bartolomeu, Sr. No. 169, fls. 38–38v, 75v. For an example of a Sudro (Sudra) resident on his land in Ambarim, see Anna de Sa, who appeared in a baptism record as the godmother of João de Sousa and his wife Antonia Fernandes's son, Roque, in 1697. Roque's godfather's caste was likewise recorded as Sudro, while Roque's parents were recorded as an entirely different caste, "Rendeiro." Thus, this baptism showed connections between three different castes. *Baptismos,* São Bartolomeu, Sr. No. 169, fl. 132.
55. *Óbitos,* São Bartolomeu, Sr. No. 147, fls. 1–173v.
56. *Óbitos,* São Bartolomeu, Sr. No. 147, fls. 45v, 52v, 66, 68, 74v, 76, 89v, 93v, 106, 124v, 141v, 144v, 173v.
57. *Óbitos,* São Bartolomeu, Sr. No. 147, fls. 89v, 93v.
58. *Óbitos,* São Bartolomeu, Sr. No. 147, fl. 8v.
59. *Óbitos,* São Bartolomeu, Sr. No. 147, fl. 13v.
60. *Óbitos,* São Bartolomeu, Sr. No. 147, fl. 8v.
61. *Óbitos,* São Bartolomeu, Sr. No. 147, 16v.
62. *Óbitos,* São Bartolomeu, Sr. No. 147, fl. 33.
63. The social significance of burial and the precarious position of slaves and freed slaves were hardly limited to Catholic Portuguese India. For burial and community recognition in the East African Muslim context, see Elisabeth McMahon, "Slave Wills along the Swahili Coast," in *African Voices on Slavery and the Slave Trade: Volume 1, the Sources,* ed. Alice Bellagamba, Sandra E. Greene,

and Martin A. Klein (Cambridge: Cambridge University Press, 2013), 511–18.

64. Processo de Diogo Soares, ANTT, IL, Processos, No. 185, fl. 109v/122v.
65. Processo de Diogo Soares, fl. 112v/125v.
66. Processo de Diogo Soares, fl. 114/127.
67. Processo de Branca de Oliveira, ANTT, IL, Processos, No. 6569, fl. 56.
68. Processo de Branca de Oliveira, fl. 62.
69. Processo de Ana de Oliveira, ANTT, IL, Processos, No. 6725, fls. 68v, 69v.
70. Maria Jaoa had to collect water for the week on those days. Processo de Ana de Oliveira, fl. 71v.
71. Processo de Diogo Soares, fl. 107/120.
72. Processo de Diogo Soares, fls. 8–8v.
73. Processo de Leonor Fernandes, ANTT, IL, Processos, No. 7631, fl. 8v.
74. See the defense inquiry testimonies of Gaspar Rodrigues, Maria Pachequa, Maria Bentes, Tome Lopez, Ines da Costa, Joam de Chaves, Lopo Vas, Joam Rodrigues, M[anoe]l Varella, Francisco Pachequo, Bras Lopez, and Margarida Lopez regarding article no. 2 of Branca de Oliveira's defense. Processo de Branca de Oliveira, fls. 27, 28, 29, 29v, 30v, 32v, 33v, 34v, 35v, 36, 36v, 37.
75. Slaveholders' resistance to marriage was not exclusive to Portuguese India. For opposition to slave marriage in Portugal, see Jorge Fonseca, "Black Africans in Portugal during Cleynaerts's Visit (1533–1538)," in *Black Africans in Renaissance Europe,* ed. T. F. Earle and K. J. P. Lowe (Cambridge: Cambridge University Press, 2005), 119, and Saunders, *Social History of Black Slaves,* 104. For Iberia more broadly, see William D. Phillips Jr., *Slavery in Medieval and Early Modern Iberia* (Philadelphia: University of Pennsylvania Press, 2014), 90–91. For the clash between marriage rights and property rights in colonial Lima, see McKinley, "Fractional Freedoms," 749–90. On the extreme end of the spectrum were Protestant slave societies, where slave marriage rights were absent. For a recent discussion, see Tera W. Hunter, *Bound in Wedlock: Slave and Free Black Marriage in the Nineteenth Century* (Cambridge, MA: Belknap Press of Harvard University Press, 2017).
76. Processo de Ana de Oliveira, fl. 8v.
77. Processo de Ana de Oliveira, fl. 24v.
78. For example, see the testimonies by Maria Pachequa, Maria Bentes, Pero Dias, and Tome Lopez, particularly regarding the fourth article. Processo de Ana de Oliveira, fls. 29–32v.

79. Processo de Ana de Oliveira, fl. 22v.
80. Processo de Ana de Oliveira, fl. 22v.
81. Processo de Ana de Oliveira, fls. 45–45v, 47.
82. Processo de Ana de Oliveira, fl. 45v.
83. Processo de Ana de Oliveira, fl. 45v.
84. Processo de Ana de Oliveira, fl. 45v.
85. Processo de Diogo Soares, fl. 20v/21v.
86. Processo de Gabriel, fls. 2v–3.
87. Processo de Paulo, ANTT, IL, Processos, No. 3672, fl. 5.
88. *Baptismos,* São Bartolomeu, Sr. No. 169, fls. 1–170v. To distinguish infants, I counted entries of individuals born to mothers whose slave status was recorded in addition to the enslaved Martinho (fl. 169), whose mother's name was recorded without her status. Each of these enslaved individuals also lacked a recorded age. Older slaves had an age listed and/or were designated as adults in the records.
89. *Baptismos,* São Bartolomeu, Sr. No. 169, fl. 130.
90. *Baptismos,* São Bartolomeu, Sr. No. 169, fl. 101.
91. *Óbitos,* São Bartolomeu, Sr. No. 147, fls. 1–173v.
92. See entries for João, Berthollameu, Francisca, Joana, Helena, and Antonia. *Óbitos,* São Bartolomeu, Sr. No. 147, fls. 98, 100, 118, 118v, 122v, 148v.
93. *Óbitos,* São Bartolomeu, Sr. No. 147, fl. 98. The precise term indicating Adrianna's slave status was *moça,* spelled "mossa" in the record.
94. *Óbitos,* São Bartolomeu, Sr. No. 147, fl. 6.
95. *Óbitos,* São Bartolomeu, Sr. No. 147, fl. 56v. An allusion to her unnamed mother's slave status was the record's comment that she was a "*negra*" in Joseph Vas's house.
96. *Óbitos,* São Bartolomeu, Sr. No. 147, fl. 13. The entry for Baltezar has an error: his father's name appeared on the left of the entry instead of his own. However, the body of the entry identified Baltezar as the son and João Rebello as the father. For an example of an exception to the pattern of recorded fathers, see the deceased Francisca who was documented in 1685 as the "daughter of Monica," a lower-caste Sudra woman who lacked a last name. *Óbitos,* São Bartolomeu, Sr. No. 147, fl. 25v.
97. *Óbitos,* São Bartolomeu, Sr. No. 147, fls. 1–173v.
98. An alternative reading of these records would be the possible documentary erasure of enslaved women's husbands in favor of listing the higher patriarchal figure, the woman's enslaver who had more authority as an owner.

99. *Óbitos,* São Bartolomeu, Sr. No. 147, fl. 8v.
100. *Óbitos,* São Bartolomeu, Sr. No. 147, fls. 13v, 14.
101. *Óbitos,* São Bartolomeu, Sr. No. 147, fl. 91v. Rangel's first name is spelled "Rafael" in this record.
102. *Baptismos,* São Bartolomeu, Sr. No. 169, fl. 101. This is the same Gonçalo whose enslaved parents were documented as married. Rangel's first name is spelled "Raphael" in this record. Both the baptism and death records list the same residence of Carebatta.
103. *Óbitos,* São Bartolomeu, Sr. No. 147, fls. 22v–23.
104. *Óbitos,* São Bartolomeu, Sr. No. 147, fls. 1–173v.
105. For an example of slaves' resistance to coerced unions elsewhere in the Portuguese Empire, see Sandra Lauderdale Graham, *Caetana Says No: Women's Stories from a Brazilian Slave Society* (Cambridge: Cambridge University Press, 2002).

CHAPTER 3: ARMING SLAVES FOR THE CATHOLIC EMPIRE

1. Processo de Gonçalo Toscano, ANTT, IL, Processos, No. 4931, fls. 2–2v. For an earlier version of this chapter, see Stephanie Hassell, "Religious Identity and Imperial Security: Arming Catholic Slaves in Sixteenth- and Seventeenth-Century Portuguese India," *Journal of Early Modern History* 26, no. 5 (2022): 403–28. For more discussion of this case, see chapter 5.
2. Locations named in his Inquisition case were Galiana and Balagate. It is likely Galiana was the city of Kalyan close to Mumbai (Bombay). Luís Filipe F. R. Thomaz, "Iranian Diaspora and the Deccan Sultanates in India: A Study of Sixteenth Century Portuguese Sources," *Studies in History* 30, no. 1 (2014): 31. Balagate's literal meaning is "the Deccan Plateau," yet the Portuguese also used the term to refer to Bijapur, one of the Deccan sultanates. Richard F. Burton, *Camoens: His Life and His Lusiads* (London: Bernard Quaritch, 1881), 1:330, 330n1; Henry Yule and A. C. Burnell, *Hobson-Jobson: A Glossary of Colloquial Anglo-Indian Words and Phrases, and of Kindred Terms, Etymological, Historical, Geographical and Discursive,* 2nd ed., ed. William Crooke (London: John Murray, 1903), s.v. "Idalcan."
3. Processo de Gonçalo Toscano, fls. 2–2v.
4. Processo de Gonçalo Toscano, fls. 3v–4.
5. J. Clancy Clements, *The Genesis of a Language: The Formation and Development of Korlai Portuguese* (Amsterdam: John Benjamins, 1996), 6; K. M. Mathew, *History of the Portuguese Navigation in India (1497–1600)* (Delhi: Mittal, 1988), 209–10; Radhey Shyam, *The Kingdom of Ahmadnagar* (Delhi: Motilal

Barnarsidass, 1966), 349. The siege of Bassein cited in Gonçalo's case was contemporaneous with the siege of Chaul.

6. Tamarind trees produced pods (also called tamarinds) with pulpy flesh utilized as a spice as well as medicine, which the Portuguese imported. James C. Boyajian, *Portuguese Trade in Asia under the Habsburgs, 1580–1640* (Baltimore: Johns Hopkins University Press, 1993), 325.
7. Processo de Gonçalo Toscano, fls. 4–4v. The currency he was carrying was an unspecified number of tangas (abbreviated as t^{gas}).
8. Processo de Gonçalo Toscano, fl. 4v.
9. Processo de Gonçalo Toscano, f. 5.
10. For the concept "peopling of empire," see Kerry Ward, *Networks of Empire: Forced Migration in the Dutch East India Company* (Cambridge: Cambridge University Press, 2009), 29–41.
11. Scholars of early modern history have noted other cases of aligning political and religious borders as well as the histories of individuals who crossed territorial borders, converted to another religion, and began new lives in a new polity. For example, Natalie Zemon Davis tracked the sixteenth-century movements, religious and geographical, of the Catholic convert Yuhanna al-Asad, also known as Leo Africanus. Eric Dursteler analyzed Mediterranean women's strategic conversions and border crossings, while Duane Corpis analyzed the movements of new converts (and those who refused to convert to a new religion) across the post-1648 Holy Roman Empire's mono- and multiconfessional localities. Natalie Zemon Davis, *Trickster Travels: A Sixteenth-Century Muslim between Worlds* (New York: Hill & Wang, 2006); Eric R. Dursteler, *Renegade Women: Gender, Identity, and Boundaries in the Early Modern Mediterranean* (Baltimore: Johns Hopkins University Press, 2011); and Duane J. Corpis, *Crossing the Boundaries of Belief: Geographies of Religious Conversion in Southern Germany, 1648–1800* (Charlottesville: University of Virginia Press, 2014).
12. Teotonio R. de Souza, *Medieval Goa: A Socio-Economic History*, 2nd ed. (Saligão, Goa: Goa, 1556, 2009), 62.
13. Délio de Mendonça, *Conversions and Citizenry: Goa under Portugal, 1510–1610* (New Delhi: Concept, 2002), 206–8. These included viceregal and crown decrees as well as decrees by the provincial council. The 1556 decree allowed the removal of Hindu "orphans" (children whose fathers had died) from their homes if they were under the age of fourteen.
14. Ricard M. Eaton, "Temple Desecration and Indo-Muslim States," in *Beyond Turk and Hindu: Rethinking Religious Identities in*

Islamicate South Asia, ed. David Gilmartin and Bruce B. Lawrence (Gainesville: University of Florida Press, 2000), 246–81; Richard M. Eaton and Phillip B. Wagoner, *Power, Memory, Architecture: Contested Sites on India's Deccan Plateau, 1300–1600* (New Delhi: Oxford University Press, 2014).

15. J. H. da Cunha Rivara, ed., *Os Concilios de Goa e o Synodo de Diamper,* issue 4 of *Archivo-Portuguez Oriental* (Nova-Goa: Imprensa Nacional, 1862), 12–14. See Decreto 9.
16. Rivara, 11. See Decreto 7.
17. Rivara, 12. See Decreto 8. This was also a religious crime punished by the Goa Tribunal of the Portuguese Inquisition.
18. Rivara, 11. See Decreto 6. *Feiticeiros* can be translated "witches," "sorcerers," or "wizards." In Inquisition case summaries, they were linked to "pagan ceremonies" and sacrifices for supplicants desiring bodily healing, treasure, or the murder of someone. For instance, in 1619 Domingas de Gouvea in Chaul allegedly consulted a *feiticeiro* for charms to kill someone, in addition to attending "pagan ceremonies" to discover treasure and cure her son. Likewise, in 1619 Dona Branca de Mello allegedly consulted *feiticeiros* "to murder her husband." João Delgado Figueira, *Reportorio geral de tres mil oito centos processos, que sam todos os despachados neste sancto Officio de Goa & mais partes da India, do anno de Mil & quinhentos & secenta & hum, que começou o dito sancto Officio até o anno de Mil & seiscentos & vinte & tres, com a lista dos Inquisidores que tem sido nelle, & dos autos publicos da Fee, que se tem celebrado na dita Cidade de Goa,* 1623, BNP, cód. 203, fls. 277 (316), 281 (324). For the definition, see Anthony Vieyra, A Dictionary of the Portuguese and English Languages, in Two Parts, Portuguese and English, and English and Portuguese, 2 vols. (London: J. Nourse, 1773), s.v. "Feiticeiro."
19. Rivara, *Concilios,* 69.
20. Rivara, 69.
21. Rivara, 121–22. See Decreto 2.
22. Rivara, 211. See Decreto 13.
23. Rivara, 72–73.
24. Rivara, 266. See Decreto 13.
25. Jan Huygen van Linschoten, *The Voyage of John Huyghen van Linschoten to the East Indies: From the Old English Translation of 1598, the First Book, Containing His Description of the East,* ed. Arthur Coke Burnell (1885; repr., San Bernardino, CA: Adamant Media, 2005), 1:222. On the other hand, Sanjay Subrahmanyam disputes this level of diversity described by Linschoten, stating that "few Muslims remained in Goa beyond the resident ambassadors of neighboring

Muslim sovereigns and their retinues." Sanjay Subrahmanyam, *Three Ways to Be Alien: Travails and Encounters in the Early Modern World* (Waltham, MA: Brandeis University Press, 2011), 27.

26. One caveat, of course, is that Inquisition cases were instances of perceived religious transgressions. A guilty verdict did not always mean that the defendant had actually committed the religious offense in question. For a discussion of the Inquisition's manufacture of religious crimes, see Carlo Ginzburg, *The Night Battles: Witchcraft and Agrarian Cults in the Sixteenth and Seventeenth Centuries,* trans. John Tedeschi and Anne Tedeschi (Baltimore: Johns Hopkins University Press, 1992). Also, for a discussion about the challenges of using Inquisition trials as evidence to untangle defendants' beliefs, see François Soyer, "'It Is Not Possible to Be Both a Jew and a Christian': *Converso* Religious Identity and the Inquisitorial Trial of Custodio Nunes (1604–5)," *Mediterranean Historical Review* 26, no. 1 (2011): 81–97.
27. Sanjay Subrahmanyam, *The Portuguese Empire in Asia, 1500–1700: A Political and Economic History,* 2nd ed. (Chichester, UK: John Wiley & Sons, 2012), 233–34.
28. According to Teotonio R. de Souza, up to fifteen hundred Portuguese settlers were concentrated in Goa. Anthony Disney suggests that the settler population constituted around two thousand from the mid-sixteenth century through the early 1600s. Souza, *Medieval Goa,* 82; A. R. Disney, *The Portuguese Empire,* vol. 2 of *A History of Portugal and the Portuguese Empire: From Beginnings to 1807* (Cambridge: Cambridge University Press, 2009), 147–49.
29. Disney, *Portuguese Empire,* 149.
30. Disney, 146; Mathew, *History of the Portuguese Navigation,* 206–8; Shyam, *Kingdom of Ahmadnagar,* 338–46.
31. Souza, *Medieval Goa,* 7–9, 16–19.
32. Subrahmanyam, *Portuguese Empire in Asia,* 154–58. For analysis of Portuguese-Ottoman relations, see also Giancarlo Casale, *The Ottoman Age of Exploration* (Oxford: Oxford University Press, 2010).
33. Disney, *Portuguese Empire,* 61, 73–74, 168–71, 221–31; Souza, *Medieval Goa,* 4–6; C. R. Boxer, *The Portuguese Seaborne Empire, 1415–1825* (Middlesex, UK: Penguin Books, 1973), 108–29.
34. Timothy J. Coates, *Convicts and Orphans: Forced and State-Sponsored Colonizers in the Portuguese Empire, 1550–1755* (Stanford, CA: Stanford University Press, 2001), 45; Michael Pearson, *The Indian Ocean* (London: Routledge, 2003), 140.
35. Coates, *Convicts and Orphans,* 88.
36. Souza, *Medieval Goa,* 87–88.

37. Coates, *Convicts and Orphans,* 87–92; Pearson, *Indian Ocean,* 125.

38. Processo de Gonçalo Toscano, fls. 18v–19. Similarly, in a 1595 trial inquisitors asked the defendant about Christians who had become Muslims in the "land of the Moors." Processo de Gabriel, fls. 7–7v.

39. Figueira, *Reportorio,* fl. 97 (5).

40. Figueira, fl. 249v (261).

41. Figueira, fl. 366 (524).

42. Coates, *Convicts and Orphans.* For a more recent discussion, see Timothy Coates, "European Forced Labor in the Early Modern Era," in *The Cambridge World History of Slavery,* ed. David Eltis and Stanley L. Engerman (Cambridge: Cambridge University Press, 2011), 3:631–49. Reliance on convict labor was neither an exclusively Portuguese nor early modern phenomenon in the Indian Ocean. See Richard B. Allen, "Slaves, Convicts, Abolitionism and the Global Origins of the Post-Emancipation Indentured Labor System," *Slavery and Abolition* 35, no. 2 (2014): 328–48; Clare Anderson, *Subaltern Lives: Biographies of Colonialism in the Indian Ocean World, 1790–1920* (Cambridge: Cambridge University Press, 2012); Clare Anderson, "Convicts, Commodities, and Connections in British Asia and the Indian Ocean, 1789–1866," *International Review of Social History* 64, no. S27 (2019): 205–27; and Anand A. Yang, *Empire of Convicts: Indian Penal Labor in Colonial Southeast Asia* (Oakland: University of California Press, 2021).

43. For the role of galleys, see Boyajian, *Portuguese Trade,* 323.

44. Figueira, *Reportorio,* fls. 94 (2)–436 (678). This sample, cited here, includes defendants sentenced from 1561 to 1623 with first names beginning with letters *A* through *J*. In this sample, 227 cases included sentences to the galleys. Not all defendants necessarily stayed in the Indian Ocean, though, as thirty were sent to the galleys of Portugal (*galés de Portugal* or *galés do Reino*).

45. Figueira, *Reportorio,* fls. 198 (136)–198v (137). The Salcete in which Bras Coelho de Sancoalle lived was part of the region of Goa, as opposed to the island of Salsette, which was part of the *Província do Norte* (Province of the North).

46. Figueira, fl. 117v (25v).

47. Figueira, fls. 106 (14), 124v (32v), 155 (63), 192 (124), 239 (240), 246 (254), 320 (420), 332v (445), 367v (527), 372v (537), 376 (544), 391 (586). They were sentenced simply to the galleys, rather than other galley labor options such as the armada of Malabar, the "armadas of the king," and the galleys of Portugal.

48. Figueira, fls. 94 (2)–436 (678). Out of a sample of 2,254 cases, thirty-eight included sentences to the gunpowder factory. Twenty-five of those cases had male defendants, while the remaining thirteen were women.
49. Figueira, fls. 94 (2)–436 (678). For example, Britis Ribeira was exiled to Daman for eight years in 1612 for having induced false testimonies, and Anna Gonçalves was sent to Daman for five years in 1623 for bigamy. Figueira, fls. 202 (144), 173 (82). Theirs were among the thirty-two cases in the sample with exiles to Daman. Another thirty-four cases produced sentences of exile to Ceylon. For examples of these, see Francisco de Figueiredo, who in 1593 was exiled for three years to Ceylon for having made a mockery of the Inquisition, and Jorge Rebello, exiled in 1585 to Ceylon for three years on account of speaking blasphemies. Figueira, fls. 317v (415), 397v (599).
50. For instance, Christovão Leitão was exiled to Angola for six years in 1613 for having committed the religious crime of bigamy. Figueira, fl. 227 (206). An example of exile to Brazil is the 1612 case of Jeronimo Nunez de Nigreiros, who was exiled six years for bigamy. Figueira, fl. 421v (649).
51. R. J. Barendse, *The Arabian Seas: The Indian Ocean World of the Seventeenth Century* (New York: Routledge, 2015), 111; Boxer, *Portuguese Seaborne Empire,* 303–4; and Subrahmanyam, *Portuguese Empire in Asia,* 240–41.
52. Ann M. Pescatello, "The African Presence in Portuguese India," *Journal of Asian History* 11, no. 1 (1977): 34.
53. P. P. Shirodkar, "Slavery in Coastal India (with Special Reference to Goa, Daman, and Diu)," *Purabhilekh-Puratatva: Journal of the Directorate of Archives, Archaeology and Museum, Panaji-Goa* 3, no. 1 (1985): 32.
54. Jeanette Pinto, *Slavery in Portuguese India, 1510–1842* (Bombay: Himalaya, 1992), 58–59.
55. Timothy Walker, "Slaves or Soldiers? African Conscripts in Portuguese India, 1857–1860," in *Slavery and South Asian History,* ed. Indrani Chatterjee and Richard M. Eaton (Bloomington: Indiana University Press, 2006), 234–61.
56. Christopher Leslie Brown, "The Arming of Slaves in Comparative Perspective," in *Arming Slaves: From Classical Times to the Modern Age,* ed. Christopher Leslie Brown and Philip D. Morgan (New Haven, CT: Yale University Press, 2006), 330–53.
57. Richard M. Eaton, "The Rise and Fall of Military Slavery in the Deccan, 1450–1650," in *Slavery and South Asian History,* ed.

Indrani Chatterjee and Richard M. Eaton (Bloomington: Indiana University Press, 2006), 115–35. See also Richard M. Eaton, "Malik Ambar (1548–1626): The Rise and Fall of Military Slavery," in *A Social History of the Deccan, 1300–1761: Eight Indian Lives* (Cambridge: Cambridge University Press, 2005), 105–28; Omar H. Ali, *Malik Ambar: Power and Slavery across the Indian Ocean* (Oxford: Oxford University Press, 2016); and Sanjay Subrahmanyam, "Between Eastern Africa and Western India, 1500–1650: Slavery, Commerce, and Elite Formation," *Comparative Studies in Society and History* 61, no. 4 (2019): 805–34. On Mughal military labor strategies, see Dirk H. A. Kolff, *Naukar, Rajput and Sepoy: The Ethnohistory of the Military Labour Market in Hindustan, 1450–1850* (Cambridge: Cambridge University Press, 1990), and John F. Richards, *The Mughal Empire* (Cambridge: Cambridge University Press, 1993).

58. Helene Basu, "Slave, Soldier, Trader, Faqir: Fragments of African Histories in Western India (Gujarat)," in *The African Diaspora in the Indian Ocean,* ed. Shihan de S. Jayasuriya and Richard Pankhurst (Trenton, NJ: Africa World, 2003), 223–50.
59. António Bocarro, *O Livro das Plantas de Todas as Fortalezas, Cidades e Povoações do Estado da Índia Oriental,* ed. Isabel Cid (Lisbon: Imprensa Nacional, 1992), 2:75.
60. Bocarro, 2:122. These were the slaves of the two hundred Portuguese Christians and the fifty Indian Christians.
61. Bocarro, 2:129.
62. Bocarro, 2:115.
63. Bocarro, 2:199.
64. Bocarro, 2:84.
65. Bocarro, 2:135.
66. Bocarro, 2:135.
67. Bocarro, 2:135–36. Bocarro stated that the number of slaves belonging to the non-Portuguese casados equated to half that population. But in one part of the description, he said there were twenty-five hundred Indian casados, while later saying that the Indian casado population was only two thousand. Since he did not state a firm number of their slaves available to fight but rather described that sector of the slave population as being "half" the number of the Indian casado population, it is not certain whether he meant the estimate to be 1,000 or 1,250 slaves who could bear arms.
68. Bocarro, 2:136.
69. Bocarro, 2:135.

70. Hendrik Kraay, "Arming Slaves in Brazil from the Seventeenth Century to the Nineteenth Century," in Brown and Morgan, *Arming Slaves,* 146–79.
71. Linschoten, *Voyage,* 1:194.
72. Carmo D'Souza, "Slavery in Goa: Legal and Historical Perspectives," in *Legacies of Slavery: Comparative Perspectives,* ed. Maria Suzette Fernandes Dias (Newcastle, UK: Cambridge Scholars, 2007), 68.
73. *The Voyage of François Pyrard of Laval to the East Indies, the Maldives, the Moluccas and Brazil,* ed. Albert Gray (London: Hakluyt Society, 1888), 2, part 1:80. The status of the Mozambican guards by Pyrard de Laval is ambiguous.
74. However, while slaves were depended upon to fight for and alongside their owners, their use of arms was restricted by law. In 1586 the viceroy decreed that slaves could not carry arms unless in their owners' company; the penalty for breaking the law was a fine of one thousand reis or a whipping consisting of thirty lashes. D'Souza, "Slavery in Goa," 67–68.
75. The following are a few examples of ethnic outsiders as military slaves in South Asia: For African military slaves in India, see Eaton, "Rise and Fall," 115–35; Eaton, "Malik Ambar," 105–28; and Ali, *Malik Ambar.* For African slave soldiers in Ceylon, see Shihan de Silva Jayasuriya, "Migrants and Mercenaries: Sri Lanka's Hidden Africans," in Jayasuriya and Angenot, *Uncovering the History of Africans,* 155–70, and Shihan de Silva Jayasuriya, "Recruiting Africans to the British Regiments in Ceylon: Spillover Effects of Abolition in the Atlantic," *African and Asian Studies* 10, no. 1 (2011): 15–31. For Turkish military slaves in South Asia, see Peter Jackson, "Turkish Slaves on Islam's Indian Frontier," in Chatterjee and Eaton, *Slavery and South Asian History,* 63–82; Sunil Kumar, "Service, Status, and Military Slavery in the Delhi Sultanate: Thirteenth and Fourteenth Centuries," in Chatterjee and Eaton, *Slavery and South Asian History,* 83–114; and André Wink, *Al Hind, the Making of the Indo-Islamic World, Volume 2: The Slave Kings and the Islamic Conquest, 11th–13th Centuries* (Leiden: Brill, 2002).
76. This Portuguese Indian pattern differed sharply from military slavery in Portuguese settlements in southern Africa, where ethnicity was emphasized. See Allen Isaacman and Derek Peterson, "Making the Chikunda: Military Slavery and Ethnicity in Southern Africa, 1750–1900," in Brown and Morgan, *Arming Slaves,* 95–119. On the Chikunda, see also Allen F. Isaacman and Barbara

Isaacman, *Slavery and Beyond: The Making of Men and Chikunda Ethnic Identities in the Unstable World of South-Central Africa, 1750–1920* (Portsmouth, NH: Heinemann, 2004). In Macau, Africans were sometimes preferred for protection in the mid-seventeenth century, as evidenced by a letter from the governor of Macau requesting African slaves for that purpose. Boxer, *Portuguese Seaborne Empire,* 304.

77. The category "pagan" is broad and could include a range of non-monotheistic religions, including Hinduism and Buddhism.
78. Rivara, *Concilios,* 18.
79. Rivara, 19.
80. Rivara, 136–37.
81. Philip II was also Spain's Philip III.
82. J. H. da Cunha Rivara, ed., *Cartas da Camara de Goa a Sua Magestade,* issue 1, part 2 of *Archivo-Portuguez Oriental* (1876; repr., New Delhi: Asian Educational Services, 1992), 126.
83. Rivara, 127.
84. Rivara, 127.
85. Rivara, 127.
86. For an alternative analysis emphasizing the ethnicity of enslaved Japanese soldiers, see Lúcio de Sousa, *The Portuguese Slave Trade in Early Modern Japan: Merchants, Jesuits and Japanese, Chinese, and Korean Slaves* (Leiden: Brill, 2019), 435–36.
87. See *Livro Vermelho,* HAG, Ms. 8792, fls. 18–19. See also *Leis a favor da Cristandade,* HAG, Ms. 7693, fls. 14–14v, as well as *Provisões a favor da Cristandade,* HAG, Ms. 9529, fls. 40v–42.
88. Shirodkar, "Slavery in Coastal India," 31.
89. For the First Provincial Council, see Rivara, *Concilios,* 9, 17–18. For the imperial law, see Rivara, 183. For the Fourth Provincial Council, see Rivara, 186. For the Fifth Provincial Council, see Rivara, 215–16.
90. Rivara, 96.
91. Figueira, *Reportorio,* fl. 367 (526).
92. Figueira, fl. 189 (118).
93. Figueira, fl. 160v (68v).
94. For analysis of the Inquisition as a state institution, see Toby Green, "Policing the Empires: A Comparative Perspective on the Institutional Trajectory of the Inquisition in the Portuguese and Spanish Overseas Territories (Sixteenth and Seventeenth Centuries)," *Hispanic Research Journal* 13, no. 1 (2012): 7–25; and Toby Green, *Inquisition: The Reign of Fear* (New York: Thomas Dunne, 2009).

95. For background information on this source, see José Alberto Rodrigues da Silva Tavim, "Um inquisidor inquirido: João Delgado Figueira e o seu Reportorio, no contexto da 'documentação sobre a Inquisição de Goa,'" *Leituras: Revista da Biblioteca Nacional,* no. 1 (Outono 1997): 183–93.
96. Figueira, *Reportorio,* fls. 94 (2)–436 (678).
97. Processo de Diogo Soares, ANTT, IL, Processos, No. 185, fl. 20v/21v.
98. Rivara, *Concilios,* 270–71.
99. Rivara, 271.
100. Titas Chakraborty, "Slave Trading and Slave Resistance in the Indian Ocean World: The Case of Early Eighteenth-Century Bengal," *Slavery and Abolition* 40, no. 4 (2019): 706–26; Alexander Geelen et al., "On the Run: Runaway Slaves and Their Social Networks in Eighteenth-Century Cochin," *Journal of Social History* 54, no. 1 (Fall 2020): 66–87; and Richard B. Allen, "A Serious and Alarming Daily Evil: *Marronage* and Its Legacy in Mauritius and the Colonial Plantation World," *Slavery and Abolition* 25, no. 2 (2004): 1–17.
101. Matthias van Rossum, Alexander Geelen, and Merve Tosun, "Enslaveability, Slavery and Global Micro Histories: Reflections through the Case of Cali," *Slavery and Abolition* 43, no. 3 (2022): 482–98.
102. Stephanie Mawson, "Escaping Empire: Philippine Mountains and Indigenous Histories of Resistance," *American Historical Review* 128, no. 3 (2023): 1211–43; and Stephanie Mawson, "Slavery, Conflict, and Empire in the Seventeenth-Century Philippines," in Allen, *Slavery and Bonded Labor,* 256–83.
103. Bocarro, *Livro das Plantas,* 2:196.
104. David Brion Davis, "Introduction," in *Arming Slaves: From Classical Times to the Modern Age,* ed. Christopher Leslie Brown and Philip D. Morgan (New Haven, CT: Yale University Press, 2006), 3.

CHAPTER 4: BONDS OF CONVERSION

1. Exile was a possible inquisitorial sentence for non-Christians. For example, in 1588 inquisitors Thomas Pinto and Ruy Sodrinho exiled and fined a Muslim woman named Bibeasilá (also known as Bibia Silia in the *Reportorio*'s index) for "perverting and impeding Christianity." João Delgado Figueira, *Reportorio geral de tres mil oito centos processos, que sam todos os despachados neste sancto Officio de Goa & mais partes da India, do anno*

de Mil & quinhentos & secenta & hum, que começou o dito sancto Officio até o anno de Mil & seiscentos & vinte & tres, com a lista dos Inquisidores que tem sido nelle, & dos autos publicos da Fee, que se tem celebrado na dita Cidade de Goa, 1623, BNP, cód. 203, fl. 188 (116). For her name listed in the document's index, see Figueira, fl. 78.

2. On inquisitorial communication, see Francisco Bethencourt, *The Inquisition: A Global History, 1478–1834,* trans. Jean Birrell (Cambridge: Cambridge University Press, 2009), 54–60. Also, for an example of intertribunal communications, see François Soyer, "'It Is Not Possible to Be Both a Jew and a Christian': *Converso* Religious Identity and the Inquisitorial Trial of Custodio Nunes (1604–5)," *Mediterranean Historical Review* 26, no. 1 (2011): 81–97. For some of the Goa Tribunal's correspondence, see António Baião, ed., *A Inquisição de Goa: Correspondencia dos Inquisidores da Índia (1569–1630)* (Coimbra: Imprensa da Universidade, 1930).
3. Processo de Gabriel, ANTT, IL, Processos, No. 4937, fls. 7–7v.
4. Figueira, *Reportorio,* fl. 108 (16).
5. Figueira, fls. 94 (2)–436 (678). This sample, cited here, includes defendants sentenced from 1561 to 1623 with first names beginning with letters *A* through *J*.
6. Sentencing these absent subjects also served as a public reminder of the shameful consequences of committing inquisitorial crimes.
7. Timothy J. Coates, *Convicts and Orphans: Forced and State-Sponsored Colonizers in the Portuguese Empire, 1550–1755* (Stanford, CA: Stanford University Press, 2001), 87.
8. For example, see the 1597 case of Gonçalo Toscano, Processo de Gonçalo Toscano, fls. 23v–24; Antonio de Barros and Marcos Gil Frazão to Inquisitor General, Goa, December 1, 1597, in Baião, *Inquisição de Goa,* 259; Antonio de Barros and Marcos Gil Frazão to Inquisitor General, December 23, 1599, in Baião, *Inquisição de Goa,* 271.
9. Figueira, *Reportorio,* fl. 306v (393).
10. Figueira, fl. 307 (394).
11. Figueira, fl. 392v (589).
12. Figueira, fl. 447 (710).
13. An inquisitorial example of runaway soldiers (and a fugitive friar) living in the "land of the Moors" appears in a 1610 denunciation. See "Treslado de huma denunciação que fes na Mesa do Santo Officio Gaspar Borges da Fonsequa . . . ," ANTT, IL, Cadernos do Promotor, Caderno 8 do Promotor, Livro 209, fls. 527–29. In

this denunciation to the Goa Tribunal, Frei Antonio de Leiria, who had fled to Vicholim in the "land of the Moors," was denounced for having made blasphemous statements in the company of fugitive soldiers.

14. Figueira, *Reportorio,* fl. 353 (498).
15. Figueira, fl. 205 (150). Because of his "pagan" status, Bodú is in the minority of people sentenced by the Inquisition from the inception of the Goa Tribunal to 1623. One way that non-Christians, such as Bodú, officially invited inquisitorial prosecution was by obstructing the spread of the Catholic faith. In the *Reportorio,* the term categorizing the offense was *impediente.* It was also used to describe impeding the work of the Inquisition.
16. The term *paganism* probably meant Hinduism in the majority of the cases involving religious crimes committed in Portuguese India. However, untangling the precise meanings of the inquisitors' category without having access to the full case records is challenging. In the *Reportorio,* Figueira coded crimes as paganism (*culpas de gentilidade*) generally without actually describing the beliefs and actions of the defendant. Clues to the category's possible meanings include the place where the religious crime occurred and the ethnic and religious background of the person committing the religious offense. For instance, if the crime of paganism occurred in Macau, then it is quite plausible (but not entirely certain) that the defendant was practicing Buddhism. Figueira's act of reading cases and then categorizing them adds a methodological challenge to using the *Reportorio.*
17. This conversion, if he persisted in it, had the possibility to radically change his lifestyle. Figueira listed Bodú's profession as a "*tangedor de bailadeiras,*" a musician presumably for female temple dancers. This would not have been a church-approved profession. Anthony Vieyra, *A Dictionary of the Portuguese and English Languages, in Two Parts, Portuguese and English, and English and Portuguese,* 2 vols. (London: J. Nourse, 1773), s.v. "Tangedor." For a discussion of *bailadeiras,* see Fatima da Silva Gracias, *Kaleidoscope of Women in Goa (1510–1961)* (New Delhi: Concept, 1996), 80–83, 104–8, 127–28. Also, Bodú was married, and he lived on the mainland outside Portuguese jurisdiction. Could he keep his profession with a new religion? If he was so adamant about his son needing to come back to the family's religious practices, how would his own family have received him upon converting to Catholicism? Did Bodú and his wife have to move to Portuguese territory after his conversion? These are post-conversion quandaries not resolved in the source material.

18. Figueira, *Reportorio,* fl. 205 (150).
19. Figueira, fl. 105 (13).
20. Figueira, fl. 447 (710).
21. Figueira, fl. 367 (526).
22. Figueira, fl. 128 (36).
23. Processo de Gabriel, fls. 1–20v. This case has been closely analyzed by different historians for different purposes. Most recently, Matteo Salvadore considered the significance of Gabriel's multiple identities and probed the level of Gabriel's agency as he self-fashioned himself through religious conversion and border crossing. The article stands out for its contextualized treatment of the Inquisition records as autobiographical sources and his attention to the inquisitorial process. Matteo Salvadore, "Between the Red Sea Trade and the Goa Inquisition: The Odyssey of Gabriel, a Sixteenth-Century Ethiopian Jew," *Journal of World History* 31, no. 2 (June 2020): 327–60. Ananya Chakravarti's analysis innovatively applies the methodology of mapping Gabriel's travels. She argues that his precise identity and intentions are inaccessible, but his travels enable us to make claims about slavery and space. She locates Goa firmly within the South Asian context, while also arguing that Gabriel's experience of slavery differed in Ahmadnagar and Portuguese territory. Ananya Chakravarti, "Mapping 'Gabriel': Space, Identity and Slavery in the Late Sixteenth-Century Indian Ocean," *Past and Present* 243, no. 1 (2019): 5–34. Patrícia Souza de Faria incorporates Gabriel's case in her discussion of border crossing, conversion, and slavery in the Portuguese Indian Ocean. Patrícia Souza de Faria, "Cruzando Fronteiras: Conversão e Mobilidades Culturais de Escravos no Império Asiático Português (Séculos XVI e XVII)," *Anais de História de Além-Mar* 17 (2016): 147–78.
24. Antonio de Barros and Marcos Gil Frazão to Inquisitor General, Goa, December 1, 1597, in Baião, *Inquisição de Goa,* 258.
25. Processo de Gabriel, fls. 6–6v; Steven Kaplan, *The Beta Israel (Falasha) in Ethiopia: From Earliest Times to the Twentieth Century* (New York: New York University Press, 1992).
26. Processo de Gabriel, fls. 2v, 6v. Chaul de Cima was also referred to as "Chaul de Riba"; see Processo de Gabriel, fl. 2v. Chaul de Cima (in English, Upper Chaul) was a Muslim city three-quarters of a mile away from the Portuguese city of Chaul. According to António Bocarro, in 1635 the city had a population of three thousand. António Bocarro, *O Livro das Plantas de Todas as Fortalezas, Cidades e Povoações do Estado da Índia Oriental,* ed. Isabel

Cid (Lisbon: Imprensa Nacional, 1992), 2:126. For the approximate distance conversion from a quarter-league to 0.75 miles, see Vieyra, *Dictionary,* s.v. "Legoa." Vieyra approximates a league to three miles. In the deposition, Gabriel said he lived in Balagate. (See Processo de Gabriel, fls. 2v–3.) Yet, in his first trial, he said he was taken to the city of Ahmadnagar. (See Processo de Gabriel, fl. 6v.) Ahmadnagar, also spelled "Ahmednagar" and rendered "Abdanaguer" in Gabriel's trial, was the capital city of the Sultanate of Ahmadnagar in the Deccan Plateau. As noted previously, Balagate's literal meaning is the Deccan Plateau, yet the Portuguese also used the term to refer to Bijapur, one of the Deccan sultanates. Richard F. Burton, *Camoens: His Life and His Lusiads* (London: Bernard Quaritch, 1881), 1:330, 330n1; Henry Yule and A. C. Burnell, *Hobson-Jobson: A Glossary of Colloquial Anglo-Indian Words and Phrases, and of Kindred Terms, Etymological, Historical, Geographical and Discursive,* 2nd ed., ed. William Crooke (London: John Murray, 1903), s.v. "Idalcan." Due to the multiple references to Ahmadnagar in Gabriel's case, I have assumed that the term "Balagate" was referring to the Deccan Plateau where Ahmadnagar was located. Gabriel's enslaver's name, Mulá Mamede, suggests that he was a teacher of Islamic law. *Mulá* meant teacher or doctor of Islamic law, and the term was the Portuguese translation of *mullah* from the Arabic term *mawla.* Sebastião Rodolfo Dalgado, *Glossário Luso-Asiático,* 2 vols. (Coimbra: Imprensa da Universidade, 1919–21), s.v. "Mula."

27. For an overview of the slave trade from Ethiopia to India, see Sanjay Subrahmanyam, "Between Eastern Africa and Western India, 1500–1650: Slavery, Commerce, and Elite Formation," *Comparative Studies in Society and History* 61, no. 4 (2019): 805–34.
28. Richard Pankhurst, "The Ethiopian Diaspora to India: The Role of Habshis and Sidis from Medieval Times to the End of the Eighteenth Century," in *The African Diaspora in the Indian Ocean,* ed. Shihan de S. Jayasuriya and Richard Pankhurst (Trenton, NJ: Africa World, 2003), 191–92.
29. Pankhurst, 199–200.
30. Kaplan, *Beta Israel,* 85.
31. Pankhurst, "Ethiopian Diaspora," 190.
32. Pankhurst, 190, 193–95. They were often referred to as "Habshis," a term that was ambiguous because other Africans received the appellation as well. However, according to Richard Pankhurst, most Habshis were likely Ethiopians (Abyssinians). For an overview of military slavery in the Deccan, see Richard M. Eaton, "The Rise

and Fall of Military Slavery in the Deccan, 1450–1650," in *Slavery and South Asian History,* ed. Indrani Chatterjee and Richard M. Eaton (Bloomington: Indiana University Press, 2006), 115–35.

33. Pankhurst, "Ethiopian Diaspora," 196–97.
34. Shanti Sadiq Ali, *The African Dispersal in the Deccan: From Medieval to Modern Times* (New Delhi: Orient Longman, 1996), 59–63; Pankhurst, "Ethiopian Diaspora," 206–7.
35. Teotonio R. de Souza, *Medieval Goa: A Socio-Economic History,* 2nd ed. (Saligão, Goa: Goa, 1556, 2009), 10; Pankhurst, "Ethiopian Diaspora," 209–10. For a discussion of Malik Ambar and military slavery in the Deccan, see Richard M. Eaton, "Malik Ambar (1548–1626): The Rise and Fall of Military Slavery," in *A Social History of the Deccan, 1300–1761: Eight Indian Lives* (Cambridge: Cambridge University Press, 2005), 105–28. For a recent biography, see Omar H. Ali, *Malik Ambar: Power and Slavery across the Indian Ocean* (Oxford: Oxford University Press, 2016).
36. Processo de Gabriel, fls. 2–2v, 4v, 8. The precise timing of his flight, in terms of the year, differed in the deposition and the trial.
37. Processo de Gabriel, fl. 2v.
38. Processo de Gabriel, fl. 6v. The word used for freedom was *liberdade.*
39. Processo de Gabriel, fl. 4v.
40. Processo de Gabriel, fls. 4v, 6v.
41. Processo de Gabriel, fls. 4v–5.
42. Processo de Gabriel, fls. 2v–3.
43. Processo de Gabriel, fls. 6v–7.
44. Processo de Gabriel, fls. 5, 8.
45. In his deposition, Gabriel referenced his owner when describing his return to Muslim territory as well as his eventual second flight from Ahmadnagar. Processo de Gabriel, fl. 3v.
46. Processo de Gabriel, fls. 3, 5v. He was circumcised in his own country.
47. Processo de Gabriel, 5v.
48. Processo de Gabriel, fls. 2–4. In the text, Sidi Reme is spelled "Sede Reme"; I have anglicized "Sede," using "Sidi," to make more obvious his categorization as an Afro-Indian. For more discussion of the term as well as alternative spellings, see Shihan de Silva Jayasuriya, "Identifying Africans in Asia: What's in a Name?," in *Uncovering the History of Africans in Asia,* ed. Shihan de Silva Jayasuriya and Jean-Pierre Angenot (Leiden: Brill, 2008), 22–25.
49. Processo de Gabriel, fls. 2, 3v, 6, 7. Gabriel gave two accounts of his return to Chaul. In his deposition, he discussed his encounter

with the soldier, who was also mentioned in the notary's description of Gabriel's appearance before the vicar. Following that timeline, he would have encountered the soldier shortly after his arrival in Chaul. In his April trial, however, he claimed that he left Ahmadnagar for Chaul two to three months prior to the trial, an assertion undisputed in the trial record. Thus, he could have arrived around January or February 1595. In either rendering of events, he would have crossed back into Chaul after the war between the Estado da Índia and Ahmadnagar ended in 1594, which included a siege of Chaul. K. M. Mathew, *History of the Portuguese Navigation in India (1497–1600)* (Delhi: Mittal, 1988), 209–11. For a description of these events placing a Portuguese chronicle in conversation with Deccan chronicles, see Sanjay Subrahmanyam, "'The Life and Actions of Mathias de Albuquerque (1547–1609)': A Portuguese Source for Deccan History," *Portuguese Studies* 11 (1995): 62–77.

50. Bocarro, *Livro das Plantas,* 2:122.
51. Vicars of the rod were appointed by the archbishop. The rod signified jurisdiction. Stefan Halikowski Smith, *Creolization and Diaspora in the Portuguese Indies: The Social World of Ayutthaya, 1640–1720* (Leiden: Brill, 2011), 109, 291. Processo de Gabriel, fl. 2.
52. Processo de Gabriel, fls. 3–3v.
53. Processo de Gabriel, fl. 2.
54. Processo de Gabriel, fls. 2v–3. This is reminiscent of the nineteenth-century Muslim community in Bahia as described by João José Reis. Within that community, Portuguese (Catholic) names were not necessarily relevant as African names were often utilized. That is to say, enslaved and freed individuals had both names, yet they did not necessarily use their Christian names among themselves. João José Reis, *Slave Rebellion in Brazil: The Muslim Uprising of 1835 in Bahia,* trans. Arthur Brakel (Baltimore: Johns Hopkins University Press, 1995), 155–56.
55. Processo de Gabriel, fls. 8v–9; Figueira, *Reportorio,* fl. 367 (526).
56. Inquisitors did not always combine the two (instruction and labor). See Figueira for sentences of "instruction"; there are over thirty defendants sentenced in this way. Figueira, *Reportorio,* fls. 94 (2)–436 (678). A few examples include the cases of Anna Leal, Catherina Pereira, Fernão de Magalhaes, and Josepho Calvo. Figueira, fls. 110 (18); 221v (195); 309v (399); 384v (573).
57. Processo de Gabriel, fl. 8v.
58. Processo de Gabriel, fl. 9.

59. Processo de Gabriel, fl. 9.
60. There is confusion about the precise date. By Gabriel's reckoning in his first session (of his second trial), he fled on August 15; witnesses, however, said he fled sometime from August 10 to August 14. Processo de Gabriel, fls. 10v, 11, 12, 15.
61. Processo de Gabriel, fl. 15. Linschoten noted that the Passo da Madre de Deus was also called the Passo de Daugijn. Jan Huygen van Linschoten, *The Voyage of John Huyghen van Linschoten to the East Indies: From the Old English Translation of 1598, the First Book, Containing His Description of the East,* ed. Arthur Coke Burnell (1885; repr., San Bernardino, CA: Adamant Media, 2005), 1:181. For a description of the *passos,* see also Souza, *Medieval Goa,* 79–80.
62. Processo de Gabriel, fl. 9v. Sixteen was his approximate age.
63. While they were freed slaves, they were also described as being in the "obligation" of the college. Processo de Gabriel, fls. 10v–11v.
64. Processo de Gabriel, fls. 10–11v. By characterizing Domingos as *ladino,* the notary pointed out his status as one who was familiar with Portuguese culture and religion rather than a new convert.
65. Processo de Gabriel, fl. 12.
66. Processo de Gabriel, fls. 10–10v.
67. Processo de Gabriel, fl. 10v.
68. Processo de Gabriel, fls. 10, 11–11v.
69. Processo de Gabriel, fl. 14.
70. Processo de Gabriel, fls. 14v–15.
71. Gabriel's interactions with Abyssinians played a central role in his narrative. These interactions raise the question of how he saw himself. Moreover, his relationships with Abyssinians reveal the social affiliations deemed appropriate by church authorities; after converting, he was placed in the household of an Abyssinian woman in Chaul. An Abyssinian man blocked the marriage to which Gabriel aspired. Later when Gabriel ran away from the College of St. Thomas, he alleged that he was looking for an Abyssinian to help him. In his final trial, his translators, including an Abyssinian, came to the rescue. For his search for an Abyssinian after fleeing the college, see Processo de Gabriel, fls. 14–14v. Antonio da Cunha was the Abyssinian translator. Processo de Gabriel, fl. 17v.
72. Processo de Gabriel, fls. 16–16v.
73. Processo de Gabriel, fls. 17–18. Unlike the witnesses who testified against Gabriel, the interpreters were older. Antonio Jorge was fifty-one years old, and Antonio da Cunha was seventy.

74. Processo de Gabriel, fls. 17v–18.
75. Processo de Gabriel, fls. 10, 11.
76. Bethencourt, *Inquisition,* 246–315. Bethencourt discusses the auto-da-fé as a public spectacle. For a personal account originally published in the seventeenth century, see Charles Dellon, *Dellon's Account of the Inquisition at Goa. Translated from the French. With an Appendix, Containing an Account of the Escape of Archibald Bower, (One of the Inquisitors) from the Inquisition, at Maçerata, in Italy* (Hull: Longman, 1812).
77. Processo de Paulo, ANTT, IL, Processos, No. 3672, fls. 3–3v. Francisco stated Paulo wore a "*toca*" [*touca*] (headgear, possibly a turban) and a *cabaia* (tunic). Other witnesses' testimonies used the terms in addition to characterizing Paulo as wearing Muslim clothing. Processo de Paulo, fls. 4–5v; Glenn J. Ames, trans. and ed., *Em Nome de Deus: The Journal of the First Voyage of Vasco da Gama to India, 1497–1499* (Leiden: Brill, 2009), 48n41; Dalgado, *Glossário Luso-Asiático,* s.v. "Cabaia"; Yule and Burnell, *Hobson-Jobson,* s.v. "Cabaya."
78. Processo de Paulo, fls. 3v–5v.
79. Processo de Paulo, fl. 3.
80. Processo de Paulo, fl. 6.
81. Processo de Paulo, fls. 6–8v.
82. Paulo was only a teenager when captured. His precise age at the time is uncertain, yet he was around fifteen or sixteen years old when baptized. Processo de Paulo, fls. 6–6v, 7v, 8v.
83. R. J. Barendse, *The Arabian Seas: The Indian Ocean World of the Seventeenth Century* (New York: Routledge, 2015), 16.
84. Barendse, 16.
85. Processo de Paulo, fls. 8v–9.
86. J. H. da Cunha Rivara, ed., *Os Concilios de Goa e o Synodo de Diamper,* issue 4 of *Archivo-Portuguez Oriental* (Nova-Goa: Imprensa Nacional, 1862), 53. See Decreto 10.
87. Rivara, 30. See Decreto 40.
88. Processo de Paulo, fl. 4v. However, in Portugal, he was variously documented as "*preto*" or "*negro.*" Processo de Paulo, fls. 2–2v, 11.
89. Processo de Paulo, fls. 3–5v.
90. Processo de Paulo, fls. 6–6v. The trial transcript labeled the first session (held on January 10, 1689) as the second session. However, this seems to be a scribal error, as there is another "second session" on January 15, 1689, beginning on fl. 8v.
91. Processo de Paulo, fl. 9.
92. Processo de Paulo, fl. 9.

93. Even in manumission records, slaveholders noted that they had purchased the captive in question to facilitate his or her conversion to Christianity. For example, see the manumission entries for Antonio and Francisco, whose enslavers expressed this sentiment in 1682. *Cartas de Alforria aos Escravos, 1682–1759,* HAG, Ms. 860, fl. 5v.
94. Processo de Paulo, fls. 8v–9.
95. Processo de Paulo, fls. 3v–5v.
96. Souza, *Medieval Goa,* 29–30; Barendse, *Arabian Seas,* 52. Surat's approximate population in 1700 potentially reached two hundred thousand residents.
97. Souza, *Medieval Goa,* 82–83; Fatima da Silva Gracias, *Health and Hygiene in Colonial Goa (1510–1961)* (New Delhi: Concept, 1994), 89–90.
98. Souza, *Medieval Goa,* 30.
99. Processo de Paulo, fl. 6v; Vieyra, *Dictionary,* s.v. "Mocadam."
100. Processo de Paulo, fls. 6v–8.
101. Processo de Paulo, fls. 3v–4, 5v, 7.
102. Processo de Paulo, fls. 3–3v.
103. Processo de Paulo, fl. 6.
104. Processo de Paulo, fl. 2.
105. Processo de Paulo, fls. 22–22v. The town was also assigned as a place of exile for other convicts. See James H. Sweet, *Domingos Álvares, African Healing, and the Intellectual History of the Atlantic World* (Chapel Hill: University of North Carolina Press, 2011), 186.
106. For example, Paulo was recorded as the "slave of Francisco Fernandes." Processo de Paulo, fl.14.
107. See chapter 3 for more discussion.
108. Figueira, *Reportorio,* fls. 96v (4v), 98v (6v). Likewise, in 1564 a Burmese slave named Bernardim who lived in Goa was sold to Portugal for having converted to Islam. Figueira, *Reportorio,* fl. 177 (94). Similarly, in 1568 a Javanese slave named Joane was sold to Portugal after being sentenced by the Goa Tribunal. Figueira, *Reportorio,* fl. 387 (578). Their sale might have been an inquisitorial tactic to ward off a potential religious relapse. As mentioned previously, inquisitors used that rationale to send the freed slave Gonçalo Toscano to Portugal. Processo de Gonçalo Toscano, fls. 23v–24; Antonio de Barros and Marcos Gil Frazão to Inquisitor General, Goa, December 1, 1597, in Baião, *Inquisição de Goa,* 259; Antonio de Barros and Marcos Gil Frazão to Inquisitor General, December 23, 1599, in Baião, *Inquisição de Goa,* 271.

109. For a discussion of the Inquisition as an upholder of slavery in Portugal, see Timothy Walker, "Sorcerers and Folkhealers: Africans and the Inquisition in Portugal (1680–1800)," *Revista Lusófona de Ciência das Religiões* 3, nos. 5–6 (2004): 83–98.
110. Processo de Paulo, fls. 4, 4v, 5v.
111. Processo de Paulo, fls. 2, 2v, 14, 16, 18, 19v, 20, 21, 22v.

CHAPTER 5: CHOOSING CATHOLIC COMMUNITY

1. For slavery, see James H. Sweet, *Recreating Africa: Culture, Kinship, and Religion in the African-Portuguese World, 1441–1770* (Chapel Hill: University of North Carolina Press, 2003), and James H. Sweet, *Domingos Álvares, African Healing, and the Intellectual History of the Atlantic World* (Chapel Hill: University of North Carolina Press, 2011). More broadly, see Carlo Ginzburg, *The Cheese and the Worms: The Cosmos of a Sixteenth-Century Miller,* trans. John Tedeschi and Anne Tedeschi (Baltimore: Johns Hopkins University Press, 1992), and Carlo Ginzburg, *The Night Battles: Witchcraft and Agrarian Cults in the Sixteenth and Seventeenth Centuries,* trans. John Tedeschi and Anne Tedeschi (Baltimore: Johns Hopkins University Press, 1992).
2. Gwyn Campbell, "Introduction: Slavery and Other Forms of Unfree Labour in the Indian Ocean World," in *The Structure of Slavery in Indian Ocean Africa and Asia,* ed. Gwyn Campbell (London: Frank Cass, 2004), xxi.
3. Campbell, xxi. See also Gwyn Campbell and Edward A. Alpers, "Introduction: Slavery, Forced Labour and Resistance in Indian Ocean Africa and Asia," in *Slavery and Resistance in Africa and Asia,* ed. Edward Alpers, Gwyn Campbell, and Michael Salman (London: Routledge, 2005), 1–19.
4. Processo de Leonor Fernandes, ANTT, IL, Processos, No. 7631, fls. 62–70A.
5. Processo de Leonor Fernandes, fl. 62. She was questioned in Goa by the bishop because the Goa Tribunal had not yet been established. The cases were ultimately decided in Lisbon.
6. In the record, the third denunciation is marked 1558 instead of 1557, but that is likely an error given that her final denunciation is marked February 1558. Processo de Leonor Fernandes, fls. 62–70v.
7. Processo de Leonor Fernandes, fl. 62v.
8. Processo de Leonor Fernandes, fls. 62v–63.
9. Processo de Leonor Fernandes, fl. 63.
10. Processo de Leonor Fernandes, fl. 63.

11. Processo de Leonor Fernandes, fl. 63.
12. Processo de Leonor Fernandes, fl. 63.
13. Processo de Leonor Fernandes, fls. 63–63v.
14. Processo de Leonor Fernandes, fl. 63v.
15. Processo de Leonor Fernandes, fl. 63v.
16. Processo de Leonor Fernandes, fls. 63v–64.
17. Processo de Leonor Fernandes, fls. 63v–64.
18. Processo de Leonor Fernandes, fl. 64.
19. Processo de Leonor Fernandes, fl. 67v.
20. Processo de Leonor Fernandes, fl. 70v.
21. Processo de Gabriel, ANTT, IL, Processos, No. 4937, fl. 9v.
22. Processo de Gabriel, fl. 10.
23. Processo de Gabriel, fl. 10.
24. Processo de Gabriel, fl. 10.
25. Processo de Gabriel, fl. 10.
26. Processo de Gabriel, fl. 10.
27. Processo de Gabriel, fl. 10.
28. Processo de Gabriel, fls. 10–10v.
29. Processo de Gabriel, fl. 10v.
30. Processo de Gabriel, fl. 10v.
31. Processo de Gabriel, fls. 10v–12.
32. Processo de Gabriel, fls. 11–11v.
33. Processo de Gabriel, fls. 11v–12.
34. Processo de Gabriel, fl. 12.
35. See chapter 4 for more of Gabriel's description of the treatment he received at the college.
36. Processo de Gonçalo Toscano, ANTT, IL, Processos, No. 4931, fls. 2–7v.
37. Processo de Gonçalo Toscano, fls. 2–2v.
38. Processo de Gonçalo Toscano, fl. 2.
39. Processo de Gonçalo Toscano, fl. 7.
40. Processo de Gonçalo Toscano, fls. 2, 19v. The ambiguous place name "Balagate" was initially used in the text. His mother's home was in Galiana (Kalyan). See chapter 3 for more discussion.
41. Processo de Gonçalo Toscano, fl. 19v. Confession was required each Lent, the forty days between Ash Wednesday and Easter.
42. Processo de Gonçalo Toscano, fls. 2–2v.
43. Processo de Gonçalo Toscano, fl. 2v.
44. *Leis a favor da Cristandade,* HAG, Ms. 7693, fls. 53v–54v; *Provisões a favor da Cristandade,* HAG, Ms. 9529, fls. 113–14; and J. H. da Cunha Rivara, ed., *Os Concilios de Goa e o Synodo de Diamper,* issue 4 of *Archivo-Portuguez Oriental* (Nova-Goa:

Imprensa Nacional, 1862), 269–70. See chapter 1 for more discussion of the violent nature of Portuguese slavery.

45. Processo de Gonçalo Toscano, fl. 2v.
46. Processo de Gonçalo Toscano, fl. 2v. Note that while Gonçalo's mother had encouraged his conversion to Islam, she was outside inquisitorial jurisdiction as she had not personally transported him to non-Christian territory. Moreover, as she was neither a baptized subject nor a resident in Portuguese territory, her own religious practices were not under the purview of the Inquisition.
47. Processo de Gonçalo Toscano, fls. 2v–3. He also described the circumcision ceremony and the prayers he prayed.
48. Processo de Gonçalo Toscano, fls. 3–3v.
49. Processo de Gonçalo Toscano, fls. 3v–4.
50. Processo de Gonçalo Toscano, fls. 9–9v. In Gonçalo's second trial session, the inquisitor said that Gonçalo was sixteen years old when he confessed his sins upon his return to Bassein. This would date his arrival in Bassein to around 1590, with his first conversion to Islam and flight to Galiana (Kalyan) in 1588.
51. Processo de Gonçalo Toscano, fl. 4. This was a very light sentence. Other enslaved individuals were given full trials for converting to Islam.
52. Rivara, *Concilios,* 270–71.
53. Processo de Gonçalo Toscano, fl. 4.
54. Processo de Gonçalo Toscano, fls. 4–4v. See also chapter 3 for more details.
55. Sanjay Subrahmanyam, *The Portuguese Empire in Asia, 1500–1700: A Political and Economic History,* 2nd ed. (Chichester, UK: John Wiley & Sons, 2012), 262.
56. Timothy J. Coates, *Convicts and Orphans: Forced and State-Sponsored Colonizers in the Portuguese Empire, 1550–1755* (Stanford, CA: Stanford University Press, 2001), 88.
57. Processo de Gonçalo Toscano, fl. 4v.
58. Processo de Gonçalo Toscano, fl. 4v.
59. Processo de Gonçalo Toscano, fl. 4v.
60. Toby Green, "Policing the Empires: A Comparative Perspective on the Institutional Trajectory of the Inquisition in the Portuguese and Spanish Overseas Territories (Sixteenth and Seventeenth Centuries)," *Hispanic Research Journal* 13, no. 1 (2012): 19–20. The *Reportorio* includes an example of prosecution for dress, as well. Francisco Furtado was prosecuted in 1618. João Delgado Figueira, *Reportorio geral de tres mil oito centos processos, que sam todos os despachados neste sancto Officio de Goa & mais partes da India, do anno de Mil & quinhentos & secenta & hum, que*

começou o dito sancto Officio até o anno de Mil & seiscentos & vinte & tres, com a lista dos Inquisidores que tem sido nelle, & dos autos publicos da Fee, que se tem celebrado na dita Cidade de Goa, 1623, BNP, cód. 203, fl. 342 (464).

61. Processo de Gonçalo Toscano, fl. 5. Burhan Nizam Shah II ruled Ahmadnagar from May 15, 1591, to April 18, 1595. On his reign, see Radhey Shyam, *The Kingdom of Ahmadnagar* (Delhi: Motilal Barnarsidass, 1966), 211–14.
62. Processo de Gonçalo Toscano, fl. 5.
63. Processo de Gonçalo Toscano, fl. 5v. Sebastião Dalgado described a *jogue* (yogi) not only as a "Hindu ascetic" but also as a "penitent and mendicant Hindu, sparingly dressed, with his body sprinkled with ashes, and with long, disheveled hair." Sebastião Rodolfo Dalgado, *Glossário Luso-Asiático,* 2 vols. (Coimbra: Imprensa da Universidade, 1919–21), s.v. "Jogue."
64. For a later description of Diu, see António Bocarro, *O Livro das Plantas de Todas as Fortalezas, Cidades e Povoações do Estado da Índia Oriental,* ed. Isabel Cid (Lisbon: Imprensa Nacional, 1992), 2:69–76.
65. Pietro della Valle recorded that every Portuguese city had a vicar "*daVara*" (or *vigário da vara*), who was entrusted with "supreme power" by the archbishop of Goa. Pietro della Valle, *The Travels of Pietro della Valle in India: From the Old English Translation of 1664,* ed. Edward Grey (1892; repr., Cambridge: Cambridge University Press, 2010), 1:133.
66. Processo de Gonçalo Toscano, fls. 5v–6. Gonçalo would have entered Gujarat, which was part of the Mughal Empire at that time. Gujarat had been incorporated in 1572. Subrahmanyam, *Portuguese Empire in Asia,* 155.
67. Processo de Gonçalo Toscano, fl. 6.
68. Processo de Gonçalo Toscano, fl. 6.
69. Processo de Gonçalo Toscano, fl. 6. On self-fashioning, see Stephen Greenblatt, *Renaissance Self-Fashioning: From More to Shakespeare* (Chicago: University of Chicago Press, 1980), and Laura Delbrugge, ed., *Self-Fashioning and Assumptions of Identity in Medieval and Early Modern Iberia* (Leiden: Brill, 2015).
70. Processo de Gonçalo Toscano, fls. 6–6v. Daman, a Portuguese city and fortress, was located on the mainland of Gujarat, which was part of the Mughal Empire. For a later description of Daman, see Bocarro, *Livro das Plantas,* 2:84–97.
71. Processo de Gonçalo Toscano, fls. 6v–7.
72. Processo de Gonçalo Toscano, fl. 1v.

73. He had seven standard sessions, followed by a special session labeled a "*curadoria.*" This last session was due to his young age; he needed a special ratification.
74. Processo de Gonçalo Toscano, fl. 2. Thus, at some point in his travels between Christendom and the "land of the Moors," he was manumitted. In his narrative, he never specified when this transition occurred. His status as a freed slave was not recorded in his entry in the *Reportorio;* in fact, there is no mention of him ever being a slave. This is a limitation of the source material: the case summaries contain an untold number of freed slaves. Figueira, *Reportorio,* fl. 367v (527).
75. Processo de Gonçalo Toscano, fls. 2–7.
76. Processo de Gonçalo Toscano, fls. 7v–10.
77. Processo de Gonçalo Toscano, fl. 8v.
78. Processo de Gonçalo Toscano, fl. 9.
79. Processo de Gonçalo Toscano, fl. 9.
80. Processo de Gonçalo Toscano, fl. 9.
81. Processo de Gonçalo Toscano, fls. 9–10.
82. Processo de Gonçalo Toscano, fls. 10–12v.
83. Processo de Gonçalo Toscano, fls. 10v–11v.
84. Processo de Gonçalo Toscano, fl. 11v.
85. Processo de Gonçalo Toscano, fl. 11v.
86. Processo de Gonçalo Toscano, fl. 12.
87. Processo de Gonçalo Toscano, fl. 13.
88. Processo de Gonçalo Toscano, fls. 13–14.
89. Processo de Gonçalo Toscano, fl. 14.
90. Figueira, *Reportorio,* fl. 429 (664). Such words the Inquisition felt necessary to police. This suggests that living conditions may have been better outside of Portuguese domains. See Coates, *Convicts and Orphans,* for discussion about the exit of soldiers who left Portuguese service and Portuguese dominions.
91. Processo de Gonçalo Toscano, fls. 14v–17v.
92. Processo de Gonçalo Toscano, fls. 14v–15.
93. Processo de Gonçalo Toscano, fls. 15–15v.
94. Processo de Gonçalo Toscano, fls. 15v–16.
95. Processo de Gonçalo Toscano, fl. 16.
96. Processo de Gonçalo Toscano, fls. 16–16v.
97. Processo de Gonçalo Toscano, fls. 16v–17.
98. Processo de Gonçalo Toscano, fl. 17.
99. Processo de Gonçalo Toscano, fl. 17.
100. Processo de Gonçalo Toscano, fl. 17.
101. Processo de Gonçalo Toscano, fls. 17v–20.

102. Processo de Gonçalo Toscano, fl. 17v.
103. Processo de Gonçalo Toscano, fls. 17v–18.
104. Processo de Gonçalo Toscano, fl. 18.
105. Processo de Gonçalo Toscano, fl. 19.
106. Processo de Gonçalo Toscano, fl. 19.
107. Processo de Gonçalo Toscano, fls. 20–22v.
108. Processo de Gonçalo Toscano, fls. 21v–22.
109. Processo de Gonçalo Toscano, fls. 22v–23v. Since Gonçalo was younger than twenty-five, Bras Mires, the bailiff of the Inquisition's jail, served as his guardian and signed the confession along with him.
110. Processo de Gonçalo Toscano, fl. 25v.
111. Processo de Gonçalo Toscano, fls. 23v–24.
112. Processo de Gonçalo Toscano, fl. 23v.
113. Processo de Gonçalo Toscano, fls. 23v–24.
114. Processo de Gonçalo Toscano, fl. 24.
115. Figueira, *Reportorio,* fl. 367v (527); Processo de Gonçalo Toscano, fls. 26–27v.
116. His departure is confirmed by two letters from the Goan inquisitors to the inquisitor general in Lisbon. Neither Gonçalo's case nor Figueira's case summary records his final sentence of exile to Portugal. Antonio de Barros and Marcos Gil Frazão to Inquisitor General, Goa, December 1, 1597, in António Baião, ed., *A Inquisição de Goa: Correspondencia dos Inquisidores da Índia (1569–1630)* (Coimbra: Imprensa da Universidade, 1930), 259; Antonio de Barros and Marcos Gil Frazão to Inquisitor General, December 23, 1599, in Baião, *Inquisição de Goa,* 271.
117. Eric R. Dursteler, *Renegade Women: Gender, Identity, and Boundaries in the Early Modern Mediterranean* (Baltimore: Johns Hopkins University Press, 2011).
118. Duane J. Corpis, *Crossing the Boundaries of Belief: Geographies of Religious Conversion in Southern Germany, 1648–1800* (Charlottesville: University of Virginia Press, 2014).
119. Natalie Zemon Davis, *Trickster Travels: A Sixteenth-Century Muslim between Worlds* (New York: Hill & Wang, 2006).
120. This framework came from the cultural retentions-creolization debate concerning the impact of slavery and the transatlantic slave trade. For an overview, see Melville J. Herskovits, *The Myth of the Negro Past* (New York: Harper & Brothers, 1941); E. Franklin Frazier, *The Negro Family in the United States,* rev. and abr. ed. (Chicago: University of Chicago Press, 1966); Sidney W. Mintz and Richard Price, *The Birth of African-American Culture: An*

Anthropological Perspective (Boston: Beacon, 1992); Michael A. Gomez, *Exchanging Our Country Marks: The Transformation of African Identities in the Colonial and Antebellum South* (Chapel Hill: University of North Carolina Press, 1998); John K. Thornton, *Africa and Africans in the Making of the Atlantic World, 1400–1800,* 2nd ed. (Cambridge: Cambridge University Press, 1998); Sweet, *Recreating Africa;* Linda M. Heywood, ed., *Central Africans and Cultural Transformations in the American Diaspora* (Cambridge: Cambridge University Press, 2002); and Linda M. Heywood and John K. Thornton, *Central Africans, Atlantic Creoles, and the Foundation of the Americas, 1585–1660* (Cambridge: Cambridge University Press, 2007). For a few examples of works on slavery and creolization in the Indian Ocean, see Robert C.-H. Shell, "The Tower of Babel: The Slave Trade and Creolization at the Cape, 1652–1834," in *Slavery in South Africa: Captive Labor on the Dutch Frontier,* ed. Elizabeth Eldredge and Fred Morton (Boulder, CO: Westview, 1994), 11–39; Megan Vaughan, *Creating the Creole Island: Slavery in Eighteenth-Century Mauritius* (Durham, NC: Duke University Press, 2005); Pier M. Larson, *Ocean of Letters: Language and Creolization in an Indian Ocean Diaspora* (Cambridge: Cambridge University Press, 2009); Shihan de Silva Jayasuriya, *African Identity in Asia: Cultural Effects of Forced Migration* (Princeton, NJ: Markus Wiener, 2009); and Françoise Vergès, "Indian-Oceanic Creolizations: Processes and Practices of Creolization on Réunion Island," in *Creolization: History, Ethnography, Theory,* ed. Charles Stewart (London: Routledge, 2016), 133–52.

121. Processo de Gonçalo Toscano, fls. 1, 2.
122. Figueira, *Reportorio,* fl. 367v (527).
123. Processo de Gonçalo Toscano, fl. 2v.
124. For example, in 1605 a Portuguese man named Ambrosio Pinheiro was prosecuted for consulting *feiticeiros* to remedy his health. Figueira, *Reportorio,* fl. 135v (43v). Nearly five hundred case summaries included paganism as a primary crime in my sample from 1561 to 1623. This figure would increase if it included related religious transgressions, such as sacrifices or pagan ceremonies, which were categorized differently by Figueira in his summaries. In terms of Gonçalo's contemporaries, one of the paganism cases concerned Francisco de Monroio from Salcete, a local Indian Christian *gaunkar* (village councilor) who was prosecuted in 1597 for paganism and faced torture, exile, and temporary servitude as a result. Figueira, *Reportorio,* fl. 321 (422). On *gaunkars*

(also spelled *ganvkars*), see Teotonio R. de Souza, *Medieval Goa: A Socio-Economic History*, 2nd ed. (Saligão, Goa: Goa, 1556, 2009), 35–38. For the larger sample of case summaries, see Figueira, *Reportorio*, fls. 94 (2)–436 (678).

125. For example, see the enslaved Angolan Manoel Francisco de Souza's 1673 denunciation in Lisbon of another man for egregiously disrespecting the sacrament of communion: "De hum Negro," ANTT, IL, Cadernos do Promotor, Caderno 51 do Promotor, Livro 248, fls. 66–66v. See also the enslaved Angolan João Rodriguez's denunciations in Lisbon in 1670 and 1671 against his New Christian enslaver, Antonio Rodriguez Marquez, as well as members of the extended family for practicing Judaism: "Denunciação de João Negro de Angola," ANTT, IL, Cadernos do Promotor, Caderno 46 do Promotor, Livro 243, fls. 212–14v, and "Outra Denunciação de João Negro de Angola . . . ," ANTT, IL, Cadernos do Promotor, Caderno 49 do Promotor, Livro 246, fls. 217–19.

CONCLUSION

1. Mayabhushan Nagvenkar, "No Genetic Quirk This: Children of Konkani Trace Their Roots to Africa," *Herald* (Panaji), February 11, 2002. The article was written on Sunday, February 10, but was published in the Monday edition of the paper. For the newspaper's city of publication, the Portuguese-styled place name, Panjim, was originally used. Panaji (Panjim) is the capital of the present-day Indian state of Goa.
2. "400 Years Later Siddhis Still Keep Konkani Close to Heart," *Navhind Times* (Panaji), February 11, 2002. Like the *Herald* article above, this report was originally written on Sunday, February 10.
3. Sérgio Mascarenhas de Almeida, "Origin of Siddhis: A Disputed Issue," Personally Speaking, *Navhind Times* (Panaji), February 18, 2002; José Colaço, "The Origin of Siddhis, Myth and Reality," Personally Speaking, *Navhind Times* (Panaji), February 25, 2002; Nagesh Karmali, "Lacing History with Sentimentalism," Personally Speaking, *Navhind Times* (Panaji), March 2, 2002; Sérgio Mascarenhas, "Portuguese History, Hiding Other Side of the Coin—I," Personally Speaking, *Navhind Times* (Panaji), March 13, 2002; Sérgio Mascarenhas, "Portuguese History, Hiding Other Side of the Coin—II," Personally Speaking, *Navhind Times* (Panaji), March 18, 2002; Shrikant Y. Ramani, "Existence of Slave Trade in Portuguese India," Personally Speaking, *Navhind Times* (Panaji), April 1, 2002; Shrikant Y. Ramani, "Slavery in Portuguese India," *Herald* (Panaji), April 10, 2002;

and Sérgio Mascarenhas de Almeida, "Biased View of History," *Herald* (Panaji), April 19, 2002. De Almeida's first name appears without the accent in this instance.

4. Beyond this debate, there is fascinating scholarly work on the community. See, for instance, Mark Sebastian Pinto, "The Forgotten Community, 'the Siddis of Uttara Kannada': How the Portuguese Indian Ocean Slave Trade Produced a Community of Indians of African Descent," *Interdisciplinary Journal of Portuguese Diaspora Studies,* 8 (2019): 165–88.
5. Ana Lucia Araujo, *Slavery in the Age of Memory: Engaging the Past* (London: Bloomsbury Academic, 2021); Amy Catlin-Jairazbhoy and Edward A. Alpers, eds., *Sidis and Scholars: Essays on African Indians* (Trenton, NJ: Red Sea, 2004); Douglas J. Hamilton, Kate Hodgson, and Joel Quirk, eds., *Slavery, Memory and Identity: National Representations and Global Legacies* (London: Routledge, 2016); Joseph E. Harris, *The African Presence in Asia: Consequences of the East African Slave Trade* (Evanston, IL: Northwestern University Press, 1971); Andreas Hofbauer, *Diáspora Africana na Índia: Sobre Castas, Raças e Lutas* (São Paulo: Editora Unesp, 2021); Shihan de Silva Jayasuriya, *African Identity in Asia: Cultural Effects of Forced Migration* (Princeton, NJ: Markus Wiener, 2009); Shihan de Silva Jayasuriya and Richard Pankhurst, eds., *The African Diaspora in the Indian Ocean* (Trenton, NJ: Africa World, 2003); Neelima Jeychandran, "Geographies of Death and Memory: Shrines Dedicated to African Saints and Spectral Deities in India," *South Asian History and Culture* 11, no. 4 (2020): 421–32; Pashington Obeng, *Shaping Membership, Defining Nation: The Cultural Politics of African Indians in South Asia* (Lanham, MD: Lexington Books, 2007); Kiran Kamal Prasad and Jean-Pierre Angenot, eds., *TADIA, the African Diaspora in Asia: Explorations on a Less Known Fact* (Bangalore: Jana Jagrati Prakashana, 2008); Shanti Sadiq Ali, *The African Dispersal in the Deccan: From Medieval to Modern Times* (New Delhi: Orient Longman, 1996); and Hideaki Suzuki, "African Diaspora in Asia," in *Oxford Research Encyclopedia of Asian History,* ed. David Ludden (Oxford: Oxford University Press, 2020), https://doi.org/10.1093/acrefore/9780190277727.013.34.
6. While ethnonyms are not always straightforward indications of origin, they do have geographical and cultural meanings. Moreover, they are significant to descendants' memories of slavery. Titas Chakraborty, "Slave Trading and Slave Resistance in the Indian Ocean World: The Case of Early Eighteenth-Century Bengal,"

Slavery and Abolition 40, no. 4 (2019): 706–26; James H. Sweet, "Mistaken Identities? Olaudah Equiano, Domingos Álvares, and the Methodological Challenges of Studying the African Diaspora," *American Historical Review* 114, no. 2 (April 2009): 279–306; Megan Vaughan, *Creating the Creole Island: Slavery in Eighteenth-Century Mauritius* (Durham, NC: Duke University Press, 2005), 91–122; and Wendy Wilson-Fall, *Memories of Madagascar and Slavery in the Black Atlantic* (Athens: Ohio University Press, 2015).

7. Paul Tiyambe Zeleza, "Rewriting the African Diaspora: Beyond the Black Atlantic," *African Affairs* 104, no. 414 (2005): 35–68.
8. For a discussion of contemporaneous forms of slavery in the Indian Ocean, see Matthias van Rossum, "Global Slavery, Local Bondage? Rethinking Slaveries as (Im)Mobilizing Regimes from the Case of the Dutch Indian Ocean and Indonesian Archipelago Worlds," *Journal of World History* 31, no. 4 (2020): 693–727.
9. An intriguing Iberian parallel is the continuation of indigenous practices of slavery in the Spanish Philippines. Stephanie Mawson, "Slavery, Conflict, and Empire in the Seventeenth-Century Philippines," in *Slavery and Bonded Labor in Asia, 1250–1900,* ed. Richard B. Allen (Leiden: Brill, 2022), 256–83.
10. This possibility would compare to enslaved individuals' access to ecclesiastical intervention elsewhere. For example, Michelle McKinley notes the role of place in her study of slave agency and ecclesiastical courts. Michelle McKinley, "Fractional Freedoms: Slavery, Legal Activism, and Ecclesiastical Courts in Colonial Lima, 1593–1689," *Law and History Review* 28, no. 3 (2010): 749–90.
11. Allen F. Isaacman and Barbara Isaacman, *Slavery and Beyond: The Making of Men and Chikunda Ethnic Identities in the Unstable World of South-Central Africa, 1750–1920* (Portsmouth, NH: Heinemann, 2004); Allen Isaacman and Derek Peterson, "Making the Chikunda: Military Slavery and Ethnicity in Southern Africa, 1750–1900," in *Arming Slaves: From Classical Times to the Modern Age,* ed. Christopher Leslie Brown and Philip D. Morgan (New Haven, CT: Yale University Press, 2006), 95–119.
12. Similarly, a connected history of global Iberian slavery has yet to be written, although there is fascinating work on the slave trade between the Spanish and Portuguese Empires. See for instance, Tatiana Seijas, *Asian Slaves in Colonial Mexico: From Chinos to Indians* (New York: Cambridge University Press, 2014). For an early conception of Iberian slavery, see Frank Tannenbaum, *Slave and Citizen* (Boston: Beacon, 1992). On the concept of Iberian

connected history, see Sanjay Subrahmanyam, "Holding the World in Balance: The Connected Histories of the Iberian Overseas Empires, 1500–1640," *American Historical Review* 112, no. 5 (2007): 1359–85.

13. A. R. Disney, *The Portuguese Empire*, vol. 2 of *A History of Portugal and the Portuguese Empire: From Beginnings to 1807* (Cambridge: Cambridge University Press, 2009). For a classic history of the empire, see C. R. Boxer, *The Portuguese Seaborne Empire, 1415–1825* (Middlesex, UK: Penguin Books, 1973).
14. On taking an imperial lens on slavery and race, see A. J. R. Russell-Wood, "Iberian Expansion and the Issue of Black Slavery: Changing Portuguese Attitudes, 1440–1770," *American Historical Review* 83, no. 1 (February 1978): 16–42.
15. Kerry Ward, *Networks of Empire: Forced Migration in the Dutch East India Company* (Cambridge: Cambridge University Press, 2009).
16. Rhondda Robinson Thomas, *Call My Name, Clemson: Documenting the Black Experience in an American University Community* (Iowa City: University of Iowa Press, 2020). Similar to remembering enslaved individuals' contributions to American universities, here is an opportunity to remembering their contributions to early modern European empires in the Indian Ocean.

Bibliography

ARCHIVAL SOURCES

Arquivo Nacional da Torre do Tombo, Lisbon (ANTT)

Inquisição de Lisboa
- Cadernos do Promotor
  - Caderno 8, Livro 209
  - Caderno 46, Livro 243
  - Caderno 49, Livro 246
  - Caderno 51, Livro 248
- Processos
  - No. 185, Processo de Diogo Soares
  - No. 360, Processo de Estevão Lopes
  - No. 2187, Processo de Lopo Soares
  - No. 3672, Processo de Paulo
  - No. 4931, Processo de Gonçalo Toscano
  - No. 4937, Processo de Gabriel
  - No. 6569, Processo de Branca de Oliveira
  - No. 6725, Processo de Ana de Oliveira
  - No. 7429, Processo de Clara Lopes
  - No. 7631, Processo de Leonor Fernandes
  - No. 11171, Processo de Guiomar de Oliveira

Biblioteca Nacional de Portugal, Lisbon (BNP)

Figueira, João Delgado. *Reportorio geral de tres mil oito centos processos, que sam todos os despachados neste sancto Officio de Goa & mais partes da India, do anno de Mil & quinhentos & secenta & hum, que começou o dito sancto Officio até o anno de Mil & seiscentos & vinte & tres, com a lista dos Inquisidores que tem sido nelle, & dos autos publicos da Fee, que se tem celebrado na dita Cidade de Goa*, 1623, Códice 203.

Historical Archives of Goa, Panaji (HAG)

Baptismos, São Bartolomeu, 1690–1702, HAG, Sr. No. 169
Cartas de Alforria aos Escravos, 1682–1759, HAG, Ms. 860
Leis a favor da Cristandade, HAG, Ms. 7693
Livro Vermelho, HAG, Ms. 8792
Óbitos, São Bartolomeu, 1682–1708, HAG, Sr. No. 147
Provisões a favor da Cristandade, HAG, Ms. 9529

PRINTED PRIMARY SOURCES

Ames, Glenn J., trans. and ed. *Em Nome de Deus: The Journal of the First Voyage of Vasco da Gama to India, 1497–1499*. Leiden: Brill, 2009.

Baião, António, ed. *A Inquisição de Goa: Correspondencia dos Inquisidores da Índia (1569–1630)*. Coimbra: Imprensa da Universidade, 1930.

Bocarro, António. *O Livro das Plantas de Todas as Fortalezas, Cidades e Povoações do Estado da Índia Oriental*. Vol. 2. Edited by Isabel Cid. Lisbon: Imprensa Nacional, 1992.

Dellon, Charles. *Dellon's Account of the Inquisition at Goa. Translated from the French. With an Appendix, Containing an Account of the Escape of Archibald Bower, (One of the Inquisitors) from the Inquisition, at Maçerata, in Italy*. Hull: Longman, 1812.

Freeman-Grenville, G. S. P., ed. and trans. *The Mombasa Rising against the Portuguese, 1631: From Sworn Evidence*. London: Oxford University Press, 1980.

Linschoten, Jan Huygen van. *The Voyage of John Huyghen van Linschoten to the East Indies: From the Old English Translation of 1598. The First Book, Containing His Description of the East in Two Volumes*. Edited by Arthur Coke Burnell. Vol. 1. 1885. Reprint, San Bernardino, CA: Adamant Media, 2005.

Pyrard, François. *The Voyage of François Pyrard of Laval to the East Indies, the Maldives, the Moluccas and Brazil*. Edited by Albert Gray. Vol. 2, part 1. London: Hakluyt Society, 1888.

Rivara, J. H. da Cunha, ed. *Cartas da Camara de Goa a Sua Magestade*. Issue 1, part 2 of *Archivo-Portuguez Oriental*. New Delhi: Asian Educational Services, 1992. First published 1876.

———, ed. *Os Concilios de Goa e o Synodo de Diamper*. Issue 4 of *Archivo-Portuguez Oriental*. Nova-Goa: Imprensa Nacional, 1862.

Valle, Pietro della. *The Travels of Pietro della Valle in India: From the Old English Translation of 1664*. Edited by Edward Grey. Vol. 1. Cambridge: Cambridge University Press, 2010. First published 1892.

Wicki, José, ed. *O Livro do 'Pai dos Cristãos.'* Lisbon: Centro de Estudos Históricos Ultramarinos, 1969.

SECONDARY SOURCES

Ali, Omar H. *Malik Ambar: Power and Slavery across the Indian Ocean.* Oxford: Oxford University Press, 2016.

Allen, Richard B. *European Slave Trading in the Indian Ocean: 1500–1850.* Athens: Ohio University Press, 2014.

———. "Exporting the Unfortunate: The European Slave Trade from India, 1500–1800." *Slavery and Abolition* 43, no. 3 (2022): 533–52.

———. "Marie Rozette and Her World: Class, Ethnicity, Gender, and Race in Late Eighteenth- and Early Nineteenth-Century Mauritius." *Journal of Social History* 45, no. 2 (Winter 2011): 345–65.

———. "Merchant Capital and Labor Migration in the Colonial Indian Ocean World." *Historia Crítica,* no. 89 (2023): 129–53.

———. "Satisfying the 'Want for Labouring People': European Slave Trading in the Indian Ocean, 1500–1850." *Journal of World History* 21, no. 1 (2010): 45–73.

———. "A Serious and Alarming Daily Evil: *Marronage* and Its Legacy in Mauritius and the Colonial Plantation World." *Slavery and Abolition* 25, no. 2 (2004): 1–17.

———. *Slave, Convict, and Indentured Labor and the Tyranny of the Particular.* Berlin: EB Verlag, 2020.

———, ed. *Slavery and Bonded Labor in Asia, 1250–1900.* Leiden: Brill, 2022.

———. "Slavery in a Remote but Global Place: The British East India Company and Bencoolen, 1685–1825." *Social and Education History* 7, no. 2 (2018): 151–76.

———. "Slaves, Convicts, Abolitionism and the Global Origins of the Post-Emancipation Indentured Labor System." *Slavery and Abolition* 35, no. 2 (2014): 328–48.

———. *Slaves, Freedmen, and Indentured Laborers in Colonial Mauritius.* Cambridge: Cambridge University Press, 1999.

Alpers, Edward A. *The Indian Ocean in World History.* Oxford: Oxford University Press, 2014.

———. *Ivory and Slaves: Changing Pattern of International Trade in East Central Africa to the Later Nineteenth Century.* Berkeley: University of California Press, 1975.

Alpers, Edward A., Gwyn Campbell, and Michael Salman, eds. *Resisting Bondage in Indian Ocean Africa and Asia.* London: Routledge, 2007.

———, eds. *Slavery and Resistance in Africa and Asia*. London: Routledge, 2005.

Ames, Glenn J. "Religious Life in the Colonial Trenches: The Role of the *Pai dos Christãos* in Seventeenth Century Portuguese India, c. 1640–1683." *Portuguese Studies Review* 16, no. 2 (2008): 1–23.

———. "Serving God, Mammon, or Both? Religious vis-à-vis Economic Priorities in the Portuguese *Estado da India*, c. 1600–1700." *Catholic Historical Review* 86, no. 2 (2000): 193–216.

Anderson, Clare. "Convicts, Commodities, and Connections in British Asia and the Indian Ocean, 1789–1866." *International Review of Social History* 64, no. S27 (2019): 205–27.

———. *Subaltern Lives: Biographies of Colonialism in the Indian Ocean World, 1790–1920*. Cambridge: Cambridge University Press, 2012.

Araujo, Ana Lucia. *Slavery in the Age of Memory: Engaging the Past*. London: Bloomsbury Academic, 2021.

Banaji, D. R. *Slavery in British India*. 2nd ed. Bombay: D. B. Taraporevala Sons, 1933.

Barendse, R. J. *The Arabian Seas: The Indian Ocean World of the Seventeenth Century*. New York: Routledge, 2015.

Basu, Helene. "Slave, Soldier, Trader, Faqir: Fragments of African Histories in Western India (Gujarat)." In *The African Diaspora in the Indian Ocean*, edited by Shihan de S. Jayasuriya and Richard Pankhurst, 223–50. Trenton, NJ: Africa World, 2003.

Bauss, Rudy. "A Demographic Study of Portuguese India and Macau as Well as Comments on Mozambique and Timor, 1750–1850." *Indian Economic and Social History Review* 34, no. 2 (1997): 199–216.

———. "The Portuguese Slave Trade from Mozambique to Portuguese India and Macau and Comments on Timor, 1750–1850: New Evidence from the Archives." *Camões Center Quarterly* 6/7, nos. 1–2 (Summer/Fall 1997): 21–26.

Bayly, Susan. *Caste, Society and Politics in India from the Eighteenth Century to the Modern Age*. Cambridge: Cambridge University Press, 2001.

Bennett, Michael D. "Slaves, Weavers, and the Peopling of East India Company Colonies, 1660–1730." In Allen, *Slavery and Bonded Labor*, 229–55.

Bethencourt, Francisco. *The Inquisition: A Global History, 1478–1834*. Translated by Jean Birrell. Cambridge: Cambridge University Press, 2009.

———. *Racisms: From the Crusades to the Twentieth Century*. Princeton, NJ: Princeton University Press, 2013.

Blackburn, Robin. *The Making of New World Slavery: From the Baroque to the Modern, 1492–1800*. London: Verso, 1997.
Blumenthal, Debra. *Enemies and Familiars: Slavery and Mastery in Fifteenth-Century Valencia*. Ithaca, NY: Cornell University Press, 2009.
Boxer, C. R. *The Church Militant and Iberian Expansion, 1440–1770*. Baltimore: Johns Hopkins University Press, 1978.
———. *The Portuguese Seaborne Empire, 1415–1825*. Middlesex, UK: Penguin Books, 1973.
Boyajian, James C. "Goa Inquisition: A New Light on the First 100 Years (1561–1660)." *Purabhilekh-Puratatva* 4, no. 1 (1986): 1–40.
———. *Portuguese Trade in Asia under the Habsburgs, 1580–1640*. Baltimore: Johns Hopkins University Press, 1993.
Brown, Christopher Leslie. "The Arming of Slaves in Comparative Perspective." In Brown and Morgan, *Arming Slaves*, 330–53.
Brown, Christopher Leslie, and Philip D. Morgan, eds. *Arming Slaves: From Classical Times to the Modern Age*. New Haven, CT: Yale University Press, 2006.
Brubaker, Rogers, and Frederick Cooper. "Beyond 'Identity.'" *Theory and Society* 29, no. 1 (February 2000): 1–47.
Burton, Richard F. *Camoens: His Life and His Lusiads*. Vol. 1. London: Bernard Quaritch, 1881.
Campbell, Gwyn. *Africa and the Indian Ocean World from Early Times to circa 1900*. Cambridge: Cambridge University Press, 2019.
———. "Introduction: Slavery and Other Forms of Unfree Labour in the Indian Ocean World." In *The Structure of Slavery in Indian Ocean Africa and Asia*, edited by Gwyn Campbell, vii–xxxii. London: Frank Cass, 2004.
———, ed. *The Structure of Slavery in Indian Ocean Africa and Asia*. London: Frank Cass, 2004.
Campbell, Gwyn, and Edward A. Alpers. "Introduction: Slavery, Forced Labour and Resistance in Indian Ocean Africa and Asia." In *Slavery and Resistance in Africa and Asia*, edited by Edward Alpers, Gwyn Campbell, and Michael Salman, 1–19. London: Routledge, 2005.
Cardoso, Hugo C. "The African Slave Population of Portuguese India: Demographics and Impact on Indo-Portuguese." *Journal of Pidgin and Creole Languages* 25, no. 1 (2010): 95–119.
———. "Convergence in the Malabar: The Case of Indo-Portuguese." *Journal of Pidgin and Creole Languages* 36, no. 2 (2021): 298–335.
Carretta, Vin. "Communications." *American Historical Review* 114, no. 3 (June 2009): 886–87.

Carretta, Vincent. *Equiano, the African: Biography of a Self-Made Man*. New York: Penguin Books, 2006.

———. "Response to Paul Lovejoy's 'Autobiography and Memory: Gustavus Vassa, alias Olaudah Equiano, the African.'" *Slavery and Abolition* 28, no. 1 (April 2007): 115–19.

Carter, Marina. "Slavery, Ethnicity, and Identity in the Indian Ocean Colonial World: A Case Study of 'Indian' Slaves on Mauritius." In *Being a Slave: Histories and Legacies of European Slavery in the Indian* Ocean, edited by Alicia Schrikker and Nira Wickramasinghe, 43–59. Leiden: Leiden University Press, 2020.

Casale, Giancarlo. *The Ottoman Age of Exploration*. Oxford: Oxford University Press, 2010.

Catao, F. X. Gomes. *The Island of Chorao: A Historical Sketch*. Alwaye, India: Mar Louis Memorial Press, 1962.

Catlin-Jairazbhoy, Amy, and Edward A. Alpers, eds. *Sidis and Scholars: Essays on African Indians*. Trenton, NJ: Red Sea, 2004.

Chakraborty, Titas. "Slave Trading and Slave Resistance in the Indian Ocean World: The Case of Early Eighteenth-Century Bengal." *Slavery and Abolition* 40, no. 4 (2019): 706–26.

Chakravarti, Ananya. *The Empire of Apostles: Religion,* Accommodatio, *and the Imagination of Empire in Early Modern Brazil and India*. New Delhi: Oxford University Press, 2018.

———. "Mapping 'Gabriel': Space, Identity and Slavery in the Late Sixteenth-Century Indian Ocean." *Past and Present* 243, no. 1 (2019): 5–34.

Chatterjee, Indrani. *Gender, Slavery and Law in Colonial India*. New Delhi: Oxford University Press, 1999.

———. "Renewed and Connected Histories: Slavery and the Historiography of South Asia." In Chatterjee and Eaton, *Slavery and South Asian History*, 17–43.

Chatterjee, Indrani, and Richard M. Eaton, eds. *Slavery and South Asian History*. Bloomington: Indiana University Press, 2006.

Chattopadhyay, Amal Kumar. *Slavery in the Bengal Presidency, 1772–1843*. London: Golden Eagle, 1977.

Clements, J. Clancy. *The Genesis of a Language: The Formation and Development of Korlai Portuguese*. Amsterdam: John Benjamins, 1996.

Coates, Timothy J. *Convicts and Orphans: Forced and State-Sponsored Colonizers in the Portuguese Empire, 1550–1755*. Stanford, CA: Stanford University Press, 2001.

———. "European Forced Labor in the Early Modern Era." In *The Cambridge World History of Slavery*, edited by David Eltis and

Stanley L. Engerman, 3:631–49. Cambridge: Cambridge University Press, 2011.

Collins, Robert O. "The African Slave Trade to Asia and the Indian Ocean Islands." In Jayasuriya and Angenot, *Uncovering the History of Africans,* 57–79.

Corpis, Duane J. *Crossing the Boundaries of Belief: Geographies of Religious Conversion in Southern Germany, 1648–1800.* Charlottesville: University of Virginia Press, 2014.

Cunha, Ana Cannas da. *A Inquisição no Estado da Índia: Origens (1539–1560).* Lisbon: Arquivos Nacionais / Torre do Tombo, 1995.

Cunningham, Lawrence S. *An Introduction to Catholicism.* Cambridge: Cambridge University Press, 2009.

Dalgado, Sebastião Rodolfo. *Glossário Luso-Asiático.* 2 vols. Coimbra: Imprensa da Universidade, 1919–21.

Davis, David Brion. "Introduction." In Brown and Morgan, *Arming Slaves,* 1–13.

Davis, Natalie Zemon. *Trickster Travels: A Sixteenth-Century Muslim between Worlds.* New York: Hill & Wang, 2006.

Delbrugge, Laura, ed. *Self-Fashioning and Assumptions of Identity in Medieval and Early Modern Iberia.* Leiden: Brill, 2015.

Díaz, Jorge Simón Izquierdo. "The Trade in Domestic Servants (Morianer) from Tranquebar for Upper Class Danish Homes in the First Half of the Seventeenth Century." *Itinerario* 43, no. 2 (2019): 194–217.

Disney, A. R. *The Portuguese Empire.* Vol. 2 of *A History of Portugal and the Portuguese Empire: From Beginnings to 1807.* Cambridge: Cambridge University Press, 2009.

D'Souza, Carmo. "Slavery in Goa: Legal and Historical Perspectives." In *Legacies of Slavery: Comparative Perspectives,* edited by Maria Suzette Fernandes Dias, 62–75. Newcastle, UK: Cambridge Scholars, 2007.

Dursteler, Eric R. *Renegade Women: Gender, Identity, and Boundaries in the Early Modern Mediterranean.* Baltimore: Johns Hopkins University Press, 2011.

Eaton, Richard M. "Introduction." In Chatterjee and Eaton, *Slavery and South Asian History,* 1–16.

———. "Malik Ambar (1548–1626): The Rise and Fall of Military Slavery." In *A Social History of the Deccan, 1300–1761: Eight Indian Lives,* 105–28. Cambridge: Cambridge University Press, 2005.

———. "The Rise and Fall of Military Slavery in the Deccan, 1450–1650." In Chatterjee and Eaton, *Slavery and South Asian History,* 115–35.

———. "Temple Desecration and Indo-Muslim States." In *Beyond Turk and Hindu: Rethinking Religious Identities in Islamicate South Asia*, edited by David Gilmartin and Bruce B. Lawrence, 246–81. Gainesville: University of Florida Press, 2000.

Eaton, Richard M., and Phillip B. Wagoner. *Power, Memory, Architecture: Contested Sites on India's Deccan Plateau, 1300–1600*. New Delhi: Oxford University Press, 2014.

Ekama, Kate. "Connected Lives: Experiences of Slavery in VOC Colombo." In *Being a Slave: Histories and Legacies of European Slavery in the Indian* Ocean, edited by Alicia Schrikker and Nira Wickramasinghe, 99–121. Leiden: Leiden University Press, 2020.

———. "Precarious Freedom: Manumission in Eighteenth-Century Colombo." *Journal of Social History* 54, no. 1 (Fall 2020): 88–108.

Ewald, Janet J. "Crossers of the Sea: Slaves, Freedmen, and Other Migrants in the Northwestern Indian Ocean, c. 1750–1914." *American Historical Review* 105, no. 1 (February 2000): 69–91.

Faria, Patrícia Souza de. "Cruzando Fronteiras: Conversão e Mobilidades Culturais de Escravos no Império Asiático Português (Séculos XVI e XVII)." *Anais de História de Além-Mar* 17 (2016): 147–78.

———. "Mais Soldados e Menos Padres: Remédios para a Preservação do Estado da Índia (1629–1636)." *História Unisinos* 16, no. 3 (2012): 357–68.

———. "O Pai dos Cristãos e as Populações Escravas de Goa: Zelo e Controle dos Cativos Convertidos (Séculos XVI e XVII)." *História,* 39 (2020): 1–30.

Finn, Margot. "Slaves out of Context: Domestic Slavery and the Anglo-Indian Family, c. 1780–1830." *Transactions of the Royal Historical Society* 19 (2009): 181–203.

Fonseca, Jorge. "Black Africans in Portugal during Cleynaerts's Visit (1533–1538)." In *Black Africans in Renaissance Europe,* edited by T. F. Earle and K. J. P. Lowe, 113–21. Cambridge: Cambridge University Press, 2005.

Fox, Colin. *A Bitter Draught: St. Helena and the Abolition of Slavery, 1792–1840*. Norfolk, UK: Society of Friends of St. Helena, 2017.

Frazier, E. Franklin. *The Negro Family in the United States*. Rev. and abr. ed. Chicago: University of Chicago Press, 1966.

Freamon, Bernard K. *Possessed by the Right Hand: The Problem of Slavery in Islamic Law and Muslim Cultures*. Leiden: Brill, 2019.

Geelen, Alexander, Bram van den Hout, Merve Tosun, Mike de Windt, and Matthias van Rossum. "On the Run: Runaway Slaves and Their Social Networks in Eighteenth-Century Cochin." *Journal of Social History* 54, no. 1 (Fall 2020): 66–87.

Genovese, Eugene D. *Roll, Jordan, Roll: The World the Slaves Made.* New York: Vintage Books, 1976.

Gerbner, Katharine. *Christian Slavery: Conversion and Race in the Protestant Atlantic World.* Philadelphia: University of Pennsylvania Press, 2018.

Ginzburg, Carlo. *The Cheese and the Worms: The Cosmos of a Sixteenth-Century Miller.* Translated by John Tedeschi and Anne Tedeschi. Baltimore: Johns Hopkins University Press, 1992.

———. *The Night Battles: Witchcraft and Agrarian Cults in the Sixteenth and Seventeenth Centuries.* Translated by John Tedeschi and Anne Tedeschi. Baltimore: Johns Hopkins University Press, 1992.

Gomez, Michael A. *Exchanging Our Country Marks: The Transformation of African Identities in the Colonial and Antebellum South.* Chapel Hill: University of North Carolina Press, 1998.

Gracias, Fatima da Silva. *Health and Hygiene in Colonial Goa (1510–1961).* New Delhi: Concept, 1994.

———. *Kaleidoscope of Women in Goa (1510–1961).* New Delhi: Concept, 1996.

Graham, Sandra Lauderdale. *Caetana Says No: Women's Stories from a Brazilian Slave Society.* Cambridge: Cambridge University Press, 2002.

Green, Toby. *Inquisition: The Reign of Fear.* New York: Thomas Dunne Books, 2009.

———. "Policing the Empires: A Comparative Perspective on the Institutional Trajectory of the Inquisition in the Portuguese and Spanish Overseas Territories (Sixteenth and Seventeenth Centuries)." *Hispanic Research Journal* 13, no. 1 (2012): 7–25.

Greenblatt, Stephen. *Renaissance Self-Fashioning: From More to Shakespeare.* Chicago: University of Chicago Press, 1980.

Gunn, Geoffrey C. *Encountering Macau: A Portuguese City-State on the Periphery of China, 1557–1999.* Boulder, CO: Westview, 1996.

Hägerdal, Hans. *Lords of the Land, Lords of the Sea: Conflict and Adaptation in Early Colonial Timor, 1600–1800.* Leiden: Brill, 2012.

———. "The Slaves of Timor: Life and Death on the Fringes of Early Colonial Society." *Itinerario* 34, no. 2 (2010): 19–44.

———. "Warfare, Bestowal, Purchase: Dutch Acquisition of Slaves in the World of Eastern Indonesia, 1650–1800." *Slavery and Abolition* 43, no. 3 (2022): 553–73.

Hamilton, Douglas J., Kate Hodgson, and Joel Quirk, eds. *Slavery, Memory and Identity: National Representations and Global Legacies.* London: Routledge, 2016.

Harris, Joseph E. *The African Presence in Asia: Consequences of the East African Slave Trade.* Evanston, IL: Northwestern University Press, 1971.

Hassell, Stephanie. "Inquisition Records from Goa as Sources for the Study of Slavery in the Eastern Domains of the Portuguese Empire." *History in Africa* 42 (2015): 397–418.

———. "Religious Identity and Imperial Security: Arming Catholic Slaves in Sixteenth- and Seventeenth-Century Portuguese India." *Journal of Early Modern History* 26, no. 5 (2022): 403–28.

Hawkley, Ethan P. "Reviving the Reconquista in Southeast Asia: Moros and the Making of the Philippines, 1565–1662." *Journal of World History* 25, nos. 2–3 (2014): 285–310.

Herskovits, Melville J. *The Myth of the Negro Past.* New York: Harper & Brothers, 1941.

Heywood, Linda M., ed. *Central Africans and Cultural Transformations in the American Diaspora.* Cambridge: Cambridge University Press, 2002.

Heywood, Linda M., and John K. Thornton. *Central Africans, Atlantic Creoles, and the Foundation of the Americas, 1585–1660.* Cambridge: Cambridge University Press, 2007.

Hofbauer, Andreas. *Diáspora Africana na Índia: Sobre Castas, Raças e Lutas.* São Paulo: Editora Unesp, 2021.

Hopper, Matthew S. *Slaves of One Master: Globalization and Slavery in Arabia in the Age of Empire.* New Haven, CT: Yale University Press, 2015.

Hunter, Tera W. *Bound in Wedlock: Slave and Free Black Marriage in the Nineteenth Century.* Cambridge, MA: Belknap Press of Harvard University Press, 2017.

Isaacman, Allen, and Derek Peterson. "Making the Chikunda: Military Slavery and Ethnicity in Southern Africa, 1750–1900." In Brown and Morgan, *Arming Slaves,* 95–119.

Isaacman, Allen F., and Barbara Isaacman. *Slavery and Beyond: The Making of Men and Chikunda Ethnic Identities in the Unstable World of South-Central Africa, 1750–1920.* Portsmouth, NH: Heinemann, 2004.

Jackson, Peter. "Turkish Slaves on Islam's Indian Frontier." In Chatterjee and Eaton, *Slavery and South Asian History,* 63–82.

Jayasuriya, Shihan de Silva. *African Identity in Asia: Cultural Effects of Forced Migration.* Princeton, NJ: Markus Wiener, 2009.

———. "East India Company in Sumatra: Cross-Cultural Interactions." *African and Asian Studies* 8, no. 3 (2009): 204–21.

———. "Identifying Africans in Asia: What's in a Name?" In Jayasuriya and Angenot, *Uncovering the History of Africans,* 7–36.

———. "Migrants and Mercenaries: Sri Lanka's Hidden Africans." In Jayasuriya and Angenot, *Uncovering the History of Africans,* 155–70.

———. "Recruiting Africans to the British Regiments in Ceylon: Spill-over Effects of Abolition in the Atlantic." *African and Asian Studies* 10, no. 1 (2011): 15–31.

Jayasuriya, Shihan de Silva, and Jean-Pierre Angenot, eds. *Uncovering the History of Africans in Asia.* Leiden: Brill, 2008.

Jayasuriya, Shihan de Silva, and Richard Pankhurst, eds. *The African Diaspora in the Indian Ocean.* Trenton, NJ: Africa World, 2003.

Jeychandran, Neelima. "Geographies of Death and Memory: Shrines Dedicated to African Saints and Spectral Deities in India." *South Asian History and Culture* 11, no. 4 (2020): 421–32.

Johnson, Walter. "On Agency." *Journal of Social History* 37, no. 1 (2003): 113–24.

———. *Soul by Soul: Life Inside the Antebellum Slave Market.* Cambridge, MA: Harvard University Press, 1999.

Jones, Eric. *Wives, Slaves, and Concubines: A History of the Female Underclass in Dutch Asia.* Ithaca, NY: Cornell University Press, 2011.

Kalb, Emma. "Slavery in South Asia." In *The Palgrave Handbook of Global Slavery throughout History,* edited by Damian A. Pargas and Juliane Schiel, 517–34. Cham, Switzerland: Palgrave Macmillan, 2023.

Kaplan, Steven. *The Beta Israel (Falasha) in Ethiopia: From Earliest Times to the Twentieth Century.* New York: New York University Press, 1992.

Karasch, Mary C. *Slave Life in Rio de Janeiro, 1808–1850.* Princeton, NJ: Princeton University Press, 1987.

Kolff, Dirk H. A. *Naukar, Rajput and Sepoy: The Ethnohistory of the Military Labour Market in Hindustan, 1450–1850.* Cambridge: Cambridge University Press, 1990.

Kraay, Hendrik. "Arming Slaves in Brazil from the Seventeenth Century to the Nineteenth Century." In Brown and Morgan, *Arming Slaves,* 146–79.

Kruijtzer, Gijs. *Xenophobia in Seventeenth-Century India.* Leiden: Leiden University Press, 2009.

Kumar, Sunil. "Service, Status, and Military Slavery in the Delhi Sultanate: Thirteenth and Fourteenth Centuries." In Chatterjee and Eaton, *Slavery and South Asian History,* 83–114.

Lahon, Didier. "Black African Slaves and Freedmen in Portugal during the Renaissance: Creating a New Pattern of Reality." In *Black Africans in Renaissance Europe,* edited by T. F. Earle and K. J. P. Lowe, 261–79. Cambridge: Cambridge University Press, 2005.

Larson, Pier M. *Ocean of Letters: Language and Creolization in an Indian Ocean Diaspora.* Cambridge: Cambridge University Press, 2009.

Levi, Scott C. "Hindus beyond the Hindu Kush: Indians in the Central Asian Slave Trade." *Journal of the Royal Asiatic Society* 12, no. 3 (2002): 277–88.

Lovejoy, Paul E. "Autobiography and Memory: Gustavus Vassa, alias Olaudah Equiano, the African." *Slavery and Abolition* 27, no. 3 (2006): 317–47.

Machado, Pedro. "A Forgotten Corner of the Indian Ocean: Gujarati Merchants, Portuguese India and the Mozambique Slave-Trade, *c.* 1730–1830." In *The Structure of Slavery in Indian Ocean Africa and Asia,* edited by Gwyn Campbell, 17–32. London: Frank Cass, 2004.

———. *Ocean of Trade: South Asian Merchants, Africa and the Indian Ocean, c. 1750–1850.* Cambridge: Cambridge University Press, 2014.

Mark, Peter, and José da Silva Horta. *The Forgotten Diaspora: Jewish Communities in West Africa and the Making of the Atlantic World.* Cambridge: Cambridge University Press, 2011.

Mason, John Edwin. *Social Death and Resurrection: Slavery and Emancipation in South Africa.* Charlottesville: University of Virginia Press, 2003.

Mathew, K. M. *History of the Portuguese Navigation in India (1497–1600).* Delhi: Mittal, 1988.

Mathew, K. S. *Portuguese Trade with India in the Sixteenth Century.* New Delhi: Manohar, 1983.

Matos, Paulo Teodoro de. "The Population of the Portuguese Estado da Índia, 1750–1820: Sources and Demographic Trends." In *The Making of the Luso-Asian World: Intricacies of Engagement.* Vol. 1 of *Portuguese and Luso-Asian Legacies in Southeast Asia, 1511–2011,* edited by Laura Jarnagin, 155–77. Singapore: Institute of Southeast Asian Studies, 2011.

Mawson, Stephanie. "Escaping Empire: Philippine Mountains and Indigenous Histories of Resistance." *American Historical Review* 128, no. 3 (2023): 1211–43.

———. *Incomplete Conquests: The Limits of Spanish Empire in the Seventeenth-Century Philippines.* Ithaca, NY: Cornell University Press, 2023.

———. "Slavery, Conflict, and Empire in the Seventeenth-Century Philippines." In Allen, *Slavery and Bonded Labor,* 256–83.

Mbeki, Linda, and Matthias van Rossum. "Private Slave Trade in the Dutch Indian Ocean World: A Study into the Networks and

Backgrounds of the Slavers and the Enslaved in South Asia and South Africa." *Slavery and Abolition* 38, no. 1 (2017): 95–116.

McKinley, Michelle A. *Fractional Freedoms: Slavery, Intimacy, and Legal Mobilization in Colonial Lima, 1600–1700.* New York: Cambridge University Press, 2016.

———. "Fractional Freedoms: Slavery, Legal Activism, and Ecclesiastical Courts in Colonial Lima, 1593–1689." *Law and History Review* 28, no. 3 (2010): 749–90.

McMahon, Elisabeth. "Slave Wills along the Swahili Coast." In *African Voices on Slavery and the Slave Trade: Volume 1, the Sources,* edited by Alice Bellagamba, Sandra E. Greene, and Martin A. Klein, 511–18. Cambridge: Cambridge University Press, 2013.

McManus, Stuart M. "*Partus Sequitur Ventrem* in Theory and Practice: Slavery and Reproduction in Early Modern Portuguese Asia." *Gender and History* 32, no. 3 (October 2020): 542–61.

Melammed, Renée Levine. "The World of Witnesses and the Holy Tribunal: Fifteenth-Century Trials of Castilian Judaizers." In *Voices from the Bench: The Narratives of Lesser Folk in Medieval Trials,* edited by Michael Goodich, 43–66. New York: Palgrave Macmillan, 2006.

Mendonça, Délio de. *Conversions and Citizenry: Goa under Portugal, 1510–1610.* New Delhi: Concept, 2002.

Mintz, Sidney W., and Richard Price. *The Birth of African-American Culture: An Anthropological Perspective.* Boston: Beacon, 1992.

Mullett, Michael A. *The Catholic Reformation.* London: Routledge, 1999.

Newitt, Malyn. *A History of Portuguese Overseas Expansion, 1400–1668.* London: Routledge, 2005.

Obeng, Pashington. *Shaping Membership, Defining Nation: The Cultural Politics of African Indians in South Asia.* Lanham, MD: Lexington Books, 2007.

O'Malley, John W. *Trent: What Happened at the Council.* Cambridge, MA: Belknap Press of Harvard University Press, 2013.

Oostindie, Gert, and Bert Paasman. "Dutch Attitudes towards Colonial Empires, Indigenous Cultures, and Slaves." *Eighteenth-Century Studies* 31, no. 3 (1998): 349–55.

Paiva, José Pedro. "The Inquisition Tribunal in Goa: Why and for What Purpose?" *Journal of Early Modern History* 21, no. 6 (2017): 565–93.

Pankhurst, Richard. "The Ethiopian Diaspora to India: The Role of Habshis and Sidis from Medieval Times to the End of the Eighteenth Century." In *The African Diaspora in the Indian Ocean,* edited by Shihan de S. Jayasuriya and Richard Pankhurst, 189–221. Trenton, NJ: Africa World, 2003.

Patnaik, Utsa, and Manjari Dingwaney, eds. *Chains of Servitude: Bondage and Slavery in India*. Madras: Sangam Books, 1985.

Patterson, Orlando. *Slavery and Social Death: A Comparative Study*. Cambridge, MA: Harvard University Press, 1982.

Peabody, Sue. *Madeleine's Children: Family, Freedom, Secrets, and Lies in France's Indian Ocean Colonies*. New York: Oxford University Press, 2017.

Pearson, Michael N. *The Indian Ocean*. London: Routledge, 2003.

———. *Port Cities and Intruders: The Swahili Coast, India, and Portugal in the Early Modern Era*. Baltimore: Johns Hopkins University Press, 1998.

———. *The Portuguese in India*. Cambridge: Cambridge University Press, 2006.

Pescatello, Ann M. "The African Presence in Portuguese India." *Journal of Asian History* 11, no. 1 (1977): 26–48.

Phillips, William D., Jr. *Slavery in Medieval and Early Modern Iberia*. Philadelphia: University of Pennsylvania Press, 2014.

Pinto, Celsa. *Trade and Finance in Portuguese India: A Study of the Portuguese Country Trade, 1770–1840*. New Delhi: Concept, 1994.

Pinto, Jeanette. *Slavery in Portuguese India, 1510–1842*. Bombay: Himalaya, 1992.

Pinto, Mark Sebastian. "The Forgotten Community, 'the Siddis of Uttara Kannada': How the Portuguese Indian Ocean Slave Trade Produced a Community of Indians of African Descent." *Interdisciplinary Journal of Portuguese Diaspora Studies* 8 (2019): 165–88.

Prasad, Kiran Kamal, and Jean-Pierre Angenot, eds. *TADIA, the African Diaspora in Asia: Explorations on a Less Known Fact*. Bangalore: Jana Jagrati Prakashana, 2008.

Priolkar, Anant Kakba. *The Goa Inquisition: Being a Quatercentenary Commemoration Study of the Inquisition in India, with Accounts Given by Dr. Dellon and Dr. Buchanan*. 2nd ed. Panaji, Goa: Rajhauns Vitaran, 2008.

Reid, Anthony. "Slavery and Forced Labour in Asia: *Status Quaestionis*." In Allen, *Slavery and Bonded Labor*, 33–48.

Reis, João José. *Slave Rebellion in Brazil: The Muslim Uprising of 1835 in Bahia*. Translated by Arthur Brakel. Baltimore: Johns Hopkins University Press, 1995.

Richards, John F. *The Mughal Empire*. Cambridge: Cambridge University Press, 1993.

Rodet, Marie. "Gender, Migration, and the End of Slavery in the Region of Kayes, French Soudan." In *African Voices on Slavery and the Slave Trade: Volume 1, the Sources,* edited by Alice Bellagamba, Sandra E. Greene, and Martin A. Klein, 319–29. Cambridge: Cambridge University Press, 2013.

Ross, Robert. *Cape of Torments: Slavery and Resistance in South Africa.* London: Routledge & Kegan Paul, 1983.

Russell-Wood, A. J. R. "Iberian Expansion and the Issue of Black Slavery: Changing Portuguese Attitudes, 1440–1770." *American Historical Review* 83, no. 1 (February 1978): 16–42.

Sadiq Ali, Shanti. *The African Dispersal in the Deccan: From Medieval to Modern Times.* New Delhi: Orient Longman, 1996.

Salvadore, Matteo. "Between the Red Sea Trade and the Goa Inquisition: The Odyssey of Gabriel, a Sixteenth-Century Ethiopian Jew." *Journal of World History* 31, no. 2 (June 2020): 327–60.

Santos, Vanicléia Silva. "Africans, Afro-Brazilians and Afro-Portuguese in the Iberian Inquisition in the Seventeenth and Eighteenth Centuries." *African and Black Diaspora: An International Journal* 5, no. 1 (2012): 49–63.

Saunders, A. C. de C. M. *A Social History of Black Slaves and Freedmen in Portugal, 1441–1555.* Cambridge: Cambridge University Press, 1982.

Scammell, G. V. "The Pillars of Empire: Indigenous Assistance and the Survival of the 'Estado da India,' c. 1600–1700." *Modern Asian Studies* 22, no. 3 (1988): 473–89.

Schoeman, Karel. *Early Slavery at the Cape of Good Hope, 1652–1717.* Pretoria: Protea Boekhuis, 2007.

Schorsch, Jonathan. *Jews and Blacks in the Early Modern World.* Cambridge: Cambridge University Press, 2004.

Schrikker, Alicia, and Nira Wickramasinghe, eds. *Being a Slave: Histories and Legacies of European Slavery in the Indian Ocean.* Leiden: Leiden University Press, 2020.

Scott, William Henry. "Filipino Class Structure in the Sixteenth Century." *Philippine Studies* 28, no. 2 (1980): 142–75.

———. *Slavery in the Spanish Philippines.* Manila: De La Salle University Press, 1991.

Seijas, Tatiana. *Asian Slaves in Colonial Mexico: From Chinos to Indians.* New York: Cambridge University Press, 2014.

Shell, Robert C.-H. *Children of Bondage: A Social History of the Slave Society at the Cape of Good Hope, 1652–1838.* Hanover, NH: Wesleyan University Press, 1994.

———. "The Tower of Babel: The Slave Trade and Creolization at the Cape, 1652–1834." In *Slavery in South Africa: Captive Labor on the Dutch Frontier,* edited by Elizabeth Eldredge and Fred Morton, 11–39. Boulder, CO: Westview, 1994.

Shirodkar, P. P. "Slavery in Coastal India (with Special Reference to Goa, Daman, and Diu)." *Purabhilekh-Puratatva* 3, no. 1 (1985): 27–43.

Shyam, Radhey. *The Kingdom of Ahmadnagar.* Delhi: Motilal Barnarsidass, 1966.

Smith, Stefan Halikowski. *Creolization and Diaspora in the Portuguese Indies: The Social World of Ayutthaya, 1640–1720.* Leiden: Brill, 2011.

Sousa, Lúcio de. *The Portuguese Slave Trade in Early Modern Japan: Merchants, Jesuits and Japanese, Chinese, and Korean Slaves.* Leiden: Brill, 2019.

Souza, Teotonio R. de. "French Slave-Trading in Portuguese Goa (1773–1791)." In *Essays in Goan History,* edited by Teotonio R. de Souza, 119–31. New Delhi: Concept, 1989.

———. "Manumission of Slaves in Goa during 1682 to 1760 as Found in Codex 860." In *TADIA, the African Diaspora in Asia: Explorations on a Less Known Fact,* edited by Kiran Kamal Prasad and Jean-Pierre Angenot, 167–81. Bangalore: Jana Jagrati Prakashana, 2008.

———. *Medieval Goa: A Socio-Economic History.* 2nd ed. Saligão, Goa: Goa, 1556, 2009.

———. "O Padroado Português do Oriente visto da Índia: Instrumentalização Política da Religião." *Revista Lusófona de Ciência das Religiões* 7, nos. 13–14 (2008): 413–30.

———. "The Voiceless in Goan Historiography: A Case for the Source-Value of Church Records in Goa." In *Indo-Portuguese History: Sources and Problems,* edited by John Correia-Afonso, 114–31. Bombay: Oxford University Press, 1981.

Soyer, François. "'It Is Not Possible to Be Both a Jew and a Christian': *Converso* Religious Identity and the Inquisitorial Trial of Custodio Nunes (1604–5)." *Mediterranean Historical Review* 26, no. 1 (2011): 81–97.

Subrahmanyam, Sanjay. "Between Eastern Africa and Western India, 1500–1650: Slavery, Commerce, and Elite Formation." *Comparative Studies in Society and History* 61, no. 4 (2019): 805–34.

———. "Holding the World in Balance: The Connected Histories of the Iberian Overseas Empires, 1500–1640." *American Historical Review* 112, no. 5 (2007): 1359–85.

———. "'The Life and Actions of Mathias de Albuquerque (1547–1609)': A Portuguese Source for Deccan History." *Portuguese Studies* 11 (1995): 62–77.

———. *The Portuguese Empire in Asia, 1500–1700: A Political and Economic History.* 2nd ed. Chichester, UK: John Wiley & Sons, 2012.

———. *Three Ways to Be Alien: Travails and Encounters in the Early Modern World*. Waltham, MA: Brandeis University Press, 2011.

Suzuki, Hideaki. "African Diaspora in Asia." In *Oxford Research Encyclopedia of Asian History*, edited by David Ludden. Oxford: Oxford University Press, 2020. https://doi.org/10.1093/acrefore/9780190277727.013.34.

Sweet, James H. "Communications." *American Historical Review* 114, no. 3 (June 2009): 887–88.

———. *Domingos Álvares, African Healing, and the Intellectual History of the Atlantic World*. Chapel Hill: University of North Carolina Press, 2011.

———. "Mistaken Identities? Olaudah Equiano, Domingos Álvares, and the Methodological Challenges of Studying the African Diaspora." *American Historical Review* 114, no. 2 (April 2009): 279–306.

———. *Recreating Africa: Culture, Kinship, and Religion in the African-Portuguese World, 1441–1770*. Chapel Hill: University of North Carolina Press, 2003.

Tannenbaum, Frank. *Slave and Citizen*. Boston: Beacon, 1992.

Tavim, José Alberto Rodrigues da Silva. "Um inquisidor inquirido: João Delgado Figueira e o seu Reportorio, no contexto da 'documentação sobre a Inquisição de Goa.'" *Leituras: Revista da Biblioteca Nacional*, no. 1 (Outono 1997): 183–93.

Teelock, Vijaya. *Bitter Sugar: Sugar and Slavery in 19th Century Mauritius*. Moka, Mauritius: Mahatma Gandhi Institute, 1998.

Thomas, Rhondda Robinson. *Call My Name, Clemson: Documenting the Black Experience in an American University Community*. Iowa City: University of Iowa Press, 2020.

Thomaz, Luís Filipe F. R. "Iranian Diaspora and the Deccan Sultanates in India: A Study of Sixteenth Century Portuguese Sources." *Studies in History* 30, no. 1 (2014): 1–42.

Thornton, John K. *Africa and Africans in the Making of the Atlantic World, 1400–1800*. 2nd ed. Cambridge: Cambridge University Press, 1998.

van Oss, Adriaan C. *Catholic Colonialism: A Parish History of Guatemala, 1524–1821*. Cambridge: Cambridge University Press, 1986.

van Rossum, Matthias. "Global Slavery, Local Bondage? Rethinking Slaveries as (Im)Mobilizing Regimes from the Case of the Dutch Indian Ocean and Indonesian Archipelago Worlds." *Journal of World History 31, no. 4 (2020): 693–727.*

van Rossum, Matthias, Alexander Geelen, Bram van den Hout, and Merve Tosun. *Testimonies of Enslavement: Sources on Slavery from the Indian Ocean World*. London: Bloomsbury Academic, 2020.

van Rossum, Matthias, Alexander Geelen, and Merve Tosun. "Enslaveability, Slavery and Global Micro Histories: Reflections through the Case of Cali." *Slavery and Abolition* 43, no. 3 (2022): 482–98.

van Welie, Rik. "Patterns of Slave Trading and Slavery in the Dutch Colonial World, 1596–1863." In Dutch Colonialism, Migration and Cultural Heritage, edited by Gert Oostindie, 155–259. Leiden: Brill, 2008.

———. "Slave Trading and Slavery in the Dutch Colonial Empire: A Global Comparison." New West Indian Guide / Nieuwe West-Indische Gids 82, nos. 1–2 (2008): 47–96

Vaughan, Megan. *Creating the Creole Island: Slavery in Eighteenth-Century Mauritius*. Durham, NC: Duke University Press, 2005.

Vergès, Françoise. "Indian-Oceanic Creolizations: Processes and Practices of Creolization on Réunion Island." In *Creolization: History, Ethnography, Theory,* edited by Charles Stewart, 133–52. London: Routledge, 2016.

Vernet, Thomas. "Slave Trade and Slavery on the Swahili Coast, 1500–1750." In *Slavery, Islam and Diaspora,* edited by Behnaz A. Mirzai, Ismael Musah Montana, and Paul E. Lovejoy, 37–76. Trenton, NJ: Africa World, 2009.

Vieyra, Anthony. *A Dictionary of the Portuguese and English Languages, in Two Parts, Portuguese and English, and English and Portuguese*. 2 vols. London: J. Nourse, 1773.

Vink, Markus. "'The World's Oldest Trade': Dutch Slavery and Slave Trade in the Indian Ocean in the Seventeenth Century." *Journal of World History* 14, no. 2 (2003): 131–77.

Walker, Timothy. "Abolishing the Slave Trade: Documentary Evidence of Popular and Official Resistance to Crown Policy, 1842–60." *Slavery and Abolition* 25, no. 2 (2004): 63–79.

———. "Slaves or Soldiers? African Conscripts in Portuguese India, 1857–1860." In Chatterjee and Eaton, *Slavery and South Asian History*, 234–61.

———. "Sorcerers and Folkhealers: Africans and the Inquisition in Portugal (1680–1800)." *Revista Lusófona de Ciência das Religiões* 3, nos. 5–6 (2004): 83–98.

Ward, Kerry. *Networks of Empire: Forced Migration in the Dutch East India Company*. Cambridge: Cambridge University Press, 2009.

Wickramasinghe, Nira. *Slave in a Palanquin: Colonial Servitude and Resistance in Sri Lanka*. New York: Columbia University Press, 2020.

Wiesner-Hanks, Merry E. *Early Modern Europe, 1450–1789*. 2nd ed. Cambridge: Cambridge University Press, 2013.

Wilson-Fall, Wendy. *Memories of Madagascar and Slavery in the Black Atlantic*. Athens: Ohio University Press, 2015.

Wink, André. *Al Hind, the Making of the Indo-Islamic World, Volume 2: The Slave Kings and the Islamic Conquest, 11th–13th Centuries*. Leiden: Brill, 2002.

Winn, Phillip. "Slavery and Cultural Creativity in the Banda Islands." *Journal of Southeast Asian Studies* 41, no. 3 (2010): 365–89.

Winterbottom, Anna. "From Hold to Foredeck: Slave Professions in the Maritime World of the East India Company, c. 1660–1720." In *Maritime History as Global History*, edited by Maria Fusaro and Amélia Polónia, 95–124. St. John's, Canada: International Maritime Economic History Association, 2010.

Worden, Nigel. *Slavery in Dutch South Africa*. Cambridge: Cambridge University Press, 1985.

Xavier, Ângela Barreto. "The Casa da Índia and the Emergence of a Science of Administration in the Portuguese Empire." *Journal of Early Modern History* 22, no. 5 (2018): 327–47.

———. *Religion and Empire in Portuguese India: Conversion, Resistance, and the Making of Goa*. Albany: State University of New York Press, 2022.

Xavier, P. D. *Goa, A Social History, 1510–1640*. Panaji, Goa: Rajhauns Vitaran, 1993.

Yang, Anand A. *Empire of Convicts: Indian Penal Labor in Colonial Southeast Asia*. Oakland: University of California Press, 2021.

Yank, Tyler. "Slave Protection and Resistance in Colonial Mauritius, 1829–1830." In *Slaving Zones: Cultural Identities, Ideologies, and Institutions in the Evolution of Global Slavery*, edited by Jeff Fynn-Paul and Damian Alan Pargas, 224–46. Leiden: Brill, 2018.

Yule, Henry, and A. C. Burnell. *Hobson-Johnson: A Glossary of Colloquial Anglo-Indian Words and Phrases, and of Kindred Terms, Etymological, Historical, Geographical and Discursive*. Edited by William Crooke. 2nd ed. London: John Murray, 1903.

Zeleza, Paul Tiyambe. "Rewriting the African Diaspora: Beyond the Black Atlantic." *African Affairs* 104, no. 414 (2005): 35–68.

Zupanov, Ines G. "Language and Culture of the Jesuit 'Early Modernity' in India during the Sixteenth Century." *Itinerario* 31, no. 2 (2007): 87–110.

Index

Page numbers followed by *t* indicate tables.